Praise for *Madam Mayor*

"An unvarnished look at public service at its most intimate, *Madam Mayor: Love and Loss in an American City* tells a story of a young woman choosing to get in the arena, solve problems, and fight for better politics and better results. Stephanie Miner shares her courage, her triumphs, and her losses in a human portrait that we could all take inspiration and guidance from right now."

**Hillary Rodham Clinton**

"I wish Stephanie Miner were mayor of Syracuse when I lived there as a graduate student. In vivid words, the first female mayor of a major New York State city takes readers inside government and inside the sometimes smarmy world of politics. She leaves us with a memorable portrait of a brave woman battling to save both her city and her lofty ideals. She succeeded as mayor despite battling female stereotypes: she's brittle, she's on edge, she's temperamental. When you finish her riveting book, you also realize she did something rare in politics: she succeeded as a human being."

**Ken Auletta**, columnist of the Annals of Communications for *The New Yorker* and author of *Hollywood Ending: Harvey Weinstein and the Culture of Silence*

"Stephanie Miner understands that local leadership is about solving problems, not playing partisan politics. Her memoir offers a behind-the-scenes look at the challenges mayors face in taking on the toughest issues facing the country— and the progress that can be made with pragmatic and fearless leadership."

**Michael R. Bloomberg**, founder of Bloomberg Philanthropies and Bloomberg L.P. and 108th Mayor of New York City

"A poignant and compelling narrative that captures the essence of public service and the profound impact of leadership on a community. As the former mayor of Syracuse, Miner's journey is a testament to resilience, dedication, and the community she loves. Her personal reflections and insightful observations offer a rare glimpse into the challenges and triumphs of governing a modern American city. I was always inspired by her unwavering commitment to Syracuse and deeply moved by her own, personal story. *Madam Mayor* is a must-read for anyone interested in the intricate balance of love, loss, and leadership in public life."

**Chuck Schumer**

"*Madam Mayor* gives readers a front-row seat at the unfathomable life of a big-city mayor trying to fix everything from pensions, to policing, to bursting water pipes, to corruption at the highest levels of government. Miner takes us on a wild ride, filled with humor, policy, politics, and deeply personal emotion. It will both destroy and restore your faith in American politics."
    **Libby Schaaf**, 50th Mayor of Oakland, California

"Stephanie Miner's book is an illuminating tale of the promise, challenges, and idealism mayors face when running a city. With passion and humor, Miner shows how the governmental system is both constructive and destructive, often at the same time. It's a story of confronting the status quo with a grinding commitment to solving problems for people. Readers interested in how things do—and do not—work in government will be fascinated."
    **Michael A. Nutter**, former Mayor of Philadelphia, Pennsylvania

"A passionate look at the joys, heartbreaks, and seamy politics of New York. Stephanie Miner, former mayor of Syracuse, skillfully invites the reader into a world that many politicians (like former New York Governor Andrew Cuomo) work hard to keep secret."
    **Eleanor Randolph**, author of *The Many Lives of Michael Bloomberg*

"Most political memoirs focus on the personal trials of running and serving. But Stephanie Miner's courageous book also includes real policy analysis and a wide-ranging treatment of the challenges facing cities and the complex interactions between different levels of government in our federal system. At times painfully honest, it should be of interest to anyone who wants to better understand urban and state politics, political ethics, corruption, public finance, and campaigns. Oh, and Andrew Cuomo too."
    **Grant Reeher**, author of *First Person Political: Legislative Life and the Meaning of Public Service*

"Miner turns the seemingly mundane aspects of local governance into a thrilling tale of intrigue as she bucked the status quo in the hurly burly, seedy world of New York politics. Rewarded with vindictiveness, pettiness, and deceit by the political status quo, *Madam Mayor* is a startling and beautiful portrayal of self-discovery by a pioneering female focused on doing the right thing with honesty and integrity amidst the contact sport of local and state politics."
    **Greg Fischer**, Mayor of Louisville, Kentucky, 2011–2022, and 75th President of the United States Conference of Mayors

# Madam Mayor

# Madam Mayor

Love and Loss in an American City

Stephanie A. Miner

UNIVERSITY PRESS OF KANSAS

Published by the University Press of Kansas (Lawrence, Kansas 66045), which was
organized by the Kansas Board of Regents and is operated and funded by Emporia State
University, Fort Hays State University, Kansas State University, Pittsburg State University,
the University of Kansas, and Wichita State University.

Library of Congress Cataloging-in-Publication Data

Names: Miner, Stephanie A., author.
Title: Madam Mayor : love and loss in an American city / Stephanie A. Miner.
Description: Lawrence, Kansas : University Press of Kansas, [2024] |
Includes bibliographical references.
Identifiers: LCCN 2024023144 (print) | LCCN 2024023145 (ebook)
| ISBN 9780700638284 (cloth) | ISBN 9780700638291 (ebook)
Subjects: LCSH: Miner, Stephanie A. | Women mayors–New York(State)–Syracuse–
Biography. | Syracuse (N.Y.)–Politics and government. | Syracuse (N.Y.)
–Biography. | BISAC: BIOGRAPHY & AUTOBIOGRAPHY / Political |
POLITICAL SCIENCE / American Government / Local
Classification: LCC F129.S8 M56 2024 (print) | LCC F129.S8 (ebook) |
DDC 974.7/66092 [B]–dc23/eng/20241024
LC record available at https://lccn.loc.gov/2024023144.
LC ebook record available at https://lccn.loc.gov/2024023145.

British Library Cataloguing-in-Publication Data is available.
Authorised Representative Details: Easy Access System Europe
Mustamäe tee 50, 10621 Tallinn, Estonia | gpsr.requests@easproject.com

He was a kid . . . from some insane place like Syracuse,
but somewhere along the line he had discovered he could say it. . . .
He had a lot to say.
*James Baldwin,* Another Country

I never had an interest in being a mayor 'cause that's a real job.
You have to produce.
*Joseph R. Biden, March 29, 2012*

To my grandmothers,
who taught me to believe

To Jack, who believed in me
even when I didn't

To the people of Syracuse,
who always believe

# Contents

*Photo gallery follows page 139.*

# Introduction

The unusual interview request from the Associated Press came about a week before the 2009 Syracuse mayoral general election. I had a miserable cold and was worried about my voice holding out for the last dash. Consequently, AP's odd request did not pique my curiosity. After I coughed through my assent to be recorded, the reporter causally said, "I've done some research, and do you know if you win you will be the first woman elected mayor in one of New York's big cities?" I did not know that and, incredibly, I had never even thought about it.

I was focused on getting elected mayor and fixated on sharing the ideas for civic solutions I believed would motivate people to support me. Lurking in my consciousness was the hope it would also compensate for my primary liability. Far from the expected politician personality, I am an introvert. While I enjoy people, I am not a backslapper or naturally gregarious. I am most comfortable as an observer, never as the star. Conquering this shortcoming, in my mind, would be the preeminent challenge to my candidacy.

I never thought about my gender as a factor. I thought it was irrelevant. I was wrong—shockingly wrong, in fact—about the role it would have throughout the race and my tenure. But I was right that the fire of my idealism would overcome my reserve and convince voters I could help them.

On that sunny fall day in 2009, though, when the AP reporter told me I would be a barrier breaker, I answered with only a mundane, "I guess you're right." Shortly after, a story ran across the country announcing I would be the first woman elected mayor of a major city in New York state. Everything changed. I would no longer be just a mayor, but a "first," and with that came unforeseen benefits and burdens.

## Syracuse, a "Mini-America"

Syracuse is synonymous with the American experience. It sits on the southern edge of Onondaga Lake, the ancestral homeland of the Onondaga Nation and the Haudenosaunee Confederacy, one of the world's oldest participatory democracies. Called a "mini-America,"[1] Syracuse's history is replete with the kinds of discoveries and ingenuity that forged our nation's economic bounty. Its economic resourcefulness dates to the 1790s, when residents commercialized salt from natural springs along Onondaga Lake. My family arrived around the 1820s to dig and dynamite the trenches that would become the Erie Canal, a public infrastructure project unleashing an era of prosperity for Syracuse, New York State, and the United States.

Innovation continued to fuel the economy in the nineteenth century, including "the Solvay Process," the name given to the creation of the efficient production of soda ash, a key ingredient in industrial products, conceived along the shores of Onondaga Lake. Like the Erie Canal, the Solvay process propelled our booming economy and transformed the world.

Syracuse became a beacon for people looking for opportunity. Immigrants from far-off lands and Black migrants from the American South[2] were drawn to the city's burgeoning economy. City Hall cheered the new residents, including more of my ancestors, with a sign above its front doors emblazoned "Syracuse Bids You Welcome."

By the early twentieth century, Syracuse's transportation infrastructure incentivized manufacturing companies to locate in the city, including the typewriter company Smith Corona, Syracuse China, and the Franklin Automobile Company. In 1921, a Syracusan described the city's prominence: "We manufacture more typewriters than any other city in the world, more soda by-products than any other city in the world, more auto parts and gears than any city in the world."

In 1937, amid the Great Depression, leaders lured Willis Carrier and his invention to cool air to Syracuse. At its peak, the Carrier Corporation employed seven thousand people in Syracuse-area factories, including my

1. Jeffrey Schmalz, "Syracuse Gets an A+ as a Test Marketplace," *New York Times*, February 22, 1984. Syracuse has a history of being one of the nation's top test markets due to its similar characteristics to the nation. See Mirror of America Report (2004) Acxiom.

2. Isabel Wilkerson, *The Warmth of Other Suns: The Epic Story of America's Great Migration* (New York: Penguin, 2020).

maternal grandfather and uncle. General Electric followed in the 1940s, opening the first of several factories, which at one point employed as many as seventeen thousand workers in the Syracuse area.

Our schools, buildings, and public spaces were imprinted with the names of the men who founded, made, and shared fortunes. Names like Crouse, Hinds, and Franklin were knit into the fabric of people's lives. The products were points of pride, too. Air conditioners were common in windows throughout Syracuse, even though the climate then rendered them superfluous. Indeed, my family had more air conditioners in storage than windows. The large, heavy machines symbolized participation in a successful economic behemoth. Similarly, expensive Nettleton shoes adorned the feet of many Syracuse men because a pair of them were given annually to each factory worker. My grandfather attributed his lifelong affection for well-made shoes to the pair of Nettleton's his aunt, a factory employee, gave him yearly.

Opportunity intertwined with our history. Syracuse became the fifth-largest city in New York state and at one point was one of the thirty largest cities in the country. Residents had good jobs, relatives lived within blocks of each other, and the public school system was one of the best in the country. Its population was largely educated, healthy, and well-off, with the average household income well above the national average.[3] Based on their own family experiences, generations of residents saw Syracuse providing the promise of a chance to climb to prosperity. It offered the fabled American dream: a job and the pride associated with being part of a successful national economy.

## Prosperity to Poverty

Syracuse's population peaked at 221,000 in 1950. That same year, signs of economic decline became apparent: Allied Chemical and General Motors closed large plants, General Electric began shrinking, and Smith Corona moved. Carrier was still a powerhouse, but it relocated to a suburban industrial park. This was in part due to the construction of the connected highway interstate system and the St. Lawrence Seaway, which began to overtake Syracuse's transportation advantage.

3. Carl Schramm, "By Forgetting Its Proud Economic History, Syracuse Loses Its Future," *Forbes*, February 26, 2013.

Community leadership, dominated by white male elites, recognized the threat and made several calamitous decisions. Believing a strong highway network could benefit Syracuse by allowing people to easily commute, a project to erect an elevated highway—Interstate 81—through the middle of the city commenced in 1956. The consequences of the decision were long-lasting and devastating. The highway destroyed a close-knit majority-Black neighborhood under the auspices of "urban renewal." It separated Syracuse in two, and spurred sprawl without growth.

By the mid-1980s, Syracuse's once vibrant manufacturing base had shrunk to the point that more people were employed in hospitals, government jobs, and service jobs. High property taxes, heavy regulation, and expensive utilities discouraged businesses from locating to the city. To respond to the downturn, Syracuse was granted a host of economic-development funding and programs. Its first economic-development zone was created 1987 and, by one official count, $2 billion in grants, tax-abatement financing, and utility benefits[4] were doled out between 1995 and 2000.

Despite the enthusiastic use of economic-development tools, there was no real economic growth. While Syracuse had historically been a low-poverty region, the number of people in poverty began growing. From 1978 to 2000, the number of jobs in the United States grew by 40 percent; in the Syracuse area (Onondaga County) jobs grew by only 12 percent. Between 1990 and 2000, the number of jobs declined.[5]

In turn, Syracuse had its own diaspora. Families saw their children move for better opportunities, and discussions about people leaving were as constant as the snow. Close-knit families who once lived within blocks of each other painfully disintegrated. Neighborhoods were drained of vitality. The sudden decline from prosperity to poverty meant people who had experienced Syracuse as a thriving community saw it deteriorate before their eyes.

By 2000, Syracuse's population had fallen to 150,000; 60 percent of its real estate was either tax-exempt or tax-abated; the property-tax rate was 3 percent of fair-market value, twice the national average; the number of actual jobs was declining; poverty was growing; and the remaining taxpayers were being squeezed to pay for services. Instead of being one of the wealthiest and healthiest cities, we confronted shocking indices of poverty

4. William Barrett, "Willis Carrier's Ghost," *Forbes*, May 29, 2000.

5. US Bureau of Labor Statistics.

and degradation, with the highest concentration of poverty among people of color and one of the largest income gaps in the nation.

The city glowingly referred to as a "mini-America" had transformed into a far different, but all too common, modern American story: a place where poverty replaced prosperity, where civic problems festered, and where government's ineffectiveness caused rampant cynicism. My family experienced it all. They dug the Erie Canal, built air conditioners, heralded economic development hope, and then reluctantly left.

When I faced the choice to stay or leave, I stayed. It was impossible not to feel people's derision when they asked the ubiquitous question of why I lived in Syracuse. I told people I liked the snow. I liked my lifestyle. I never told them the full truth, because contemptuously asking someone why she lives in her hometown reveals a profound lack of empathy.

I stayed because I belonged. The streets I walked were the same ones trod by generations of my family. In Syracuse, people confuse my great-grandparents with my grandparents, stumble over who is an uncle or a cousin, and conflate longtime friends with family. This continuity created a deep personal history, leading me to want to make Syracuse a welcoming place—just as it had been for the people who came before me.

## Betty, Genevieve, and Mario

The seeds of that desire were lovingly planted by my grandmothers. As the oldest of five children, my frequent visits to both of my grandmothers were respites. The time with them was just about me—nirvana. While different in many ways, my grandmothers shared an idealism about our history and an ability to laugh at human folly. My visits were marked by the arrival of the daily newspapers. Whether I was in Syracuse with my maternal grandmother, Betty Cooney, or in Binghamton with my paternal grandmother, Genevieve Miner, all activity stopped to read the morning and afternoon newspapers cover to cover. As soon as I was able, I started reading the newspaper to be like them.

Throughout those reading sessions, each would point out people she admired. Strong, opinionated people with a sense of justice: Barbara Jordan, Daniel Inouye, and, of course, the Kennedys. Frequently, the news was shared with a personal revelation and punctuated with peals of laughter. My grandmother Miner shared she was enthralled by President Kennedy's hair when she sat behind him at an Army-Navy football game. My grandmother Cooney boasted she knew Lyndon Baines Johnson because when he came to Syracuse to deliver the Gulf of Tonkin speech, Air Force One flew so close to her house, he saw her waving the American flag in her yard.

I ran to the library to read about the events they discussed. Biographies and history tomes filled my head (and backpack) with stories united by the theme of a leader rising to conquer a crisis and helping his (it was always a man) people prosper. At some point, one of them gave me *Profiles in Courage.* The notion of courage as the benchmark for a successful leader became my romantic ideal. It was only after serving as an elected official that I remembered Kennedy said he wrote the book because of the obstacles to courageous behavior inherent in our political system. But, of course, by that time my indoctrination was long completed.

My unusual interest in history and politics was well-known. When I was twelve, a friend told her father during my visit that I was going to be governor. He cynically laughed and said, "That will never happen because she doesn't have a gun." I did not understand what he meant but was troubled enough that I mentioned the remark to my parents. My mother explained "gun" meant a penis and made it clear she thought it was a stupid comment. My father agreed. It was never discussed again, but the comment was so searing that to this day, I can picture exactly where I was and can hear him say the words.

On a summer night when I was fourteen, I saw Mario Cuomo give his "Tale of Two Cities" speech on a small black-and-white television precariously placed on a porch ledge at a camp on Oneida Lake. That night, Cuomo sealed my love for politics. I wanted to be part of it somehow. The seed my grandmothers planted grew, and I studied political science at Syracuse University, determined to work in politics.

Through luck, I would go to work for Mario Cuomo in my twenties. I bantered with him in his signature Socratic style, always losing whatever battle of words we engaged in. I watched as he fought for ideas, convinced they would win in the public arena, and I listened as he argued about policy with integrity. My front-row seat allowed me to see him govern with a certainty that ideas were sacrosanct. In the process, he reinforced my idealism about politics and our democracy and demonstrated that a cerebral person could be a politician.

With an unshakable belief in our political system, I entered the arena as a city councilor and, eventually, as the mayor of the city. I would follow my grandmothers' inspiration and Mario Cuomo's model and use ideas to make Syracuse better.

## Madam Mayor: Love and Loss

Being the mayor put me in the eye of a constant, complicated storm that forced me to evaluate, question, and reevaluate everything I believed. Throughout my volatile tenure, I grappled with my belief I could make a difference. My love for politics became brittle, but my struggles forged it into a fuller understanding of public service.

This book describes the clash between ideals and the reality of governing, as well as the personal rewards and tolls. It details the process of trying to make a constructive difference in a complex civic system, addressing issues like fiscal management, infrastructure, and community relationships. It illustrates the constant tension in governing: why local public administration requires intricate bargains with state and national bureaucracies; how the celebration of the private sector often undercuts civic problem-solving; and the consequences of a political culture trumpeting superficial answers.

My biggest challenge, of course, was to get elected mayor. As with other cities, Syracuse's local leadership structure was composed largely of white men who had traditionally recruited candidates from their own networks, which were mostly devoid of women.[6] Like other idealist female candidates, I ran for mayor to make my city better.[7]

My gender marked me as the rarest of creatures: an elected female executive.[8] In 2009, the year I ran, only about 15 percent of the women who ran

6. Melody Crowder-Meyer, "Gendered Recruitment Without Trying: How local party recruiters affect women's representation," *Politics & Gender* 9 (2013): 390–413.

7. See Andreea-Nicoleta Voina, "Gendered Experience in Local Governance: Views of U.S. Female Mayors," in *Sustainable Development and Resilience of Local Communities and Public Sector Organizations*, ed. Cristina Haruţa, Cristina Hinţea, and Octavian Moldovan (Cluj-Napoca: Accent, 2019), 754–769.

8. Fernando Ferreira and Joseph Gyourko, "Does Gender Matter for Political Leadership? The Case of U.S. Mayors," National Bureau of Economic Research, Working paper 17671, December 2011, Figure 1 & 2, https://www.nber.org/system/files/working_papers/w17671/w17671.pdf.

for mayor in the United States were elected. Women are underrepresented in local government throughout the United States. The reasons behind this gap have not been the subject of a great deal of research.[9] I hope my experiences detailed here as a candidate and mayor will be a foundational piece in a growing area of study.

Mounting a political campaign is always an enormous effort, but I had willed myself to believe that Syracuse's recent experience with female candidates and its progressive reputation would ameliorate gender as a factor in the race. But I was wrong. I became trapped in a familiar "double bind."[10] My opponents, with the media willingly in tow, criticized me almost exclusively for my temperament. I wasn't passionate, I was abrasive; I wasn't assertive, I was aggressive. It may not have been said out loud, but the message was clear: I was, like so many women who dared to enter the political arena, a "bitch." Throughout my tenure, my demeanor, my appearance, my authenticity, and my positions were all seen through the lens of gender.

A deep reservoir of idealism and a passion for public service convinced me that by becoming a local political leader, I could make a constructive difference in people's lives.[11] I took office just as the ravages of the Great Recession of 2007–2008 started bearing down on municipal governments. My stewardship became consumed by avoiding bankruptcy. The byzantine issue of pension funding demonstrated the challenge of implementing sustainable solutions in a system driven by short-term demands. Adding a note of Shakespearean drama, my primary antagonist throughout my tenure would be Mario Cuomo's eldest son, Andrew.

As state and federal governments disregarded local governments, I learned to maximize partnerships with the private sector and philanthropic organizations to bridge the gap. Initially, IBM Smarter Cities showed us how data could solve a chronic tax-collection problem. By implementing that solution, we fixed a revenue issue and enabled the creation of one of the most successful land banks in the state. Building upon the work with IBM, we were awarded an "Innovation Team" grant from Bloomberg Philanthropies. The grant represented one of the greatest potentials for public-private

9. Mirya R. Holman, "Women in Local Government: What We Know and Where We Go from Here," *State & Local Government Review* 49, no. 4 (December 2017): 285–296.

10. Kathleen Hall Jamieson, *Beyond the Double Bind* (Oxford: Oxford University Press, 1995), 5, 6, 38.

11. Voina, "Gendered Experience in Local Governance."

partnerships and helped us address failures in our critical systems, including essential infrastructure.

Yet, partnerships held peril, too. While many urged governments to contract with the private sector to bring efficiency and much needed capital to government services, I found such arrangements often involved false promises put forward to escape the responsibilities of providing services equitably. Syracuse's failing educational system was a death knell for both the city and its families. I worked to implement education-reform efforts and partnered with a philanthropic organization to provide college scholarships for graduating high school students. Despite the private sector's commitment, I learned that incremental progress in education is arduous, transformational change illusory, and support transitory.

Reforming police practices and improving relationships between the police and neighbors was also grueling. In one of the most important missions of city government—keeping its citizens safe—my administration confronted an environment rife with guns, deep-seated bias, and skepticism. Police viewed themselves as warriors, while many citizens saw them as aggressive outsiders. Both groups needed one another, yet their very different experiences set public safety and justice on a collision course.

Entrenched politicians' willingness to champion superficial answers to complex problems complicated our challenges. This was especially clear in matters of economic development. An inside view of an objectively foolish project, "Hollywood [coming] to Onondaga," drove home the damaging consequences of a transactional political culture. The developer of the project was, at one time, a close friend. The area's vested stakeholders became loud supporters, while I was a lonely opponent. The celebration of superficial economic-development announcements while problems continued to fester provided an object lesson in how bad policy creates civic cynicism.

This book is a firsthand account of breaking barriers and stereotypes while attempting to solve common American problems in our political system. It's an outsider's tale intended to illustrate the strengths and weaknesses of our political process through the exploration of policy, gender, power, and corruption. It details the intractable challenges faced by hundreds of cities like Syracuse and shares the lessons, trials, and tribulations of making city government function, as well as the unexpected, and often unbelievable, joys of public service.

As the first woman elected mayor in any of New York state's Big 5 cities and one the few women who has served as a mayor in America, the book is a unique contribution to the understanding of contemporary American public policy. I hope readers who are interested in urban public policy or want an inside look at the workings of our political system—and perhaps those looking for a light in these dark times—will find it enjoyable.

# Ideals

## Front-Seat Socrates

When I get nervous, I get red. Beet red. The red flush starts at my ribs, moves to my face, and even colors my ears. On a lovely, temperate autumn morning, standing on the tarmac of a private air hanger, the volcano inside me erupted as a small plane taxied toward me. The plane carried Governor Mario Cuomo and I was to meet him for the first time. The plane door opened, he bounded down the steps, wearing the type of clothing I associated with my grandfathers—a small-brimmed hat and a dark blue overcoat hanging to his knees. I assumed someone had determined a fall day in Syracuse required a coat and hat. Cuomo briskly walked to a nondescript four-door sedan, which normally served as a state police officer's unmarked car, and got into the front seat. I hadn't been told what the protocol was and expected to brief him before we got in the car. Realizing my error, I hurried to catch up with him. When I did, I quickly got into the backseat. As Cuomo put on his seat belt, without turning his head, he said, "How are things, Stephanie?" Knowing full well my crimson complexion belied my answer, I caught my breath and said, "Fine, governor."

I was twenty-three and had been hired days before by the Cuomo administration to fill a position in Syracuse to represent the governor. Cuomo was seeking a fourth term and upstate New York was sure to be battleground for a tough campaign. Cuomo's competition was a little-known state senator named George Pataki who had succeeded in consolidating the support of the Republican Party's moderate and conservative wings, as well everyone tired of twelve years of Cuomo's rule. Senator Alfonse D'Amato, a pugnacious Long Island Republican, summed up the opposition by saying the state had become "the taxasaurus and spendasaurus capital of the nation."[1] Pataki's platform was little more than a promise to cut taxes and the fact he was not Cuomo.

I worshipped Cuomo from afar. Two years earlier, in 1991, at the end of a summer college program in the state legislature, I was invited to an event for interns on the second floor—the governor's floor—of the capitol building. When I arrived, I was put in the standing section in the back of the room with no view of the stage. As I stood craning my neck, I overheard Cuomo's staffers identify interns with powerful family connections and escort them to the front. When the governor came into the room, everyone stood to clap, further obstructing my view. All I could do was listen. He exhorted the young people who filled the room to enter government to serve the public by doing good, meaningful work. He was not talking directly to me, but I felt like he was. I knew I would heed his call, but I had no inkling I'd be working for him a few years later.

I continued to follow Cuomo's career. By 1991, I had accumulated enough credits to take a semester off from Syracuse University, and I'd decided to go to New Hampshire to volunteer for Cuomo's presumed presidential campaign. In December, after months of tortuous deliberations, Cuomo announced he was not running, famously leaving a plane chartered to take him to New Hampshire idling on the tarmac.[2] Disappointed but still eager to be involved, I drove to Manchester, New Hampshire, in January and volunteered for Nebraska senator Bob Kerrey's presidential campaign.

New Hampshire was great fun, even though Kerrey came in a disappointing third. I was offered a low-pay, no-guarantee traveling job with the campaign. I made a gleeful late-night phone call to my parents to tell them I'd been offered a job. Their succinct questions punctured my elation. My father pointedly asked, "Don't you want to graduate from college? How much will they pay you? How long will it last?" After that conversation, I reluctantly said goodbye to the traveling political circus to return to Syracuse University to finish my work and graduate.

Back in Syracuse, I started working on Geraldine Ferraro's Senate campaign, which included traveling with her when she came upstate. She was

1. James Dao, "D'Amato, Raising Funds, Assails Cuomo's Record as Governor," *New York Times*, September 28, 1993.

2. Kevin Sack, "Cuomo Says He Will Not Run for President in '92," *New York Times*, December 21, 1991.

warm, charming, and charismatic—and she knew it. I always had the sense she felt she could get anyone to vote for her if she could just talk to them. There was always a lot of "Ohh, honey," and "Oh my gosh, so good to see you!" and a big smile and accompanying laugh for each person she spoke to. She seemed focused almost exclusively on the personal interactions campaigning required and less interested in policy. It was not a winning formula for Democratic primary voters that year.

The day after Ferraro lost her close primary to Robert Abrams, I was hungover in LaGuardia Airport, waiting to fly back to Syracuse. As a bout of nausea hit, I ran to a trash can in the terminal and wretched. I shamefully lifted my head, hoping no one noticed me, and saw a middle-aged white guy running toward me and two airport workers. As he came closer, he yelled at the workers, "Where's the shuttle to DC?" They pointed to the terminal right in front of the guy. One then said to the other, "That asshole wants to be mayor of New York and he can't even find his way to the shuttle." For the first and last time, I was thankful for the distraction of Rudy Giuliani, who, at the time, was plotting a second mayoral run after his unsuccessful 1989 race.

Sometime after the election, Ferraro came to an event in Syracuse to thank volunteers. I was standing with her when she grabbed a pen from her wallet and a newspaper clipping fell out. I bent down to pick it up and saw it was a *New York Times* graphic showing the counties she'd won in the 1992 Senate primary. When I handed it to her, she seemed embarrassed that I had seen it and said, "It's silly really that I keep this, isn't it?" I don't think I said anything, but I was struck by what that map must have meant to her to keep it that close. I realized then that politics and elections scar people.

## Front-Seat Socrates

After Ferraro lost, a staff member from Cuomo's office asked if I was interested in working for him. I was, of course. Shortly after, I was hired to be his Central New York regional representative, which meant staffing the governor when he was in the five counties in the center of the state—Onondaga, Cortland, Oswego, Cayuga, and Madison. The job required briefing the governor on local views, arranging meetings, and identifying issues. I was learning to use the state phone system when I answered a call from a man who never gave me his name, commanding me to "staff the governor" the next day. When I asked what that meant, he told me to make sure I had ten turkey sandwiches with no mayo for the governor and the traveling staff. "Mrs. Cuomo thinks he's getting fat, so no mayo," the voice barked. I asked again for more information, the voice said, "He knows everything," and the line went dead. I hung up the unfamiliar phone in the unfamiliar office and felt myself familiarly turning red.

The phone rang again and, this time, a man who identified himself as the state trooper assigned to drive the governor the next day said: "Don't worry about the 'butt board.' I have a couple in my trunk." I confessed I had no idea what he meant, and he kindly explained that the governor had a bad back, and when it bothered him a wood board was placed on his chair seat. It was portable and imprinted with the state seal and the governor's signature to make it look official, but it was called the "butt board."

When I asked the trooper for more guidance, he told me to know the location of the men's bathroom at every venue and to have black markers and large index cards on hand. When I inquired about the turkey sandwiches, the trooper laughed and said only the staff were interested in the sandwiches. "I don't think I've ever seen Cuomo eat one, but the traveling staff does." He told me to get them donated, but I ended up buying them.

During that first meeting, as Cuomo settled in for the ride, I dutifully tried to brief him on local events, but he paid no attention. Instead, he fired off questions on various topics, including sports, the law, and human behavior. Everything was game and anyone in the car could be called upon to answer.

When the radio played an advertisement for the Oneida Nation's Turning Stone bingo casino, he asked, "Stephanie, can Indians vote?" With great trepidation, I answered that they were members of a sovereign nation, but they also were residents of the United States, and "that's the rub of it." He laughed at my obvious lack of confidence and said, "Yup, and you rubbed right into it."

He would keep pushing to see how far he could take a discussion until the other person gave up. It was never mean-spirited, just a test to put you through your paces. If it was basketball season, there was always discussion about the Big East league and prospects for Syracuse and St. John's University. One time, he was so pleased by a St. John's player, he joked that he was going to appoint him to the New York State Supreme Court. Then he asked, does the governor of New York have the power to appoint people to the Supreme Court? Could he appoint a person without a law degree? Who was the last Division One basketball player to serve on the bench? Which governor appointed him? What decision was he famous for getting right? Wrong? . . . And on and on it would go until you admitted defeat.

Sometimes something he saw would serve as a catalyst. Once we drove by the long-polluted Onondaga Lake[3] and he asked me why the state should be responsible for cleaning a lake contaminated by others. "I was just the friendly uncle sitting at home watching television, while you all went out, had a great time, and drove the car into the lake. Now I have to clean it up," he said by way of framing the argument.

Other times, it was existential such as when he asked me how I would define faith. I don't remember how I answered, but he said to everyone in the car, "I tell my kids, I cannot be absolutely sure their mother is faithful to me, but I believe it with every fiber of my being." And then he said faith "is believing in something with your very being even when you don't have absolute proof it exists." When I told this story to another Cuomo worker, he said to me, "Have you seen his kids? They look exactly like him! No faith necessary."

On another visit, we were driving to the site of a new factory being built in Oswego. Oswego is rural and, like much of upstate New York, had been beset by tough economic times. As we drove the forty-five minutes from Syracuse to the factory site, we passed some road-construction workers and the governor said, "Every time you pass by a construction crew, there is always one guy standing around talking. Why is that?" Whenever I pass a road crew, I look to see if this Mario rule is in effect, and most of the time, it is.

The night was cold and dark. The factory was half-built and seemed far away from any evidence of civilization. We did not have a home-field advantage given the economic realities and an ever-present upstate-downstate divide. The governor did not want to wear an overcoat because the workers were not wearing coats. But they were upstaters used to working outside in the cold and had clothes appropriate for the weather.

As I watched the governor on the temporary platform, I kept thinking

3. Starting in the 1800s and continuing for more than one hundred years, industries discharged industrial waste into Onondaga Lake, causing it to become the most polluted lake in the United States. New York State Department of Environmental Conservation, Onondaga Lake, www.dec.nys.gov.

about the cold, wondering whether I should do something and silently pleading for the event to end quickly. I saw the governor's head tilted close to the construction worker seated next to him. He was paying no attention to the ceremony and, instead, listening raptly to the worker.

My imagination was running wild with all the ways I had failed to protect the governor when Joseph Percoco came striding toward me with an intense scowl. Percoco was Cuomo's downstate advance guy but was filling in for the upstate guy. I'd met him for the first time at the dry run a couple of days before the event.

Built like a linebacker, he started barking orders, as if everyone worked for him: "This room is not acceptable. We will need a clean trailer that only we have access to with a phone and fax dedicated to us from noon until the governor leaves. These slats on the ground must be removed and more steady flooring put on the ground for the governor," and on and on.

I suggested to Percoco that we did not bark orders in this part of the state and, perhaps, doing so during a reelection campaign might be counterproductive. He scoffed and told me I would learn how it was done. It was my first encounter with Percoco, but it would not be my last.

Percoco asked me who the governor was talking to on the stage. I shrugged because I didn't know. He responded by giving me a death stare, and it was clear I would be answerable for the consequences of the horrible seating arrangement. The plant bigwigs had asked me to have the steward for the Ironworkers Union sit next to the governor. Without any thought about this crucial detail, I had instantly agreed to the request. I knew only that the steward had a good reputation. I assumed my failure to control this detail would result in me being fired.

Eventually, the governor offered his remarks. People crowded to get pictures and shake his hand. We left the cold, muddy site and got into the car, with the all-important turkey sandwiches in hand. I braced myself for the governor's reaction. He turned to me in the back seat and with a grin on his face said, "Stephanie, that Gary Robb, what a great guy." It took me a second to remember the steward's name was "Gary."

Robb told the governor he'd spent some time in the seminary. The governor challenged him to prove it by delivering the Suscipiat, a Latin prayer traditionally chanted at Roman Catholic Mass that's notoriously difficult to say. The governor and Robb had been having a great time reciting it to each other, seeing how far each could get before making a mistake. It was what can only be described as a Catholic Boy-Off, but it ensured my job was safe.

The fact that I had been part of executing an event where the governor enjoyed himself was gold. To be looked upon with favor by the governor was how people in the administration measured themselves and each other. I was happy to be in the glow for the simple reason it kept Percoco from barking at me.

Some months later, I was summoned to Albany, along with the rest of the state's regional representatives, to attend a meeting at the governor's mansion about the upcoming election. It was my first time in the mansion, and approximately twenty of us were seated around a large dining table. I was told to sit at the last seat on the corner. I was grateful to be off to the side because I was still uncomfortable with my role.

After we sat down, the governor entered and took his seat in the middle of the table. He congratulated one of my fellow representatives on the recent birth of his son by wishing him "mazel tov." I thought it was interesting he was comfortable with both Latin and Yiddish and I heard him say, "Where's Stephanie?" A hush fell over the table and every head turned my way.

Trying to keep my voice steady, I said, "Right here, governor."

"Stephanie, tell me three things I could do in Central New York to get more votes," Cuomo said.

I felt a flush creeping up my neck. I had planned to stay invisible in the meeting, not be an active participant—much less the first one questioned.

I took a deep breath and said I would have a robust job-retraining program for the thousand workers who had just learned they were going to be losing their jobs at Miller brewing facility in 1994, and then I tried to expand that suggestion into two more proposals. He interrupted me, laughing, and said, "No, that's the same as the first one." He was right. I smiled to acknowledge it, and the conversation moved on to someone else. A friend sitting next to me dropped her head and whispered, "Girllll, he likes you," and then, sounding concerned, she said, "Are you all right? You're really red."

Cuomo was widely admired for his oratory, but he was a terrific retail politician, too. And he did it by being exactly who he was—a guy from working-class Queens. Once, a Black woman with a Caribbean lilt came running up to him, saying, "Governor, I'm from Jamaica," and without missing a beat, the governor responded, "Me too." (Jamaica, Queens, that is.)

I watched him interact with all kinds of people—from union leaders talking about the redistribution of wealth and affluent donors asking for more tax breaks to city dwellers concerned about public safety and rural folks worried about family farms—and he always seemed eminently comfortable in his own skin and never tried to be something he was not.

Watching him was a high point of the job. Hearing him say "thankyouverymuch" as if it were one word was a tell he was about to exercise his famous speaking talent. Hearing him incorporate something I'd mentioned into his remarks was thrilling because it indicated he respected my opinion. After speeches, he would often ask my opinion. Usually I'd think, "You're widely held to be one of the best orators of our time. What could I possibly say to that question?" Nevertheless, I would dutifully report on the comments I'd heard from the audience or which points got the best response.

During a break toward the end of one jam-packed day, the governor and his traveling staff, including me, were in a hotel suite waiting to go to an evening event. I moved toward a TV to listen to a newscast covering the governor's events earlier in the day. The governor stopped me and in a fatherly tone told me to go back and finish the sandwich I was eating. He responded to my surprised look by saying it had been a long day and I needed to eat.

Another time, we'd arrived at a picnic and union leaders met us at the car to present the governor with a T-shirt bearing the union insignia. The governor started to take off his dress shirt to put on the T-shirt, and I was overcome by panic. The first rule of my job was never to leave the governor's side, and there was a media photographer present. But as the only woman in the group, I was uncomfortable standing next to the governor as he took his shirt off. While the union guys cheered his undressing, the governor silently gave me a look giving me permission to step away. He then gave the photographer a death stare, after which the camera was put away. It was not the first time I saw that Cuomo could take care of himself.

Cuomo's political skills were clear when you saw the ease and energy he brought to any argument of ideas. In October 1994, he was to attend an editorial board meeting with the *Syracuse Post Standard/Herald Journal*. The joint leadership of the newspapers had historically leaned conservative. The paper's editorial section was taken with Pataki's plan to cut state personal-income taxes. In one column, the editorial board wrote: "Pataki has struck a chord that is elegant in its simplicity and is sure to resonate

with an electorate fed up with costly political gimmickry of recent years."[4]
The governor, in turn, viewed Pataki's plan as irresponsible and lacking
substance.

On the appointed day, we were ushered into an elegant conference
room. I took a seat on the perimeter of the room and the governor sat in the
middle of a large conference table. The newspaper's reporters and editors
came in, armed with pens and notebooks, and shook the governor's hand.
After everyone was seated, the meeting began with a softball question for
the governor. Just as he was about to answer, the door swung open, and the
publisher, Steve Rogers, entered the room with dramatic flair. Rogers, who
seemed to me to be in his sixties, was short and rotund and had a full head
of white hair. He was legendary in Syracuse for the power he exerted in the
region and had a tempestuous history with the governor.

Rogers dismissively greeted the governor and, instead of sitting at the
table, walked over to a coffee station along the wall and poured himself a
glass of water. As people sitting at the table murmured in a weak attempt to
start the discussion, the governor leaned back in his seat and acknowledged
Rogers with a brusque "Steve." The room had so much tension I started getting red. In the most aggressive tone I had ever heard him take, the governor
started saying it was amazing what Pataki "can say and get away with." He
continued that he took his responsibility seriously and said, "Where's the
bullshit? Where's the reality?" It was the only time I ever heard him swear.
"It's all a matter of facts. If you stay on the surface, you can say and believe
a lot of things," Cuomo said, implying that Rogers' reasoning behind his
support of Pataki was superficial.

Rogers pummeled Cuomo on the state of the economy and taxes. The
governor responded that every time he came to Syracuse, Rogers was asking
for more state money for economic development projects. He was always
begging for state money and then complaining about taxes. I thought the
metaphorical heat might incinerate me until I saw the publisher pick his
nose. At which point, Rogers became all too human, and I realized how
fortunate I was to have a first-hand seat at this rhetorical clash.

At the end of the meeting, the governor stood up and grinned from ear

4. Editorial, "Pataki's Challenge—The GOP Candidate's Tax-Cut Proposal Has an Elegant Simplicity That Is Refreshing and Welcome," *Post-Standard*, September 30, 1994.

to ear. "Boy, that was fun." He meant it, but while he enjoyed himself, it was not enough to get the paper's endorsement that year.

As I got more comfortable with my role, I would suggest things the governor might change: maybe don't put your hand on your chest when describing the mammogram machine, maybe don't lean in like you're getting a mammogram; maybe don't say, "My tie—made by my Jewish son-in-law!"

Once when he was asked by a television reporter about the criminal justice system, the governor all but said it was a mess. After the interview, when he asked me what I thought, I gingerly said a sitting governor running for reelection should not, perhaps, say the criminal justice system he oversees is a mess. "But it is, Stephanie," he said matter-of-factly.

I took from his example that the civic arena was a place where ideas should be presented and debated, and the best idea would win. The notion that one would intellectually compromise for a political win was what lesser people did. Those who were noble, and would ultimately triumph, were those who were true to the power of discourse and rational thought. That's how problems got solved in a democracy. People deserved public servants who respected them and would give them honest answers. The fact that the political arena was a minefield for such beliefs made the victories more important and sweeter.

It was a message that resonated with me. I was an introverted nerd. I loved history and saw it as the story of great biographies. My grandmothers' infatuation with smart, iconoclastic leaders indoctrinated in me the idea of politics as a place where justice was fought over and ultimately prevailed. With Cuomo as an example, I thought there was room in politics for someone like me—a person who loved ideas and solving problems. The fact that there were not a lot of politicians who looked like me was something I assumed would change sooner rather than later in our democracy. It was the thinking of an idealistic twenty-three-year-old American.

Late in his reelection campaign, I staffed Cuomo at a big fundraiser in Syracuse. As he got ready to speak, he looked at his notes and asked, "Stephanie, what should I say to these people?" I said, "Tell them why they should be proud to be Democrats. It's not easy here."

To my delight, he scrapped the prepared notes and riffed about what it meant to be a Democrat: to even the playing field, give all people a chance, not just the lucky few. He told the audience that although he had done well in law school, no one would hire him. Someone suggested it might help if he changed his name to Mark Conrad. He held up his giant hands and said, "Can you imagine me, Mark Conrad?" People roared.

There were plenty of signs of Cuomo fatigue, like older Italian American voters suggesting that they'd had enough of him; the constant struggle to fill rooms for political events he was headlining; even a union head shouting that Cuomo hadn't done enough for his members. I ignored these signs because it was inconceivable to me that a force like Cuomo, with his intellect and charisma, could be beaten by a lightweight, relatively unknown state senator. I told myself if I worked hard and helped spread the message, people would vote for him. They had to—after all, he was Mario Cuomo. He had the best mind, ideas, and intentions.

One evening during the campaign, after another Cuomo staffer and I had finished an interview, a radio reporter casually asked what our plans were if he lost. I was dumbfounded because it was disloyal to even think about that possibility. When I said as much to the radio reporter, he gave me a quizzical look.

Election Day 1994 arrived, and around six in the evening, traditionally a peak time for Democrats to vote, an urgent call went out saying that Andrew Cuomo, the governor's older son, was ordering the phone script for the get-out-the-vote efforts to be changed. It was a bad sign.

I did not know Andrew Cuomo. He was long ensconced in Washington in the Clinton administration when I joined his father's administration. Despite his physical absence, Andrew was always a spectral presence. Commonly referred to as "The Prince of Darkness," he was notorious for being overly demanding. He was also recognized as a shrewd political strategist.

The demand to change the script was followed by whispered calls saying Andrew was furious with Congressman Charles Rangel because his Harlem constituents, reliable Democratic voters, had not gone to the polls in large numbers. Before I left the board of elections that night, I received a call that the governor had lost. The Republican Revolution was born, and I was out of the best job I was sure I would ever have.

Early next morning, my grandmother Betty Cooney showed up at my apartment to console me, saying loss was a part of politics. A few days later, I stopped at a local coffee shop and saw several people who'd led me to believe they were supporters of the governor huddled around a phone book. As I moved closer to say hello, I saw they had circled names and were writing lists. Turns out they were writing down the names of people who would soon be fired and lists of jobs soon to be available. It was a painful lesson in the old adage that in politics, there are no permanent friends or enemies, just permanent interests.

Mario Cuomo made an indelible impression on me. He was the epitome of how a person should conduct themself as a political figure—take the responsibility seriously, fight over ideas, and respect the people you represent. He made me believe that politics was a higher calling, grounded in ideals and marked by inspiring battles. He was my guiding star.

After the election loss, I decided to follow Mario Cuomo's example and go to law school at the University of Buffalo. Upon graduation, I joined Blitman & King, a labor law firm in Syracuse that represented many of the union leaders I had met when I worked for the governor. As was standard for the time, most labor organizations were run by men.

I struggled with the fact that I did not look the part of a traditional attorney. I was female, young, and even younger looking. Most of the time, my gender was never directly addressed, but there were times when it awkwardly arose: attending meetings in union halls decorated with calendars of scantily clad women, men telling sexual jokes until they realized I was in the room, and being asked directly how old I was.

Eventually, because I genuinely liked the clients, I learned how to deliver a message and keep the relationships functional. I would stand by the ubiquitous calendars with attractive women splayed over cars and admire the car. "I've always loved Mustangs," I'd say.

## Rites of Passage?

Upon my return to Syracuse as a duly licensed and employed lawyer, I joined the Onondaga County Democratic Committee. At one of my ward committee's regular meetings, two incumbent city councilors failed, after being pressed, to justify a foolish vote. In a moment of irritation, I concluded I could do a better job. Almost immediately after that meeting, an at-large city council seat opened. While my firm's partners weren't thrilled with the idea, they didn't prevent me from running.

Instead of representing districts, at-large councilmembers represent the city as a whole. There are typically four candidates (two Democrats and two Republicans) vying for two seats. The top two vote-getters get elected.

When I decided to run, there was one Democratic incumbent, a longtime community activist, and no strong Republican candidates on the ballot.

That changed shortly after I announced my candidacy. The son of a well-known, popular Republican state senator announced he was running for the seat, too. In an instant, I went from a likely second-place finisher to a certain loser. Even people who wanted to be supportive told me that losing would be a good learning experience.

At thirty-one years old, conventional wisdom was I was too young and had no name recognition to beat either candidate. I was demoralized and decided my only option was to work myself to exhaustion just to stave off regret about my impulsive decision to run. I made it a point to stay away from the folks who claimed to be experts on Syracuse politics, because they depressed me with their patronizing, "better luck next time" certainty about the upcoming election results. Soon I was viewed not only as a certain loser but also as an outsider who did not welcome the self-proclaimed experts' advice.

A few people reminded me I was not without strengths. I knew how to put together campaigns; I could carry a message of change; and while I had no name recognition, I could rectify that by going door-to-door and raising money. I embraced a punishing schedule. I worked at the law firm, changed my shoes at the end of the workday, left the office, and knocked on doors across the city. My plan was to knock on thousands of doors so no one would be able to say I hadn't worked hard.

Every night I was in a different neighborhood. Sometimes I had company. My friend Pete Kavanaugh, a retired high-school principal, would often join me. On many occasions, the person who opened the door and saw him would say, "Mr. Kavanaugh, I am a much better person now. I have a house and children." Without missing a beat, Kavanaugh would say, "Well then, I need you to vote for this lady, Stephanie Miner." And the homeowner would say, "Oh, absolutely, Mr. Kavanaugh. You can count on me." I would stand and smile.

My friends helped organized small-dollar fundraising events. The firm's clients were generous, as were several unions. My grandfather Ralph Miner attended one house party. I had the impression he was donating because he loved me but thought my candidacy was a flight of fancy. After the event, he excitedly told me he was surprised to learn the head of the teachers union was supporting me. "They only support good candidates," he proclaimed, and beamed at the notion I was a serious candidate.

We raised enough money to allow us to hire the innovative and creative local ad agency Romanelli Communication. Romanelli determined that one cost-effective way to raise my name recognition was to buy billboard space, and if we committed to buy them early, they'd be cheap. Weeks after making the commitment, almost forty billboards with a five-foot-high cropped headshot of me next to the slogan "Elect a Real Fighter to the Common Council" went up across Syracuse.

The day the billboards appeared, my campaign manager called me from a car, unable to speak through her laughter. All I could hear her say to the car's driver was, "Turn around, go by it again." Between guffaws, she said she had fielded lots of calls about one billboard in a "great location" on one of Syracuse's busiest roads, but, she said, "It's next to Adult World."

She explained that the billboard's position made it look as if my huge face and slogan were advertising Adult World, a porn-video emporium—not an ideal association for a female candidate. Others asked jokingly what type of voter I was seeking to attract. I don't remember how we dealt with the situation, but I do remember the constant laughter it inspired.

I was pleased when the first media interview, including a photo taken by the weekly outlet's photographer, was published, until I learned people were calling the picture "the babe shot." There was no discussion about the interview. While the picture was just a headshot, it was used to objectify me. It made me uncomfortable, but I didn't know how to react.

Later, my then website, stephanieminer.com, was hacked. The links to the state and county parties were changed to take users to a porn site advertising the services of teenage Asian girls. I look back with some chagrin that I played it off as amusing. "It's somewhat laughable, but still irritating,"[5] I told the daily newspaper. I did not file a police report and had no idea who hacked the site. I thought it was low-key dirty tricks and, perhaps, evidence I was being seen as a real threat. I never thought about it as evidence of misogyny or as particularly unfair.

My youth and my introverted nature made me something of an outsider

---

5. Michelle Breidenbach, "Council Hopeful's Web Site Hacked," *Post-Standard*, October 25, 2001.

to people deeply ensconced in Syracuse's political universe. I never thought it was related to my gender. Women had successfully run for the city council for almost thirty years. The teasing about the billboard location, the objectification, and the hacking was evidence, I told myself at the time, that I was being subjected to hardball tactics. Looking back, I think I used laughter to deflect because I didn't know how to confront sexism. I was afraid if I did bring attention to it people would not like me and not vote for me. Sadly, as I think about it today, I think the choice is still the same. I'm not sure that if I had called attention to the objectification, it would have mattered. It may have cost me votes by giving my opponents the opportunity to say I was "too sensitive" for political office. I wanted to be elected and join the club of elected officials. Then, as now, female candidates were expected to endure sexism as a price of admission. It's unfair, but, in my view, it is the reality of the system.

## Underdogs Bite

Romanelli created fifteen-second commercials to be shown on local cable stations, using my tagline "Paid for by Friends of Miner, like me." Since there was also a hotly contested mayoral primary happening that year, we decided to unveil my television commercials the day of the primary, when everybody would be watching the results on television.

It was a beautiful September day, and I was working in my law office when I got a call from the senior partner in New York City. When I got on the phone, he asked me a question about a legal matter and then said, "Something has happened here. A plane flew into a building; it's very strange." I hung up, and within moments, the office manager came around to tell us planes had flown into the World Trade Center and our office was closing.

The world changed that moment, and my campaign commercials were the last thing on my mind. Over the next couple of weeks, I watched a lot of television, I went to memorials, and I learned about people connected to the Syracuse community who died in the attacks.

It seemed the only thing to do was to try to re-create some normalcy, and I went back to campaigning with a heavier heart and more uncertainty than ever. One day I was by myself, walking door to door, and I saw a gentleman in his late sixties working in his yard. We talked about the neighborhood and the state of the city, and I gave him my pitch. He looked me and said, "Everyone always says they are going to change things, but they never do." With no other material left, I said to him, "I'll tell you what, do I look like everyone else?" And he laughingly said, "You sure don't." I continued, "Just give me a chance." He shook his head and said he would think about it.

I gave that campaign my all. I was a definite underdog, and after the election, I didn't want to feel there was more I could have done. The final weekend before Election Day, I made hundreds of calls reminding people to vote. I received several pleasant responses from people saying they would vote for me because I was personally calling.

After an exhausting seventy-two hours of get-out-the-vote efforts, I went home, played my answering machine, and heard my own voice exhorting me to vote for me in the upcoming election. I had been so tired I hadn't even realized I'd called and left a message on my own answering machine.

Two other first-time candidates, Marty Masterpole and Rory McMahon, ran that year. The three of us campaigned together, and I often saw more of them than their wives did—something I'd be reminded of when each asked me discreetly not to mention to their wives how much fun we were having.

The general election finally arrived on November 6, 2001. On Election Day in Syracuse, there is a tradition of candidates, officeholders, and the community gathering to end the campaign with a pasta lunch in the basement of a Catholic grammar school. It's a lovely event, but I was too nervous to enjoy it. All I could muster was to push food around my plate.

I was sitting with Masterpole and McMahon. Like me, McMahon was anxious—not only was he on the ballot, but his wife was days away from giving birth to their first child. When McMahon and I failed to respond to Masterpole's cheerful banter, he suggested we leave and go to a bar. Immediately, we agreed. As we left the packed room of politicians, wannabes, and community organizers, we each sputtered separate fictions of events we needed to attend.

When we convened at the bar, Masterpole regaled us with a story about a sound truck he had rented that day to travel his district telling people to vote for him, which had, unsurprisingly, gotten him in trouble with a police officer who reminded him there was a noise ordinance prohibiting sound trucks. McMahon kept looking at his phone, and I tried to be supportive by telling him that everything was going to be fine, meaning with his pregnant wife.

McMahon nodded and said he wished there was another week of the campaign because he thought he could win with more time, and he predicted that I would win. I told him not only would I lose, but I wouldn't survive another day of a campaign. Masterpole cheerfully interrupted our gloom, saying, "I think I'm going to win!" That night when the votes were counted, McMahon had eked out an upset victory, and Masterpole's race was too close to call.[6] Masterpole was eventually declared the winner and spent the next couple of years being called "Landslide."

I had waited for the results at a friend's house. The house was filled with excitement, but I was decidedly queasy. I asked John F. X. Mannion what he thought would happen. Jack, as he was called, was an insurance executive who had been active in democratic politics for years. Completely separately, though, he was someone who was becoming exceedingly important to me. What I wanted him to tell me was that I would win. Instead, he said, "I think it's all going to be fine." I told him that wasn't what I wanted him to say, and he replied, "Well, that's what I think." His candor made his opinion carry more weight, and it's one of the reasons I would eventually marry him.

My college friend Michele Gerroir, who had come to the party to support me, recognized my unease and escorted me out of the house. It was a dark, clear night, and flowering mums and Halloween decorations were illuminated on the porches and stoops of the surrounding houses. It was warm enough that we weren't wearing jackets, but I knew by the smell of the air that would soon change. As we crunched over dead leaves on the sidewalk to a street corner out of sight of my election party, Gerroir asked how I was feeling. I said I was exhausted, but "there is nothing else I could have done. If I lose, I know I did my best." She nodded.

We walked back to the house, and I thought the frost would come soon and the long hours of my campaign had robbed my opportunity to enjoy autumn. I crossed the threshold into a light-filled room and heard the television announcer say, "In one of the biggest surprises of the night, newcomer

6. Luis Perez and Maureen Sieh, "Democrats Stampede to City Council—They'll Have 7–2 Majority, Bea Gonzalez First Hispanic Elected to Council," *Post-Standard*, November 7, 2001.

Stephanie Miner is the top vote getter in the councilor at-large race."[7] A huge, spontaneous cheer filled the house as the announcer went on to say I had shocked conventional wisdom by beating a well-liked incumbent and the state senator's son.

I was stunned. Jack looked at me and said, "I told you you would win." He had not. But he was right, too. I was, as I had told Mario Cuomo seven years earlier, fine, and this time the red flush was from excitement.

7. Dan Cummings, WSYR-TV, November 6, 2001.

# Election

## Becoming Madam Mayor

Standing in front of the door, I reminded myself to focus and then knocked. Knocking on doors, debates, forums, neighborhood meetings, house parties, and events—a thousand, maybe ten thousand, personal interactions determining if I was worthy of a vote. The homeowner, an older gentleman, came to the door and I introduced myself. He took a long look and said, "You're not a dragon; you're a little girl." I responded that I was a lot younger looking when I started running for mayor. He laughed and gestured for me to sit down.

It was a successful interaction, but I knew my frenetic grassroots campaigning, trying to convince one voter at a time, was not a successful strategy. The scale of the mayoral campaign was too big. I would have to write my own playbook to defeat the stereotypes being employed by my opponents to become "Madam Mayor."

## Syracuse 2009

With a total area of 25.6 square miles, Syracuse is a condensed, old city composed of distinct neighborhoods encircling a downtown. Incorporated as a city in 1848, its history is replete with indices of ingenuity helping to build the United States—the Erie Canal, the Solvay process, and Carrier Air Conditioning.

Yet by 2009, while still the fifth-largest city in New York State, it had lost one-third of its population since 1950.[1] Syracuse's tax revenues were growing at an anemic 3.7 percent while its expenditures were growing an average rate of 4 percent. The city had difficulty raising revenue from property tax because nearly half of its property was tax-exempt, and a significant number of the remaining properties were tax-delinquent.

The once flourishing manufacturing base, with its high-paying jobs, had been replaced by lower-paying service jobs, primarily in the education and health sectors.[2] At least 25 percent of the families living in the city were living in poverty, the second-highest rate for any city in the state. The unemployment rate, at almost 9 percent, was higher than the statewide rate.

People may not have known the poverty rates, but residents witnessed the change in economic circumstances. We knew people who were struggling financially. We worried about crime. We lived with a school system struggling to graduate students. We participated in discussions about people leaving. Where once each unique neighborhood was dense and primarily owner-occupied, vacant buildings were now common, as was rental property. These were the realities of a city that had been on a long and steady slide in the wrong direction.

The mayoral election of 2009 would be an open contest. The Democratic incumbent, Matthew J. Driscoll, had exhausted the city's two-term limit. The Syracuse mayor's seat is considered a Democratic seat, but a Republican was elected in 1997 and held office as recently as 2001. The last race had been the closest mayoral election in eighty years, with the Democratic incumbent ultimately prevailing by a margin of 3.6 percent.[3] The mayor's office was important, and recent history indicated that a candidate from either party could prevail.

I would like to say I engaged in a thoughtful, rational process to decide to run for mayor, but I did not. It was an alchemy of instincts, feelings, and

1. In 2009, the population was approximately 145,170. Office of the New York State Comptroller. "New York Cities: An Economic and Fiscal Analysis 1980–2010," September 2012, p. 2. https://www.osc.state.ny.us/files/local-government/publications/pdf/nyc report2012.pdf.

2. Federal Reserve Bank of New York, "Syracuse Metro Area," https://www.newyorkfed .org/regional-economy/profiles/Syracuse.

3. Frederic Pierce and John Mariani, "Driscoll Survives—It's the Closest Syracuse Mayor's Race in 80 years," *Post Standard*, November 9, 2005.

personal preferences. By this time, 2008, Jack and I were married. I first met Jack when I worked for Mario Cuomo. As a prominent Cuomo supporter, I was tasked by my bosses with personally inviting Jack to gubernatorial visits or relaying messages. While friendly and charming, Jack was simply another personality to keep happy during a tough gubernatorial campaign.

After Cuomo's loss, Jack suggested I could work at Unity Mutual Life Insurance Company. With few options, I accepted the offer and briefly worked for his son Patrick before I left to go to law school in Buffalo. While Jack was the chief executive officer, my interactions with him were limited to occasional discussions about politics.

During law school, for reasons I don't remember, the conversations started becoming more frequent. He was smart, unpredictable, charming, and the most interesting person I had ever met. And he knew he was all of those things, but somehow, he was still intriguing and gracious. Somewhere during these conversations, a real and deep friendship was born. I cared about him and wanted and needed his opinions. I looked forward to the daily calls and made mental reminders to tell of my triumphs and disasters. He made each better.

Given the thirty-eight-year age difference, I never consciously realized the relationship was evolving into something more intense. It seemed impossible, but it had changed. I was certain of two things: he had become the most important person in my life and second it scared me. While I felt like he had dropped a bomb in my life, he made it seem simple. We loved each other and what else mattered, but, of course, a lot of things did matter. It was unconventional and would and did subject us to ridicule. Some people would never understand, some people would never try to understand, and some people would just be mean. Being with Jack was the craziest thing I ever contemplated, but the alternative, being without him, was inconceivable. While I knew it was never going to be easy, there simply could be no me without him.

By 2008, I'd also become a partner at my law firm, Blitman & King, but security was not excitement. In my two terms on the city council, I experienced the despair of defeat and the exaltation of victory—especially with the improbably named "Destiny USA" project. After my surprise election to the city council in 2001, I was thrown into a political cauldron over a $1.7 billion mall development plan. Destiny USA was being touted as the largest retail mall in the country. Supporters of the project, including almost every elected official at every level of government, business interest group, and local media outlets, urged city officials to provide forty-five years of tax breaks and subsidies worth hundreds of millions of dollars to the Pyramid companies, a local developer, to build this eye-popping project.

After a quick and scarring learning curve, I realized the developer had not made any enforceable commitment to build the promised Taj Mahal–like edifice. In a bruising eight-year battle, I strenuously argued, often alone, that the project was corporate welfare and the developer's promises illusory. I lost several searing battles and, ultimately, the war,[4] when the developer received all its requested benefits. Many predicted at the time, in 2006, that my opposition to Destiny signaled the end of my nascent political career, but I was sure the developer was taking advantage of the community's hopes for economic revitalization.

As so often happens in politics, the perception of my political fortune changed after the developer repeatedly failed to deliver anything resembling its public promises. More egregiously, the developer continued collecting huge public subsidies.[5] By 2009, I had become a David who fought Goliath. My advocacy was perceived as courageous and correct. With that perception came recruitment efforts for me to run for the state legislature, Congress, and county executive.

I would be lying if I said I wasn't flattered by the attention. Jack suggested I focus on the job I wanted, not the political campaign others were encouraging me to make. While local government is not glamorous, it was fascinating to me and impacted the front lines of people's lives—the roads they drove, the schools their children attended, the safety of their neighborhoods. I learned ideas mattered in small ways, like solving a school-busing issue for a constituent, and large ways, such as fighting the behemoth Destiny project. Both were consequential and rewarding.

In city government, there was always something new to learn about the people you saw in grocery stores, ran into in restaurants, and lived next to as neighbors. I enjoyed listening to people explain the issues, untangling

4. Marnie Eisenstadt, "Stephanie Miner, Out on a Limb—Can a Contentious Policy Wonk Who Deflects Questions About Her Marriage Be Elected Mayor? This Born Public Servant May Be Driven Enough to Find Out," *Post-Standard*, December 3, 2006.

5. Mike McAndrew and Jeff Rea, "Without Promised Expansions, Pyramid Collects Millions—Congel, Partners Gather $9 Million a Year in Tax Breaks on Malls in Syracuse, Watertown, and Utica," *Post-Standard*, October 1, 2006.

the components of a problem, and getting instant feedback on proposed solutions. I took deep dives into policy reading lots of academic studies on municipal governance, learned about policy wonks advocating successful civic solutions, and signed up for think tank publications. I was voracious in an effort to find civic solutions by reviewing academic, best practices, and any other theory that came to my attention.

I was interested in the work, and Destiny had demonstrated to me that once I felt strongly about a position, I would be outspoken regardless of the strength of the opposition. My reserved nature did not qualify me as a natural politician, but I felt my bookish sensibility could compensate in a city desperate for new ideas. With all of this in mind, I decided to run for mayor.

Absent from my thought process was the role my gender would play in a campaign. Syracuse was a relatively progressive city, several women had been elected to the city council since 1970, and a female county executive was elected in 2007. In both 2001 and 2005, a woman had been a serious contender for the mayor's office. Given these facts, I thought my gender would not pose a significant challenge to getting elected.

If I had researched the issue, I would have discovered that the percentage of women who won mayoral elections was about 15 percent nationwide.[6] Thus, winning the mayoral election would make me an outlier,[7] something I'd never considered myself to be.

Syracuse is an old city with a rich history. That history is revealing, but it can also be stultifying. While some women had been elected, for much of its history, Syracuse was governed by the same types of people:[8] white men with fathers and grandfathers who'd once held office.[9] It was not

---

6. Fernand Ferreira and Joseph Gyourko, "Does Gender Matter for Political Leadership? The Case of U.S. Mayors," *National Bureau of Economic Research* 1767 (December 2011): figure 1 and 2, https://www.nber.org/system/files/working_papers/w17671/w17671.pdf.

7. Mirya R. Holman, "Women in Local Government: What We Know and Where We Go from Here," *State and Local Government Review* 49, no. 4 (December 2017): 285–296.

8. This phenomenon is not unique to Syracuse. Political parties engage in "gendered recruitment," limiting the number of women recruited for office—even when the local parties are open to women running, because local party leaders are largely men who recruit from networks of people they know, which are mostly men. Melody Crowder-Meyer, "Gendered Recruitment Without Trying," *Politics & Gender* 9 (2013): 390–413.

9. Research has found local politics are dominated by white elites. Jessica Trounstine, "Dominant Regimes and the Demise of Urban Democracy," *Journal of Politic* 68 (2006): 879–893.

uncommon to see the same last names on ballots—Hancock, Walsh, and Young.

This resulted in a government led by people with the same predictable voices and experiences. At some point, those voices turned into a choir embracing and trumpeting easy solutions. It was a political version of a get-rich-quick scheme: chase a business or project and claim it would bring about a transformational change for the community when the deal was announced. But that transformation rarely happened.

The Destiny USA project was just one example of this flawed approach. Even though the promised project never materialized, the developers were able to become even more wealthy on public benefits, and the single largest piece of taxable property in Syracuse was granted tax-free status for forty-five years. The most obvious losers were the children who attended the Syracuse City School District, which had lost millions of dollars in public funding. In exchange, Syracuse got a standard mall, which would eventually confront bankruptcy.

It was just one of a series of legislative decisions that failed to benefit the people of Syracuse. Between 1995 and 2000, $2 billion in grants, tax-abatement financing, and utility benefits were given to business interests. Despite the promises of revitalization, economic growth rarely followed. Since 2000, residents had been told the Destiny project would create wholesale economic revitalization, every city school system building would be renovated, and there would be a modernized airport. By 2009, none had occurred. After so many disappointments, residents had understandably developed a deep-seated cynicism about local government.

I wanted to show a different way. Syracuse had the ingredients to become a modern and innovative city. It was home to several colleges and universities, had a highly educated, hardworking population, and a history of ingenuity. Even Syracuse's relatively small size, a population of just under 150,000, was an asset. I envisioned making civic change almost in terms of an equation: establish goals, measure the progress, tweak a policy to ensure successful outcomes, or change it altogether if it was not meeting benchmarks.

I wanted to build a candidacy around ideas: an efficient, modern government utilizing creative public policy; smart economic development, not corporate welfare; an education system offering opportunity to everyone, not the lucky few; and overall innovation in the design and execution of municipal policy to benefit the entire community. While I knew that trying to do things differently would challenge the system, it was what I'd been indoctrinated to believe good leaders did. They challenged the status quo with new ideas, solved problems, and, in the process, fulfilled the promise of democracy.

## The Team

The open mayoral seat would attract serious challengers. I needed a strong team to get elected. I wanted my friend and fellow city councilor Bill Ryan to be a part of that team. In politics, the concept of friendship is anything but simple. I talked with Ryan about all things political, but he was a potential candidate, too. Jack suggested I talk to Ryan about the obvious issue, and I reluctantly agreed.

The fateful day arrived for the difficult discussion. As soon as Ryan and I sat down for lunch, I tried to start, but Ryan interrupted, saying, "I don't even know why I look at the menu, I always get the same thing." I nodded and tried again, only to have the waitress arrive to take our order. After she left, I got as far as, "Bill . . ." and he interrupted again. It was not going to plan. With no other options, I blurted out, "I want to be friends, but I've decided to run for mayor. If you run, I understand, and I just want you to know I'd like us to be friends when it's over." With an effortless laugh, he said, "I know. I'm not going to run; I'm going to support you." Relieved, I asked why he made me struggle. He said, "I've been waiting for you to ask me." It proved to be an excellent lesson that one should never presume support and people deserve to be explicitly asked for it.

Ryan went on to tell me I needed to ask for "Bruce's support." The "Bruce" he was referring to was Bruce Connor, a retired firefighter, a locksmith, the owner of a car-detailing business, and a respected leader in Syracuse's Black community. On any given day, you could see his locksmith van at a host of locations, where he was working and, most importantly, talking to people. If all politics is truly local, everyone needs a Bruce Connor.

The Black community in Syracuse had a long history of being taken advantage of, ignored, and marginalized by power brokers, decision-makers, and elected officials.[10] There were three people of color who had announced

---

10. Carmela Monk, "15th Ward's Legacy—Black Community Lost to '60s Urban Renewal," *Post Standard*, February 23, 1989.

they were going to run in the Democratic primary.[11] I was not going to take the community for granted, nor was I going to cede the community to other candidates. To get support, I needed the right people associated with me to talk, listen, and relay messages.

I knew Connor and liked him, but Ryan was right. I needed to ask him to help me. When Ryan and I met with Connor, I told Connor I wanted and needed his help to get elected. He just nodded and said that because I had Ryan's blessing, he would think about it. I was crestfallen until Ryan gleefully explained Connor would test me to see if I would return his calls, listen to his advice, and allow him to be a full member of the team. When I said that's what I told him I would do, Ryan responded that most people say they will, but they don't. "You will," he said.

Sure enough, Connor and I began meeting every morning and he called me throughout the day to relay information. He told me which leaders I needed to call, which ones I needed to sit down and meet, and those who could be trusted. To know a community is to know who to approach, when to listen, and when to ask.

I thought as a city councilor I knew the important leaders in the Black community, but I did not. Leaders are present in all walks of life. They come in different shapes and sizes and from multiple places. Connor guided me through the leaders from the entire community: the pastors, coaches, barbers, matriarchs, renowned athletes, and business owners. To a person, everyone in the Black community I reached out to would respond, "Bruce's friend?" It was never city councilor, mayor hopeful, or lady candidate, just "Bruce's friend."

When I affirmed, indeed, I was "Bruce's friend," a meeting would be scheduled. At the meeting, I would listen and answer questions. I could never read people's reactions to get a sense of how a meeting went and would have to wait for Connor to tell me if I passed. If I did, I would get invited to meet the leader's group at the block party, the graduation party, the breakfast clutch, anniversary celebrations, and, of course, church.

Being asked to come to church was a big deal, because it meant the pastor deemed me worthy of the opportunity to address the congregation. I was explicitly told Black folks in church have the highest expectations for the service. The best music, the best speakers, the best suits and hats, the best

11. Alfonso Davis, Carmen Harlow, and Bea Gonzalez.

announcements, the best dancing, the best clapping, and, if you are lucky, afterward, the best food.

As a Catholic, I was used to the forty-five-minute obligation on Sunday. Black churches, in contrast, believed that if people are going to congregate to worship God, the service should be joyously compelling. It had to be to keep people worshipping for hours at a time.

At my first invitation to address a congregation, I sat on the edge of the pew and the service came and went without the expected invitation for me to speak. After the service ended, the pastor told Connor I looked so nervous he felt bad putting me on the spot. When the next invitation came, I tried not to look as nervous as I felt. When I was called to speak, the choir head introduced me and pulled down the microphone at the podium for me to use. It was to become my signature move. I got to the microphone and paraphrased a line from a B. B. King song saying, "I'd like to live the love you sing about," and the congregation cheered with a force of love and positivity I would never forget. I was hooked and started looking forward, for the first time in my life, to going to church. Connor laughed and said, "I was catching the spirit."

Sunday at a traditional Black church was also a lesson in how campaigning could make you a better person and, hopefully, a better public servant. To witness the service, the community, and the love was to understand how foundational the church was in the lives of its members. My presence and acceptance in Black churches ensured I was not a stranger in their world, and, in turn, they were not strangers in mine. With that as a basis, we could form relationships to enable me to ascertain and represent their interests.

My team was in immediate need of a policy person and a campaign manager. There was only one person I thought could fill the policy role. With flaming red hair, a full red beard, freckles, and a skinny body as if he gave his last potato to his mother, Andrew Moynihan Maxwell, age twenty-five, was a poster boy for policy wonks. He worked in the city's community development department, an office I regularly criticized for mismanaging budgets, development projects, and personnel. Yet he was knowledgeable and always composed, even under my harshest scrutiny.

One night, during a contentious neighborhood meeting, I observed Maxwell endure the residents' ire with City Hall. It was clear they respected Maxwell but not his bosses. When I told him he was doing a good job, he gave me a forlorn smile. I asked him if he would meet me to talk about the city.

We met shortly after, and I opened our meeting by asking him how he thought city government could be better. Like a dam was breached, he poured forth ideas and examples from the country and across the world. Making a passionate speech about Syracuse, he said he wanted to, and knew he could, make things better if someone would listen. He finished with, "I'd like to help you if I can." A week later, I told him I wanted him to put together all my policy positions, but I could not pay him. He shocked me by answering, "Don't worry about that."

As for a campaign manager, it is an important and difficult position to fill. You're asking someone to uproot their life for a year, work impossibly long hours for a candidate who may not be able to raise money, run a good campaign, or even pay you, and, in the end, shoulder the blame for a loss. A candidate always gets credit for the win and a campaign manager responsibility for the loss. Great work, if you can get it!

As I was searching, I got a phone call about a potential manager from Geneva, New York, who had worked on a couple of unsuccessful congressional campaigns upstate. I sent him an email and we arranged an early morning breakfast meeting.

The morning of the meeting, central New York got hit by a snowstorm. As Jack and I drove to a diner near Syracuse University, I assumed the meeting would get canceled because of the weather. Jack looked out the window and said, "There's your guy." Standing next to an old Saab was a young guy with no winter jacket, wearing a suit that was too tight and smoking a cigarette.

Indeed, that guy walked into the diner and introduced himself as Dan McNally. When I said I thought we'd have to cancel because of the weather, he said he left his home early to make sure that didn't happen. McNally told us about his political management experience, which was thin, and told us what he would expect for a salary. When we ended the meeting, I told him I would be in touch.

As we walked to our car, Jack asked me what I thought. "He doesn't have a lot of experience and I don't know how to pay him," I said. Jack responded, "You should snatch him up right now, today. He's a superstar, don't wait." Taken aback, I probed Jack about how, after such a short interaction, he was so sure McNally was a talent. Jack pointed to McNally planning to avoid the snowstorm, his use of language at our meeting, and his overall focus. McNally, Jack said, wanted the job; he was smart, and he would do what was necessary to win. It was clear to Jack, and it turned out he was right.

When I offered him the job, McNally accepted instantly. He grew a beard to match Maxwell's and they became known as "black beard and red beard." Ryan quickly nicknamed the team "the kids." When I pointed out he was on the team, too, he told me his wife had accused him of being a kid more than once.

## Campaign Plan

Shortly after getting "the kids" onboard, I left Blitman & King to focus exclusively on my campaign. The race for mayor would have three parts: the designation by the Democratic Party, the primary election, and the general election. The designated candidate would be the person who successfully received a simple majority of weighted votes[12] by members of the Syracuse Democratic Committee. Given the importance of the office, the low barrier to force a primary, and our unruly nature as Democrats, it was a forgone conclusion there would be a primary.

The primary was the most important part of the race. Democrats outnumbered Republicans by a margin of three-to-one and the primary was held in September, a few weeks before the general election.[13] These two factors meant the Democrat who won the primary was presumed to be the likely winner of the general election. But Republicans had won in Syracuse, so winning was a presumption, not a guarantee.

I skipped a big announcement in favor of simply telling the newspaper I intended to run. The next order of business was putting together the all-important campaign plan grounded in an attainable budget. While I had raised money as a city council candidate, raising it for the mayor's race would be on a completely different scale. I'd raised about $60,000 for the

12. Each committee person has an assigned number of votes based on the votes the Democratic candidate for governor receives in a general election in the committee person's election district. Thus, the Democratic areas have more "weight" in the designation process because each person has more assigned votes.

13. Onondaga County Board of Elections, City of Syracuse Enrollment Data. http://on gov.net/elections/Statistics.html.

first of my two city council races; for the mayoral race, I'd have to raise at least $300,000.

I couldn't fathom how I was going to raise that much money. When confronted with these facts, Jack was optimistic, telling me, "It will be tough, but I think we can do it." On occasion, he would punctuate that with, "You're the best candidate; people will recognize that." I wasn't so sure.

McNally put together a draft budget projecting the campaign would raise $27,000 a month and keeping expenses level at $4,600 a month, meaning I'd have to raise $302,000 by the primary, or $900 a day.

The earliest expensive item was a benchmark poll that cost $26,500. This poll provides important data before the real campaign begins. The information helps the campaign design a successful narrative. While some campaigns spend hundreds of thousands of dollars to conduct weekly polls, if we met our audacious budget goals, we would execute three polls: the all-important benchmark; one in midsummer to see if my message was resonating with voters; and assuming I won the primary, one right before the general to see if I was on track to win.

The benchmark poll of likely Democratic voters was conducted in early April, and it revealed that most voters didn't know who I was. More important, it showed voters were looking for someone who understood their concerns, could implement effective change, and be tough enough to get the job done.

Voters' desires lined up with why I wanted to be mayor. I believed I was a person who advocated for people's interests, understood issues, and could bring change by implementing smart policies. This reinforced my belief that voters wanted the type of leader I thought I could be: a person who challenges the status quo.

For me to win, the poll found I needed to convey this message:

Supporters of Stephanie Miner say the city needs a mayor who can bring new energy and new ideas to city government and will be tough enough to make the changes that need to be made. Stephanie Miner has earned a reputation as a tough, no-nonsense leader. She has not been afraid to stand up for what she believes in and has consistently fought to protect the interests of average city residents and taxpayers. We need a tough leader like Stephanie Miner who can bring a new outlook to city hall and who can be counted on to demand accountability and results.

The other major early expense was access to a voter contact system called the Voter Activation Network (VAN), a voter database software program and web-hosting service used by Democratic campaigns and nonprofit organizations. The company that created this tool was founded in 2001 and had become by 2009 the largest partisan provider of campaign-compliance software.[14] It is available across the country and the subscriber tailors it to a specific district.

The VAN was a revolutionary technological tool that provided a wealth of information for our campaign. We could build lists of the right voters to contact—those who vote in Democratic primaries, and those who vote only in general elections. These names could be sorted into lists by neighborhood and street. We could even use it for fundraising by seeing who had donated to local campaigns in the past. Not surprisingly, the VAN program was expensive.

We needed to pay for the poll and the VAN early, when we had the least amount of money. In addition, we needed money for computers, paper, phones, and salaries. The biggest expense, almost half of our goal of $300,000, would be budgeted for television ads and direct mail. Virtually the entire budget was aimed at getting my message to voters. If we could raise the necessary money, we could get the story out and I would win. If we failed, I would lose.

## Mother's Milk

People give money to candidates for a variety of reasons. Some are noble: they believe the candidate is a good person, will do a good job, and has good ideas. Those donors usually in give in small amounts, $20 or $50, matching the donor's capacity to give or level of interest in local government.

On the other hand, the people who donate the most money do it on the basis of self-interest. This is a particularly stark divide in local elections. People seldom have a passion for local government policy. Sure, they want good, open, and transparent government, but it's easier to motivate someone to give money based on their feelings about immigration, reproductive freedom, or health-care policy than zoning rules.

Yet, zoning and planning regulations impact real estate developers.

14. NGP VAN. https://www.ngpvan.com/about/.

Consequently, they tend to be the biggest donors in local elections. They will, of course, say they give lots of money to ensure good government and may even admit they want access to the officeholder. Given my fierce opposition to the developers of the Destiny USA project, I started from a losing position in the money race.

Our goal was to raise sufficient money to spend exactly enough on the right things and not a penny more. I watched McNally agonize over spending $100 on paper for the printer, comparison shop for phone lines, and ask for donations of computers and phones. I listened to my campaign treasurer, Martha Maywalt, give advance warnings about bills coming due. Our donated campaign headquarters was nicknamed "the cave." To save money, the staff wore gloves and wrapped themselves in blankets instead of turning on the heat.

To raise money, I needed to engage in "call time." This is when a candidate for office calls potential donors personally to ask for money. My campaign would sort through campaign finance reports, then through the VAN program, and eventually use internet searches to identify potential donors. I got a list with a person's name, work, home, and cell phone numbers, along with a little information about them. But essentially, I was a stranger asking people for money. One-third of our money was to be raised this way, which meant performing call time for several hours every day.

I was asking a lot of people to do things for me, so I needed to make the calls. I sat down with the first list—people who had previously donated to Syracuse mayoral campaigns—and started calling. I was thankful when the first batch of names did not answer, and I could just leave a message. The next batch consisted mainly of wrong numbers. When I finally got a potential donor on the phone, I choked and couldn't ask for money. Instead, I asked the would-be donor, in this case a local construction company, if I could see their porous asphalt products. At the visit, I also failed to ask for a donation, though I could tell my hosts expected to be asked.

This cycle of failing to ask for money, and instead asking for a tour or coffee, continued. I knew I was choking, but I couldn't find it in me to ask a stranger for money. It was antithetical to who I was and felt immoral. It was such a block that Jack would ask me every time we talked if I had asked someone for money. McNally heard me sheepishly say no and said to me, "One day you're going to get tired of having coffee."

As I struggled during call time, Jack was putting together his own strategy. He sent a letter to hundreds of his contacts asking for a campaign donation. Shortly after the letter was mailed, the campaign started receiving checks and notes from a host of people who had little connection to Syracuse but a bond with Jack. Jack had a host of passionate beliefs; insurance reform, a united Ireland, immigration, All Hallows High School, and Notre Dame, to name a few. Through these causes, he had assembled a huge and diverse network, which he called upon to financially support my candidacy. While it made me cringe to think about him asking people to donate to my campaign, it had the opposite effect on him. It was a way for him to talk me up, and how could that be embarrassing? This fundraising project and the transfer of the money I had left over in my council account ($110,000) was lucrative enough to help carry the campaign through the beginning months when I was struggling to ask for money.

## Challengers

Carmen Harlow, a former county legislator, and Alfonso Davis, a community activist, both announced they would be running in the Democratic primary. While neither of them had a record of garnering the level of support necessary to be a serious contender in a citywide race, politics always offers surprises.

The biggest surprise so far was the early withdrawal of the city council president Bethaida "Bea" Gonzalez. She was the first candidate to officially declare she was running for mayor in October 2008, but by February 2009, her campaign had stalled, and she dropped out of the race in March. Despite this, she would have an outsize role in the campaign.

In early spring, my only remaining serious Democrat opponent was Joseph Nicoletti. Nicoletti had been a staple of Syracuse politics since the 1970s, when he started working in Syracuse's parks department for the charming and hugely popular mayor at the time, Lee Alexander.[15]

Preternaturally gregarious, Nicoletti always seemed to be running for office. He had run or threatened to run for mayor in 1985, 1993, and

15. Lee Alexander, a legend in Syracuse, was mayor from 1970 to 1985. During those years, he was regarded as a telegenic spokesman for urban America. After leaving office, Alexander was convicted for racketeering, tax evasion, and conspiracy related to a $1.5 million kickback scheme conducted while he was in office. Lawrence Van Gelder, "Lee Alexander, 69, Mayor Whose Career Ended in Jail," New York Times, December 27, 1996.

2001.[16] He did not promulgate any new ideas or vision about the city; he just wanted to be mayor. Yet he was formidable. He had huge name recognition, knew the political system intimately, and had raised copious amounts of money.

In early spring, several people said they had received calls asking them to participate in a mayoral poll. While the pollster wasn't identified, it was clear it was on Nicoletti's behalf. The poll tested several messages, including responses to questions about my temperament, insinuating I was shrill and could not get along with anyone. I was somewhat gleeful when I heard this. I thought it would backfire, since it was the definition of sexism to imply (or state outright) that a woman is not fit for office because of her temperament.

Nicoletti, in my view, was spending lots of money on a fatal campaign strategy. I assumed I wouldn't have to deal with the issue because the public reaction would immediately stop the message and it would rebound to my benefit. The reality was that the issue of gender would be relevant in ways I could not fathom.

## Hanging My Soul on the Back of the Door

McNally told me he had an idea to make call time more successful. He wanted to have someone in the room with me who would keep it on track. I bristled at the thought that I needed a babysitter, but I was in no position to fight because I was failing. He suggested our first intern, Ashley Sulewski, for the role.

Sulewski came into the call-time room, and I told her, "I feel like I close the door and hang my soul on the back of it." To relieve the pressure, I'd decided to compartmentalize the part of myself making the "asks" from the version of myself I was most comfortable with. This separation was not something I wanted anyone to witness, I told her, but since she had to be there, nothing I said or did could be shared outside the room.

She agreed and handed me the first list and mentioned that the person on the top had given $5,000[17] to a Democratic congressional candidate and

16.  Tim Knauss, "Joe Nicoletti Joins Syracuse Mayor's Race, Touting His Experience," February 23, 2017. https://www.syracuse.com/news/2017/02/joe_nicoletti_joins_syracu se_mayors_race_touting_his_experience.html.

17.  While $5,000 would have broken campaign finance laws for an individual contrib- uting, many people give the maximum amount in their individual name, and then have

that he should give me at least a thousand. "You're absolutely right," I said as I picked up the phone to call the potential donor. I got through my pitch and with the $5,000 number in my mind, I asked for a $1,000. The donor said he would give me $500 to start and more later if my performance merited it.

I'm not sure there really was a $5,000 donation. I think it was a McNally and Sulewski strategy to tap my competitive streak. In any event, it worked. To relieve my stress during these calls, I let loose with a string of four-letter expletives when I was unsuccessful on a call and grinned from ear-to-ear when I snagged a donation. When the session ended, we would celebrate the yeses and minimize the refusals, but discussing my actual behavior during call time was still off-limits.

Gradually, the sessions became more lucrative. My first successes were with donors who were familiar with my reputation of refusing to be bought. Early donations, they seemed to feel, would keep open possibility of a good relationship. I got better at making pitches, better at asking, better at trying to turn a no into a maybe. While eventually I became comfortable with the fundraising process, I never got over the feeling I was hanging my soul on the door.

One time during the primary, McNally was driving me and Jack to a campaign event. While he drove, McNally told me a long-promised dona- tion had not materialized. I grabbed my phone and motioned for quiet in the car.

The voice on the other end of the phone line said, "Hey, Stephanie. This is a surprise. What's going on?"

"What's going on?" I answered. "You promised me $1,000 over a month ago and still no check. I know you donated to Nicoletti, so don't bullshit me. I want my check."

The real estate developer stammered, "I'm good for it. I'd do it tonight, but I have to go to a family wake."

I replied, "I know about the wake. Bring the check and give it to Elizabeth."

Astonished, he said, "You want me to bring a campaign check to a wake?" "Exactly," I answered and hung up. I told McNally to make sure we got the check. Sensing my mood, he answered succinctly, "Yes, boss."

their spouse and their children give the maximum amount, too. Such a practice whereby one person is responsible for getting other people to donate is known as "bundling" donations.

From the back seat, Jack piped up, "My God. What's happened to my wife?"

"She's trying to get elected mayor," I barked. It was a far cry from the person who'd drunk gallons of coffee to avoid asking for money.

As I became seen as a leading candidate, the campaign office's phone started ringing with people requesting to meet me with the implicit promise of donating money. Sulewski and McNally vetted the callers to ensure they merited a meeting.

One day McNally told me he had set up a meeting with a man named Jerry Weiss. Weiss's name was unfamiliar to me. McNally said he was a big political player in Albany and, while he could not find out exactly what he did, filings showed he was responsible for bundling up to $40,000 in donations. I knew few people who would donate that kind of money.

To receive that largesse early in the campaign is a huge advantage. Funding campaigns is a perverse cycle. The money is needed early in the campaign when you haven't raised enough to pay staff, retain consultants, and media expenses. At the end of the campaign, if you're doing things right, there's not enough time to spend money effectively. A large donation in the summer would allow us to front-load our all-important advertising budget.

McNally dropped me off for the meeting with Weiss with the parting words, "Boss, this could be important." I walked to the coffee shop and saw a middle-aged white man, slightly overweight, with a nice suit and an overall look that said successful. I approached and apologized because it was clear he had been waiting. He told me he always arrived early for important meetings. I sat down thinking it was a good sign he thought our meeting was important.

He started by saying that while we had never met, people told him I was going to be the next mayor. Another good sign. He asked me what I knew about him, and I answered truthfully "Not much, but you donate to campaigns." He smiled and said he represented a lot of people who did work around the state, including in Syracuse. The work they did was important, so they were interested in who would be mayor. I nodded. He said he gave money to ensure they had work. He then mentioned a law firm that did work for the Syracuse Industrial Development Agency.

I stopped nodding and must have given him a quizzical look because his next sentence was explicit: "I'm not going to donate money unless I know you're going to give them the work." My immediate thought was that it was such a blatant crime he was proposing—campaign donations for a promise of municipal work—that maybe he was wearing a wire for an investigation. The next second, I was filled with disgust and wanted to get away as quickly as possible without making a scene. I said, "I'm not going to do that." He leaned back and said that was disappointing.

The meeting was clearly over. As he stood up from the table, he told me he knew Nicoletti and had supported him in the past. In fact, Nicoletti had been begging for a meeting with him for months. I stood up shook his hand, and we parted. When McNally picked me up, he told me I looked like I had seen a ghost. I told him I never wanted to see or hear Weiss's name again.

Later, I checked Nicoletti's filing and saw that Weiss had given him $5,000 and, I assumed, was responsible for other donations. At the end of the campaign, when it was clear I was going to win, Weiss contributed $5,000 to me. A far cry from the $40,000 he was said to be able to arrange. He did this hoping, I assume, that I wasn't offended by his earlier proposition. I could almost hear him say, "Congratulations. Nothing personal, my clients do great work."

After my interaction with Weiss, I made a habit of checking candidates' early filings to see if Weiss was a donor. He often was. It didn't mean those candidates were doing anything illegal. His proposition to me could have been a one-off or, more likely, he didn't have to be so explicit with others because there was an unspoken understanding of what was needed for candidates to get donations and donors to give money.

A little over a year after his interaction with me, Weiss settled a legal claim regarding actions he and a high-profile Albany lobbyist took to get a $13 million investment from a New York City pension fund. While admitting no wrongdoing, Weiss agreed to pay the state $78,000, a $26,000 fine, and forgo fees. He was not banned from lobbying public officials.[18]

## Query Ideas?

In keeping with my desire to run an idea-based campaign, I wanted a detailed policy plan to share with the public. Maxwell worked diligently to put the ideas into a usable form, with the quotidian name the "50-point plan." In an introduction drafted by Maxwell to be used under my name, the plan set

18. Jimmy Vielkind, "Jerry Weiss Settles, Too," *Times Union*, December 8, 2010.

forth why I was running and what I intended to do: "As mayor, I will strive
to improve the quality of life in the city of Syracuse by developing and implementing progressive policies steeped in innovation, transparency, community engagement, and a zeal for bold, equitable leadership that provides
21st Century responses to Syracuse's 21st Century challenges and opportunities." The document set forth broad goals and specific strategies to execute
my vision. It was done with the aim of providing the framework to usher in
innovation and vigor in city government. It was an impressive document, a
blueprint for my candidacy and (potentially) my administration. And the
media ignored it.

It was frustrating. Syracuse desperately needed new ideas and energy,
but the media was not interested in writing about those issues. It regularly
covered the amount of money each candidate raised and personal attacks,
two categories that favor entrenched, traditional candidates. Perhaps it was
cynical. The media knew the strength of a candidate is highly related to the
amount of money he or she raises. Or it is an easier story to cover than the
nuances of urban public policy. Regardless, discussions about policy and
ideas were rare in the media's coverage.

Our fundraising efforts started to bear fruit in the early summer. With
my call-time sessions, Jack's list, and small neighborhood fundraisers, by
the July filing we had raised more money than our benchmark goal. We filed
early, showing we had $241,848, 70 percent of which was raised through
donations under $200. It was a strong number, reflecting a wide breadth of
support.

I was amazed we had accomplished a feat that seemed impossible a few
short months before. To celebrate, we took our team to lunch at the Dino-
saur BBQ. Even at a restaurant notorious for being loud, our small band of
warriors was so rambunctious the waitress asked what we were celebrating.
The table turned to me, and I said simply, "We met an important goal."
When the waitress walked away, Jack said I should have said that I was going
to be the next mayor. McNally jumped in saying everyone would know that
tomorrow and another round of toasts and cheers followed.

## Three Part Disharmony, Part 1: Designation

By mid-March, the designation process was in full swing, and it was apparent the race was between me and Nicoletti. The Democratic Party's process

dictated the designation would be decided by a formal vote of the members of the Syracuse Democratic Committee. Members of the committee were supposed to support good candidates with a vote to give the designation. Once a candidate was designated, members were to collect signatures to enable the candidate to get on the ballot and work to get the person elected.

The committee was an insular group dominated by people who were appointed because of a vested interest in local government, usually a family relationship or job with an elected Democrat. This was rounded out with a few people with an interest in grassroots issues. While there were mechanisms in place to challenge the committee member appointment process, it rarely happened.

The committee itself was particularly weak. Many members had not been seen in years, only cast absentee ballots, or were even rumored to have moved out of the area. Others were placed on the committee to do the bidding of the incumbent mayor, and since he was not running, they were resigning from the committee. A committee that was supposed to have several hundred members from all over the city had closer to a hundred, and many of those people were more interested in personal issues than policy.

Despite this, I never thought about passing up the designation process and going straight to the primary election. I was a party person and wanted to support the process, even if it was imperfect. I wanted to show that the party could support and embrace change agents. As a nontraditional candidate, I thought the designation of the party would be an imprimatur of institutional support. I relished the challenge even though I knew it would be a bruising battle.

When I sat down to focus on the members of committee, it was obvious Nicoletti had been planning to run for more than a year. Some members were friends of his and his prior campaigns. While I had been busy with other things, Nicoletti had been ingratiating himself and getting his people appointed to vacant slots. I assumed Nicoletti graciously offered to help build the committee for the good of the party. From the party perspective, it's best to have a slot occupied. It was not unfair or illegal; it was how the game was played.

I took the committee list and started making countless phone calls, pencil in hand, jotting down notes next to each member's name. I had lots of individual meetings, often while walking through neighborhoods. The list became an extension of my being. It was always with me and on my mind.

When I got a committee person to commit to vote for me, we entered the information into a spreadsheet with a "1" by the name. If the committee member told me he or she was voting for another candidate, the person was assigned a "5." A person leaning toward me was a "2," toward another candidate a "4," and undecided was a "3." This is, of course, an imperfect science and why I used a pencil. It is hard to tell someone something they don't want to hear. It's much easier to be vaguely misleading, or even just lie since it was a secret ballot. In her day, my grandmother, a member of the committee, would tell candidates, "I will give it every consideration." When I asked her what that meant, she said, "Honey, if they can't figure that out, then they're not smart enough to be in office."

It was difficult to be a "1" on my list. We had a lot of strong "2's." We regularly asked people to help us gently verify a certain member was voting for me. Sometimes the answers that came back were completely different from the answers I had and "1's" became "5's." I kept calling everyone except the lost cause "5's."

There were several committee members I would call repeatedly and even stop by their homes but never received any response from. There was one committee member I called twenty times, always leaving a message, and I never heard back. I started calling them "ghosts."

Bruce Connor overheard me talking about a "ghost" and said he knew him and to give him a day. That night, Connor came into the campaign office with his hand around a young man's collar and said, "He's ready to talk to you." We started running each of the ghost's names by Connor.

Connor would get the name and come back with a real phone number, an explanation of relationships, and the committee member's leanings. He would say something like, "I know him, his mother goes to my church, and his father went to high school with my nephew. I'll talk to him and tell you when to call." We soon started calling Connor the "fisher of men." We made our way through this category realizing that even if they supported us, if they "ghosted" when the vote came, it would all be for naught.

Another group of committee people were interested only in jobs—keeping a city job, keeping a loved one employed by the city, or, most often, getting a promotion. When a committee member hinted at such a swap, I would gently ignore it. Nicoletti did not take the same approach. The same members who'd been warm and friendly with me when hinting about a job promise would stop returning my calls. Soon I heard the same people saying, "Joe promised to make me DPW commissioner." For some inexplicable reason, it was always the Department of Public Works commissioner.

Such promises are unethical and illegal, but there are no consequences because it can easily be denied. When I confronted Nicoletti about it, he laughed, saying, "I don't know what you're talking about." It was a classic old-school political move, and it irritated me that it seemed to work.

## Field Warriors

In the late spring, the Working Families Party (WFP) offered to supply and pay people to go door-to-door for me. The WFP was a small but active third party in the state focused on bringing progressive issues to the forefront of political debate. I had worked with the party during my tenure on the city council. Most of its success had been downstate, and supporting my candidacy would give WFP a chance to establish a foothold upstate. I readily accepted the offer.

The Working Families Party interviewed hundreds of people to become organizers and canvassers. The people who made the final cut were a motley crew of young progressives, old hippies, and people wanting a summer job. The canvassers received lessons on my record and how to discuss policy, and then honed a campaign pitch about me. Finally, they were given clipboards with lists of voters by street, pens to mark the responses, and pieces of my campaign literature.

Every day, they would gather at the campaign office around nine thirty in the morning to get an assignment. Some would be drinking coffee and eating donuts; others would be talking about politics. One worker practiced tai chi on the sidewalk in front of the office. Returning around four o'clock sweaty and tired, they would be filled with stories of unleashed dogs, mothers in parks, and the general happenings in Syracuse that day. Their returned lists would be entered into a database that allowed us to measure our progress in meeting the audacious goal of contacting every primary voter face-to-face at least twice. It was my own scrappy army,[19] systematically spreading my message to every part of the city.

---

19. The scrappiness brought its own challenges. One WFP canvasser stole McCluskey's purse, and another one, when pulled over by a police officer, proceeded to swallow a vial of crack and tell the officer he worked for the Miner for Mayor campaign.

## Hustings

A crucial element of the delegation process was candidate presentations at neighborhood ward meetings. These meetings were held to give candidates a forum to make a speech, entertain questions, and, in the process, give the committee members an opportunity to see how we performed on the stump. The first meeting was held by the biggest and most powerful Democratic ward in Syracuse, the 17th. Thinking I'd be fine on instinct alone, I didn't spend any time preparing. It showed.

I was a disaster: halting, verbose, and visibly flushing red. In contrast, Nicoletti was smooth, walking through the audience, and deflecting all tough questions. As the meeting broke up, I could hear people whisper how well Nicoletti had done and how shocked they were at how poorly I had done. Jack kept asking me what happened.

The next day, my young communications director Lindsay McCluskey told me I needed to be better. I nodded and she said nervously, "You know . . . like . . . you shouldn't use the word 'heretofore' in a stump speech. Um, you need to practice." I agreed.

The next meeting combined three wards of Syracuse's northside. We learned Nicoletti and his team were going to be testing the argument that I didn't have "the right temperament to be mayor." The plan, we were warned, was to make me angry to illustrate I had a temperament problem.

While I was somewhat worried about Nicoletti's likely taunting, I was more concerned about having a good presentation. My last one was so bad it had hobbled my projection as a strong candidate and likely mayor. After the 17th ward debacle, I started practicing a stump speech, first by myself in front of mirrors, then in the car as I traveled, and finally testing out phrases with the kids. Initially, I felt self-conscious, even goofy, but it was making my presentation stronger. By the Saturday morning of the northside wards meeting, I was ready to give a good presentation.

The room was packed when we arrived. Jack, his eleven-year-old granddaughter Maggie, and McNally, armed with a video recorder, took the last open seats in the back. The atmosphere in the room was tense. I tried to ignore the pressure, and the moderator called the meeting to order. Reminding everyone to be civil and saying he was going to be strict in enforcing the rules, the moderator turned the floor over to us, and each candidate gave a brief opening statement. I gave my stump speech and could tell by the nodding heads I did well. I looked at Jack and he discreetly confirmed it.

I focused on having a professionally detached look as Nicoletti gave his presentation. I wanted to avoid looking angry or surprised if he taunted me, which he didn't do in his opening remarks. When the floor opened for questions, a committee member named John Copanas jumped to his feet and directed the first question to Nicoletti. In many ways, this was an emblematic confrontation in local politics.

Copanas, the Syracuse city clerk, was an insider, a longtime Democratic Party activist, and a onetime supporter of Nicoletti. Now Copanas was saying he was diametrically opposed to him. Adding to the mix of emotions, Nicoletti's closest advisor was Copanas's uncle. It was so personal, people wondered if Copanas would flip to support Nicoletti.

Not knowing what to expect, and in an attempt to appear professionally respectful, I set my sights on a pair of perfectly manicured, rather obese feet in open-toed sandals in the front row. As I was pondering the feet, I heard, "With all of that how can we trust you, Joe?" I looked up to see Nicoletti throwing folding chairs out of his way and charging Copanas. As he did, he yelled, "I know what you've been saying about me, John!"

The entire front row jumped out of their seats. Folding chairs were falling in every direction. I stood stoically, astonished by the melee, as the moderator ran toward Nicoletti. Screaming "break it up," he and several other men grabbed Nicoletti and demanded he calm down. After a brief recess, the meeting continued in name only. It was effectively over because everyone was in shock at what had happened.

When I joined Jack and McNally in a car to leave, I said what was on everyone's mind, "*I'm* the person with the temperament problem?" McNally then sheepishly admitted he had failed to capture the kerfuffle on video, because he was getting a donut when the whole thing broke loose. As we laughed, Maggie excitedly asked, "Stephanie, are all the meetings like this?"

In the immediate aftermath, Nicoletti's supporters dismissed his chair throwing as a "boys will be boys" nonevent. At the same time, it had become clear that Nicoletti's team was in the full throes of a whisper campaign that I had a temperament problem. He and his supporters would never say it with attribution; instead, they would quietly share it with ward members, potential donors, and the media. Many of those people, in turn, would ask me and my supporters about it.

I dismissed the accusation with a hand wave or rolling my eyes. I felt I had no other way to handle it. If I became angry or charged sexism, I assumed the Nicoletti supporters would say, "See what we mean?" Then they would gleefully continue to repeat these stereotypes. I refused to think about it and reminded myself: if you're responding, you're losing. Engaging on the "temperament" issue would distract from communicating my message.

Several of my female supporters were outraged at Nicoletti's insinuation and infuriated at his chair-throwing performance. Allowing him to suggest I had a temperament problem while dismissing his aggressive behavior seemed to be an illustration of a dangerous and damaging double standard. Unbeknownst to me, one of my supporters had decided to put the issue squarely to Nicoletti at the next ward meeting in the valley, a diverse working-class neighborhood composed mostly of older homeowners.

The valley neighborhood was the den of one of Syracuse's legendary insiders, Susan McSweeney. I had known her for years. She had gotten her start in politics working for Mayor Alexander and worshipped him. McSweeney would bemoan the state of the local party, comparing it to better times, when Alexander made sure everyone working at city hall donated to the local party to stay employed. When I gingerly told her that was illegal, she shook her head and waved me off as if I was wet behind the ears.

McSweeney now worked for Assemblyman William Magnarelli, who had assured me he and his staff would stay neutral during the designation process. She frequently told me in a quiet voice, "You know I love you and I've always supported you." I wanted to believe her.

When the opening statements finished at the valley meeting, the first questioner, a longtime activist with National Organization of Women (NOW) and a supporter of mine asked Nicoletti why he was saying I had a temperament problem. Before he could answer, McSweeney jumped up and loudly interrupted, saying, "That's not fair. Joe has been good to all of us, and we need to just move past what happened."

Nicoletti then asked for another question. When I protested that Nicoletti should have to answer the question, the moderator, a Nicoletti supporter, told me it was not necessary and called on another questioner. I could not protest strongly because I would have been accused of not having "the right temperament." In addition to allowing Nicoletti to dodge responsibility for the whisper campaign, McSweeney's comments effectively told everyone she (and by implication Magnarelli) was supporting Nicoletti. It was a stunning betrayal—procedurally, substantively, and personally.

As I was leaving the meeting, as if to assuage her conscience, McSweeney said, "Honey, we just need to stop this divisiveness. I'm just so tired of it." Once again, because of the temperament issue, I could not confront her directly about her duplicity. I just stared at her, which made it uncomfortable. Without any succor from me or my supporters, she walked away muttering about me having to "get over it."

The next day, a representative of SEIU 1199, the health-care workers union, which had endorsed me, called and asked me about the meeting. When I relayed the details, the representative grunted, thanked me, and hung up. A couple of hours later, McNally, sporting a huge smile and a conspiratorial laugh, presented me with a telephone message from Magnarelli, urgently looking to speak with me.

McNally explained SEIU 1199 had called Magnarelli to express its displeasure with McSweeney's behavior. The union representative told Magnarelli it would not buy a table of tickets (which cost thousands of dollars) for his upcoming annual fundraiser because of the behavior. When I returned Magnarelli's call, he was a complete gentleman. McSweeney, he said, made a mistake. He wanted me to be his guest at his fundraiser, where he promised to introduce me, the implication being it would send the message he was supportive of my candidacy.

The next day, when I walked into the Grand Ballroom in the Hotel Syracuse for the fundraiser, I saw Sheldon Silver, the Speaker of the Assembly and Destiny USA's mastermind Bob Congel seated prominently at the main table. Congel, who always had a smile and a lie on his lips, had spent gobs of money and time making my life difficult during the Destiny debates. The perfidy of McSweeney coupled with the reminder of the Destiny tricks was overwhelming. As Magnarelli and McSweeney jumped to their feet to greet me, I grabbed my phone, turned, and walked away to take a fake call.

As I did, I collided with Assemblyman Richard Brodsky. An irascible character with a penchant for quoting the "Godfather" movies, Brodsky was a friend I referred to as my own "Hyman Roth," a nickname he loved. With his typical accusatory bark of a greeting, he said, "What are you doing!" I told him about recent events, said I did not have the stomach for it, and I was leaving.

Like a proverbial slap in the face, he said, "Stop being a little girl!" Now he had my attention. "You're going to walk into that room like you have the biggest balls here and go over and greet Congel. Remember: big brass balls!" I took a deep breath and turned around and did exactly what Brodsky said. I shook Congel's hand, greeted the Speaker of the Assembly with a smile, and thought about of having the biggest balls in the room. Brodsky's admonition made me laugh for days after.

In the final days before the designation voting was to start, there was one outstanding committee person we could not contact, Peg Barone. Barone had a significant number of votes. Rory McMahon, the former city councilor who had been elected the first time with me, called and said he had grown up with Barone's son. Telling me to meet him that Sunday, he said we would drive to her house and get her support.

On the designated Sunday, I climbed into McMahon's SUV with a bunch of flowers in hand. He derisively asked what they were for and pointed to a case of beer in the back. We arrived at Barone's compact house at the end of a dead-end street. As I rang the doorbell, McMahon stood in the driveway shouting her name. There was no response. Just as we decided to leave, we heard the garage door open. We turned to see Barone walk onto the driveway in a long tank top, blue eye shadow, and little else.

She grabbed the beer McMahon gave her, hugged it to her body, and apologized for being underdressed. I had to tell myself not to say, "Then why did you come out." I stood in silence, awkwardly holding the flowers and unable to make eye contact. McMahon quickly filled the void, telling her he was supporting me because he had a young daughter, and he had another child on the way. I was the only one he trusted to do a good job. He finished with a strong, "I need you to support Stephanie to help me."

I handed Barone the flowers, which she quickly cast aside on the hood of a car. McMahon told her to give his best to her son and we left. We rode back to my car in silence. All I could think was, "This is how one gets elected mayor—by giving a case of beer to a semi-clad, middle-aged, white woman in a driveway?" McMahon dropped me off, smiled, and said, "I think you'll get her vote."

Finally, the evening arrived when the designation vote of the committee would be announced. The voting was done on paper ballots and would be calculated by an independent auditor. Each campaign was represented at the unveiling of the results by a staffer, in my case, McNally. Based on our spreadsheets, we thought we'd be able to win outright on the first ballot, but there was always room for games and dishonesty, so we couldn't be certain.

I decided to wait for the results with Jack at city hall, just around the corner from where the ballots were being tabulated. Jack and I sat in a public hallway under a gallery of portraits of previous mayors. Minutes passed that seemed like hours. It was so intense, I told Jack I wasn't sure I could take the waiting. He told me I was being dramatic. Just as I was about to bark at him, McNally's number flashed on my phone. I picked it up with my heart in my throat. "Seventy percent," he said. "You got 70 percent, and Nicoletti got 30."

## The All-Important Television Commercial

After months of asking, scrimping, and saving, the campaign started writing checks to execute our media plan. We estimated that the essential television campaign would cost $121,000 for two different commercials to run in the two weeks before the primary. This was the bare minimum we needed.

While I had never done commercials, I knew I was too reserved to be a natural. I had little choice but to trust the producer, Paul Novak, to help me overcome my liabilities. Novak ran a one-man operation out of Rochester. He was an experienced television advertising expert. He, too, seemed to be quiet and reserved and I felt he understood what I was trying to do and would be able to project it in a thirty-second commercial.

On the appointed day in early July, I was told to bring six different outfit changes to a rented hotel meeting room. When I arrived, I was greeted by a gracious woman who told me she would pick the outfits and do my makeup and hair. She made me comfortable in an uncomfortable role.

Novak put me in a chair with a flag behind me and I started reciting written lines over and over. But try as I did, I sounded rehearsed and flat. It was painfully obvious I was terrible. After about twenty different takes reciting the thirty-second script multiple ways, I was told to do another outfit change and come back in five minutes.

While clearly uncomfortable, I was also distracted by the morning news speculating that Syracuse's current mayor, Matthew Driscoll, was on Governor David Paterson's short list to become his lieutenant governor. If Driscoll was picked, he would leave the mayor's office early, immediately throwing a huge monkey wrench into the campaign. I could not escape the idea my campaign was about to spend hundreds of thousands of dollars in a race that would be turned upside down the next day.

During the break, I escaped to the bathroom and called someone in the governor's office, asking about the choice and reiterating my situation. The answer I got was a telling but still cryptic, "That's not the direction I think the governor's going." Relieved, I changed into another outfit.

When I returned to filming, Novak suggested trying something different. Instead of hewing to a script, Novak asked me questions. My spontaneous answers illustrated my genuineness and passion on video. Churning through more outfits, I answered a host of questions, including ones that anticipated me having to respond to a city emergency, like a natural catastrophe, Nicoletti going negative, and other hypotheticals. Filming is expensive and time-consuming, so it's best to think through every possibility and have all sorts of video ready to respond to a campaign need.

When we finished, I could tell by everyone's reaction I had supplied good material, not trite, rehearsed sound bites. The next day, I learned the governor had selected Richard Ravitch, a wise man of state politics widely credited with rescuing New York City from bankruptcy and saving its mass transit system, as his lieutenant governor.[20] I didn't know it at the time, but Ravitch would become a mentor and close friend.

## Disharmony, Part 2: The Primary

Earning the party designation meant each member of the Democratic committee was responsible for gathering about twenty signatures of eligible registered Democrats on a petition authorizing me to become the Democratic Party's designated candidate for mayor. The goal of the designation fight was supposed to be seizing the resources of hundreds of committee members to collect signatures on my behalf. Unfortunately, as we learned, a number of those members were ghosts or not interested in actively supporting me. We couldn't assume the committee would be able to get the requisite signatures, so the campaign would lead, track, and have volunteers get signatures, too.

To force a primary, Nicoletti would have to gather the signatures of one thousand registered Democrats in Syracuse demanding a primary. While Davis and Harlowe had not been able to put together formidable campaigns,

20. Sam Roberts, "Richard Ravitch, Rescuer of the Subways and New York's Finances Dies at 89," *New York Times*, June 26, 2023.

they both announced they'd be gathering signatures to force a primary. This meant there would be four campaigns frenetically racing to get the signatures of at least one thousand registered Democrats in Syracuse.

To sustain the perception of front-runner status and fend off any argument we lacked support, we had the additional burden of ensuring we got the most signatures of any of the campaigns. Every day and evening, the campaign sent out dozens of volunteers with clipboards, petitions, and VAN-created neighborhood maps with lists of eligible voters.

The volunteers would return to campaign headquarters each evening with completed petitions. The petitions would be "scrubbed" by the VAN, using the program to ensure the signee was an eligible Democrat. If they met the criteria, their name was entered into our database.

Volunteers would regale us with tales of their adventures gathering signatures. We got back a blood-stained petition thanks to a voter who opened a door after having just cut himself with a knife and our volunteer bartered with him by saying, "Sign and I'll help you." Reticent signers were convinced by volunteers who shoved a foot in the door jam and pleaded with them. Volunteers snuck into apartment buildings and knocked on every door, flouting the posted rules. Unchained dogs gave chase to volunteers, and they received offers of beer, bathrooms, and indiscreet invitations by the barely clothed. It was humanity in all its richness. We laughed every night as we successfully climbed the mountain ensuring we got the most signatures.

## Dog Whistle for a Cat Fight

As our petition strategy started, Nicoletti was gearing up to announce a major endorsement from the former mayoral candidate and current city council president Bea Gonzalez. On the day of the endorsement announcement, McCluskey pulled me out of a public event. With a grim face, she said Gonzalez had made damaging remarks about me, and the press was in a frenzy, meaning we had to leave before the media arrived.

I soon discovered that while standing next to Nicoletti, Gonzalez had said, "We've all seen Councilor Miner in her public persona and I'm looking for leadership that is more even-tempered and has a sense of fairness that I have not always seen in my colleague."[21] The entire event was Gonzalez

21. Meghan Rubado, "Syracuse Council President Bea Gonzalez Won't Get on the Stephanie Miner Bandwagon," *Post-Standard*, September 29, 2009.

attacking my personality. Not only was Nicoletti no longer engaged in a whisper campaign, but he found a woman to explicitly say what he wanted. Male and female reporters alike were agog with the personal and blistering attack on me and were falling all over themselves to get me to respond.

One prominent television moderator wrote that "a shot fired across the bow this morning in the race for Mayor of Syracuse or was it the Democrats beginning to form a circular firing squad? Former mayoral candidate and current City Council President Bea Gonzalez endorsed former councilor Joe Nicoletti. . . . The words without the tone do not tell the whole story. There was nearly a wink that came with the words 'even-tempered.' It wasn't a reach to interpret the comment as personally critical of Miner."[22]

Nicoletti used Gonzalez to set the public trap for me. He was employing time-worn tropes about how a woman is supposed to behave.[23] Conventional wisdom suggests they be "nice" and viewed as stupid or be tough and viewed as a "bitch," meaning without the appropriate temperament to be a leader, leaving women leaders stuck in an untenable situation.

When a woman engages in hackneyed stereotypes about another women, it allows everyone to freely engage in, while not acknowledging outright, the hideous sexism behind such comments. Gonzalez's use of the word "tone" was a dog whistle making it easy for people to publicly engage in the discourse that assertive women should not be in leadership positions.

My predicament was not unique. Almost every woman of a certain age has faced what has been called a "double bind," a socially constructed trap for women interpreted to be stepping out of appropriate female roles. At its core, it's a strategy used by those in power against those without.

The California senator Barbara Boxer described her experience as a woman in politics in 1972 as "masochistic" and "a series of setbacks without rewards." In a particularly resonate comment, Boxer wrote in her 1994 memoir, "If I was strong in my expression of the issues, I was strident."[24] I was aware of the nature of the double bind, but ignorantly, I thought it was history. Yet I confronted the phenomenon thirty-seven years after Boxer

22. Matt Mulcahy, "Race for Syracuse Mayor," May 27, 2009. http://www.mattsmemo .com/2009/05/.

23. Nancy A. Nichols, "Whatever Happened to Rosie the Riveter?" *Harvard Business Review* (July–August 1993): 60.

24. Barbara Boxer and Nicole Boxer, *Stranger in the Senate: Politics and the New Revolution of Women in America* (Washington, DC: National Press Books, 1993), 73.

encountered it, where my passionate advocacy, which could be character-ized as articulate, ambitious, or aggressive depending on your point of view, was used as a tool to paint me as unfit for a leadership role.[25]

Many people recognized the sexism behind the accusations, but the media refused to address it. Collectively, the media was more interested in a woman tearing down another woman. It was easy to write about and would get attention. Sexism remains alive and well because many in society encourage it, the media covers it, and women cannot escape it.

When asked, I refused to respond to Nicoletti and Gonzalez's characterizations. It was difficult. I wanted to point out Gonzalez never cited a position, policy, stance, or vote where my temperament somehow interfered with serving the public. But engaging in that type of discussion only allows the destructive stereotype to proliferate. Others said on my behalf that she had a right to endorse who she wanted.

I am not sure Gonzalez understood she was undercutting something she professed to believe in—feminism and equality—but she was. She became a regular source of excoriating personal criticism of me devoid of any substance. According to her, I was arrogant, and "conversations with [me] never went well," and she was "concerned about how [I] behave in public and private."[26]

She didn't provide any specifics, but the way she chose to communicate that message undercut women and kept harmful myths alive. But being on the receiving end of sexist tropes wasn't all bad—it strengthened my resolve to be comfortable with myself and taught me to control my reactions to other people's views.

## Message Kicks In

By the end of July, our direct-mail plan was in place. At a cost of about $82,000, the campaign planned to send people likely to vote in the primary at least five direct-mail pieces, one piece for each of the five weeks leading up to the election.

25. Kathleen Hall Jamieson, *Beyond the Double Bind: Women and Leadership* (Oxford: Oxford University Press, 1995), 5, 6, 38, 39, 69.

26. Meghan Rubado, "Why One Endorsement Escapes Miner—After Eight Years, Bea Gonzalez Is Disenchanted with Democrats, Politics, and a Mayoral Candidate," *The Post-Standard*, September 29, 2009.

The first two pieces were testimonials from constituents about how I had helped solve a problem when no one else would (message: Miner understands people like me); the next two focused on the work I had done to help Syracuse students go to college (strong on education); on how I would oversee economic development differently (change); and an unplanned last piece, made possible because of a fundraising windfall, on how I would "Renew the Promise of Syracuse" (take the city in a new direction). As soon as the pieces hit the mailboxes, I would hear how good they were from residents and supporters alike. The mail effort was supplemented by volunteers knocking on doors, my public appearances, and, beginning at the end of August, my television commercials.

The strategy was to communicate directly with voters that I would be a strong mayor implementing needed change, and we executed our plan. Our polling results showed Nicoletti's campaign was not persuading voters—our polling showed the "temperament issue" was not compelling to voters and my experience in meeting voters suggested the same, but I wondered if that would be the case if the personal attacks were the only conversation the media covered.

Were elections just about raising the requisite amount of money to create a narrative? If I had not raised the necessary money to communicate my message, would the harmful stereotypes have triumphed? Shouldn't someone in power call sexist campaign tactics unacceptable?

Even if my poll was right about the temperament issue, would Gonzalez's words and actions allow the media to continue to hammer the issue long past the election? Would I be forced to soften my arguments in anticipation of sexist retaliation? If so, can you be an effective leader if you must restrain your strengths and personality because of a flawed stereotype?

At the end of the campaign, I was exhausted, battling a persistent cold, and tired of having to restrain my reactions so I would not be labeled "temperamental." One night I arrived at the campaign headquarters after a full day and evening of activities. Early the next morning, I was scheduled to film a new commercial, which was possible because of our fundraising success.

When I walked into the office, McCluskey reminded me to wear my contacts, not my glasses, because of the filming. Moments later Sulewski, too, reminded me to wear my contacts. Seconds after that, McNally said,

"Boss, don't wear your glasses tomorrow." At which point, I yelled, "If another fucking person mentions my glasses, I'm going to lose it. I'm not an idiot."

Clearly, I had lost it. As soon as I finished my profanity-laced rant, I saw the kids looking shocked and likely worried such an outburst would leak and confirm all the worst suspicions about my temperament. I followed their glances to two witnesses of the outburst shyly looking at me. McNally whispered they were two of our best volunteers. With my head hung low, I walked over to them and apologized. "Don't worry," the volunteer named Matt Jackson said. Smiling and pointing to his girlfriend, Maureen, the other witness, he continued, "She says much worse to me all the time."

I knew days before the primary, courtesy of our tracking poll, that I had a significant lead over Nicoletti. On primary night, we gathered at Nibsy's Pub, which we decided to call a family restaurant in our press release, and watched the returns with family, friends, and supporters. With a typically small turnout in an off-year election, I won by a margin of 44 percent to 36 percent.[27] My winning coalition[28] was made up of young voters, educated voters, and liberal homeowners living on the east side of the city. Nicoletti led among older voters, Italian voters, and non-college-educated women.

## Disharmony Part 3: All Over but the Shouting

Winning the primary was tantamount to getting elected mayor because registered Democrats significantly outnumber registered Republicans. Steve Kimatian, the Republican candidate, was a political newcomer and a former television news executive. The short time between the primary and the November 3 general election meant Kimatian's only chance was to raise and spend an unprecedented amount of money. He did not, but he did work hard. I continued to campaign as if I was in a tough race.

The night of the general election, we were in a suite at the Sheraton University Hotel. Unlike primary night, a small group of insiders watched the returns from the private suite and others gathered in a large ballroom

27. Michelle Breidenbach and John Stith, "Dougherty Wins GOP Nod to Run for Legislature in Clay," *Post-Standard*, September 16, 2009.

28. There were no exit polls, but this information is based on the map of the primary results and the poll we did after the primary and before the general election.

room below us. As we waited for the polls to close, we watched the Lemoyne College men's basketball team upset the hugely favored Syracuse team. I looked at Jack, hoping it was not an omen of upsets. As the game ended, the polls closed, and the initial numbers showed Kimatian winning. As I looked on, Jack kicked McNally out of the seat in front of the computer, but as more precincts began reporting full results, the numbers changed to match our predictions. I ended up winning by a margin of 50.1 percent to 39.2 percent.[29] My primary emotion was relief, not happiness.

When I went downstairs to greet people in the packed ballroom decorated with balloons and bunting, I was overwhelmed. I took the microphone to try to say something. I was humbled looking out at the crowd of people who had made my election possible and attempted to thank everyone, including the voters who did not support me. Out of the corner of my eye, I saw Jack and I was inspired to thank the "men who have decided to get involved with temperamental women." A cheer erupted, and it was only then that I began to feel happy. I was to become "Madam Mayor," a role that would challenge everything I knew about myself and the world around me.

29. Meghan Rubado, "Stephanie Miner Elected Syracuse's First Female Mayor," *Post-Standard*, November 4, 2009.

# Holding Office

## Fiscal and Other Constant Crises

On my sixth day as mayor, I was in Albany for a command appearance at Governor David Paterson's State of the State address. I had been assigned a state trooper to escort me to the event by the governor's office. My three-person entourage included Jack's eldest son, Patrick, an insurance executive, who attended the speech to meet with industry regulators.

A female state trooper met us at the Capitol building entrance and ushered us in. At the security screening stop, the trooper motioned to the guard and whispered. The guard nodded, cleared his throat, and authoritatively stated, "Clear the way. I have the mayor of Syracuse here." He then looked at Patrick and said, "Right this way, sir." After a frozen moment, Patrick said, "I'm not the mayor, she is," and pointed to me.

With a broad grin, the female state trooper said to me, "Don't worry, they'll get used to you."

## Mayor with an "O," Miner with an "E"

The time between Election Day and the first month in office is a blur. I was flying blind but kept making decisions, because if I didn't, I was told the wheels of government would stop moving. My world became filled with sycophants who told me they knew everything, treated me as a conquering hero, and offered self-interested advice. Jack, my three sisters, and old friends were quick to remind me I was just a person who won an election. I kept thinking I would get a call telling me how to be a good mayor, but it never came. It seemed bizarre that I would take over such an important role with no training or expertise, but that was exactly what I did.[1] I realized I'd have to figure out how to do the job, solicit constructive criticism, and find reassurance on my own.

The most immediate decisions involved staffing. The morning after I won, our campaign office phones rang incessantly with people looking for jobs; in the afternoon, the mail was filled with résumés; and by the evening, every person known to be associated with our campaign had been approached by someone looking for work.

Weeks after the election, I heard Elizabeth DeJoseph, one of my campaign "kids," on the phone saying, "I'll check our database. Yes, we have your résumé on file. Let me put you on hold and transfer you." At which point, in the freezing office, she laughingly put her mittened hand on the telephone receiver and handed the phone to another staff member. When I quizzically looked at her, she explained that to seem professional, she'd created a fake database and phone transfer system.

Everywhere I looked, there were piles of résumés, fat envelopes addressed "personal and confidential" to "Mayor Minor," and phone messages of congratulations from people looking to speak to me, which I quickly learned meant they were fishing for a job. Overwhelmed by the sheer volume of job seekers and the fawning adulation, I proclaimed we would filter them by only responding to those who recognized "it's Mayor with an 'o' and Miner with an 'e.'"

I needed a deputy mayor whom I could trust and who could deal with bureaucracy to manage this process. If I was to execute my goals, I needed a good support team composed of committed, creative, and smart people around me. Sycophants or people given a job as a political favor could not and would not move a lumbering city bureaucracy forward.

I turned to the recently retired chief of the Syracuse Fire Department, John Cowin, for my deputy mayor. Cowin knew Syracuse and city government, and his oft-repeated motto was, "As long as it's not illegal, we will do it." He never hesitated to give me information I didn't want to hear when I was on the city council, another trait I felt was vital to successfully implementing change. Combined with his legendary sense of humor, I believed we'd be able to work toward my goals and have fun doing it.

1. While sporadic programs for mayors existed, I was not aware of anything systematic at the time I was elected. Years later, the Bloomberg Harvard City Leadership Initiative program was created to fill this gap and I participated in the program as a mayoral coach.

The night of the announcement of Cowin's appointment, he and I attended a Christmas tree lighting ceremony in the Tipperary Hill neighborhood of Syracuse. As dozens of children gathered to celebrate the season, we watched Syracuse's legendary restaurateur and big personality Pete Coleman dressed as Santa Claus race up the street in a golf cart. Cowin turned to me and whispered that golf carts were not legal on city streets. I told him his first job as my deputy mayor was to tell that to Coleman. As Cowin rolled his eyes at me, Coleman drove the cart to us, jumped out, started handing out candy canes to the throngs of children surrounding him, and loudly said, "John, I'm so FUCKING glad she named you deputy mayor." It was a welcome, if rather unconventional, indication I was making good decisions as the mayor-elect.

My plans required new leadership in the city's various departments. An awkward part of a transition of power is the abrupt change in management. One day you have one boss, and twenty-four hours later, you have a different boss with different goals. In early December, my advisors and I discussed how to let certain employees know their services would no longer be needed. The dilemma was whether targeted employees should be told when they arrived at the office on January 1, my first day as mayor, or be told earlier that they would not be employed in the new administration. There was no easy way to deliver the news, and I decided the employees should be told as soon as possible. Cowin volunteered to be the bearer of bad news.

The first employees to be let go were the people on my predecessor's staff, the commissioners of several departments, and most of the people in the community development office. We felt it should come as no surprise, because it's standard for a new mayor to surround himself, or herself in this case, with her own people in the role of scheduler, press secretary, and personal assistants. These would be the people closest to me, and I needed to trust them completely; they also needed to understand my quirks and be passionate about accomplishing the goals I'd set forth.

The same held true for the leadership of city departments. As a city councilor, I had expressed frustration with the priorities and outcomes of several departments, particularly the community development department. When I looked closely at the office, it seemed to be a soft-landing spot for political appointees, with little thought given to ideas for investing in the community. There were rumors that some employees had difficulty describing their jobs and others didn't come to work at all.

Andrew Maxwell, the red-beard campaign policy "kid," and Paul Driscoll,[2] the current deputy commissioner, were two bright stars in the department who had been stifled. I decided to make Paul the new community development commissioner and reorganize the department. Paul was a classic absent-minded-professor type known to forget his voicemail code for weeks and had been asked more than once if he'd brushed his hair in the past month. But he knew how to deploy federal regulations and funding for community development initiatives, housing goals, and poverty mitigation. Most important, he had a passion for helping people.

When we told Paul we were going to let employees in community development know they would be terminated effective January 1, he insisted he should be the one to let them know. On the fateful day, Paul realized a birthday celebration for one of the employees was scheduled. He decided to follow the usual practice of bringing in donuts to celebrate. When the staff gathered to celebrate the birthday, Paul announced they would not have jobs with the new administration. After a second of stunned silence, the employee with the birthday flung the box of donuts in the air and said, "Happy fucking birthday to me!"

When Cowin told the mayor's staff they would not be hired in January, employees rushed out of the room, and one emailed the outgoing mayor, Matt Driscoll, who was out of town, to say she had been fired. Driscoll promptly called Cowin and gave him a withering dressing-down for firing his staff while he was still mayor.

The next day, the newspaper ran a front-page story with the headline, "PURGE."[3] Jack read the story and simply said, "Not ideal." I agreed. I had made the decision with the best of intentions but had overstepped my bounds. I had made an unforced error, but I hoped the news I was making changes would be viewed positively, even if I had done it in a clumsy manner.

I officially became mayor on Friday, January 1, 2010, at the ripe age of thirty-nine years old. My first test was to handle a major snowstorm predicted to hit on Monday, January 4. Syracuse has exacting standards when it comes to dealing with snowstorms; it does not shut down. I'd never get a

2. No relation to the former mayor Matthew Driscoll.

3. Meghan Rubado, "PURGE: Miner Fires 20 Syracuse Workers—Some Who Were Let Go Say They Were Told in 'Short,' 'Cold' Meetings," *Post-Standard*, December 16, 2009.

second chance to make a first impression about how I'd run the city. It was exceedingly important that the snow be cleared and the city continue to run.

I called my newly named commissioner of the department of public works, Pete O'Connor. "Commissioner," I said. "I can't have a snowstorm screw up the city the first Monday I'm mayor." He answered, "Don't worry, boss. We've got you covered." As we hung up, I remembered the sign in the DPW garage that said: "Through these doors pass the best snow fighters in the USA."

The snowstorm came and went without a hitch. To personally express my thanks, I arranged to visit the DPW facilities. O'Connor met me and Cowin at the department's main door and walked us through the office introducing us to the staff, a few of whom were women. He then led us through the rest of the facilities, which were occupied only by men. He explained traffic-control technology, sign-making capabilities, and asphalt manufacturing.

He took us into a large, open garage where the snowplows and other pieces of equipment were maintained. Bundled up in a coat and gloves for a typical January day in Syracuse, I watched dozens of men clad only in sweatshirts work on snowplows, pickup trucks, engines, and other equipment. The entire process was fascinating, especially the expertise required to keep the vehicles operating, which ensured the city could run. As I listened to the explanations, I realized how integral these employees' roles were in ensuring I would be successful. Without their dedication to making the city function daily, I couldn't focus on my goals.

As we headed back into the building, O'Connor quickly moved past a large open room. I stopped and asked what the room was, and he said it was the parts shop, where workers got the equipment required for maintenance. Just then I saw a young man walk from the back of the room toward me. As he got closer, I saw he wore an unbuttoned work shirt with a T-shirt underneath. O'Connor introduced him, and I saw his T-shirt read, "Overworked and Underfucked." Wondering how wearing that T-shirt solved either of those problems, I asked the employee a couple of innocuous equipment questions, studiously avoiding the T-shirt's message. I felt Cowin and O'Connor on either side of me dying—Cowin with laughter and O'Connor with embarrassment. I wrapped up the conversation and walked toward the exit and saw one more room.

O'Connor said to me, "Mayor, you don't want to go in there." Poor Pete,

I thought, it's gone so well up to the last part of the visit. My instinct told me there were likely calendars with scantily clad women or worse in the forbidden room. Managing people meant balancing interests, and in this case, O'Connor and his team had done good work. I decided to let O'Connor fix it, telling him I would be back soon to see the room. A visibly relieved O'Connor exhaled and said he understood. Cowin and I laughed about the T-shirt all the way back to city hall.

## Learning to Wear the Cape

My first name, "Stephanie," disappeared the night I was elected, replaced immediately by "Mayor." At first, I thought it was because "Mayor Miner" was almost poetic, but I began to realize it was more than the name's alliteration. I sensed people used the title to communicate their expectations that I would solve their problems. It didn't matter what the problem was: a shortage of physicians, an abundance of deer, or income inequality. If it impacted my constituents, they expected me to deal with it.

I was the elected official they would see daily in the news and, if they wanted, they could walk into my office in city hall. To be a good mayor meant I would be accessible, focused on their interests, and accountable to them. In turn, people acted as if the title bestowed the superpower of giving them a shot at a better life. After all, I was mayor of the city that was the economic, cultural, and intellectual hub of the central part of New York State.

As my first city address, scheduled twenty-seven days after I took office, was put together, I was learning that I'd inherited an inefficient operation with antiquated systems: offices that communicated by fax and used dot-matrix printers, and a phone system that hadn't been substantively updated since around 1982.

Not only were our internal operations inefficient, but our provision of services was too. Under the existing system of issuing permits, sets of drawings were shipped for review sometimes to six different departments spread across the city. The process involved too many people, which delayed approvals and was costly and frustrating to everyone from homeowners trying to add a deck to developers renovating commercial space. Almost everywhere we looked, we saw basic services desperately in need of modernization.

That first week in January, as we hustled to move in and start running a city, Cowin came into my office and uncharacteristically closed the door behind him. With a foreboding air, he said he needed to talk to me. The FBI had contacted him and said they wanted to meet him regarding "a crime committed against the city." He finished by silently staring at me. I sputtered, "John, I haven't done anything." He responded, "Yeah, I know. I just wanted to check." We couldn't understand why they called him, not me, or what this "crime against the city" might be.

Cowin returned from his FBI meeting the next day, came into my office, and, once again, closed the door. Only this time, he could barely control his laughter. The FBI told Cowin that at least $700,000 in quarters, dimes, and nickels had been stolen from Syracuse's parking meters between 2000 and 2005.[4] The agent had contacted Cowin because they'd met before.

The FBI explained an embarrassingly simple caper. The city hired a private company to collect and deposit the parking meter money. One of the company's employees had copied a key to the meters and used it to publicly empty the meters, sometimes into his own pants pockets, and deposit the coins in his personal bank account. While routine scrutiny of the falling revenue from parking meters should have alerted the city to the crime, the people in charge[5] had assumed revenue was decreasing because so many meters were old and breaking.

The scam was effectively stopped when the city started replacing single-space meters with pay stations. Even then, there was a pattern of strange vandalism occurring at the new pay stations, but there was no investigation. The scammers had been attempting to disable the new pay meters to keep their illegal cash flowing. It was only when the FBI was tipped off by an informant that the caper was stopped. Federal authorities could not charge anyone for the thefts because the statute of limitations had expired.

One of the first substantive questions I asked when I became mayor was, "How many vacant houses do we have?" While I was campaigning, I met dozens of residents who pointed to a vacant house on their street, one on the corner, or one they suspected would soon be vacant, and desperately asked me to do something before the abandoned homes destroyed their

---

4. Robert A. Baker, "Man Admits He Had Stolen Cash—Case Involves $700K Taken from Syracuse Parking Meters Over 6 Years," *Post-Standard*, October 22, 2010.

5. In 2012, the budget director found an unexplained drop in receipts from parking garages. Her questions led to the discovery of a scheme to embezzle money. We referred the matter to the Onondaga County District Attorney's office.

neighborhood. Like many Rust Belt cities, Syracuse had seen an outmigration of jobs, with people leaving vacant properties in their wake. One vacant house led to another, causing property values to fall and neighborhoods to tumble from stable to marginal or worse.

People in nearly every neighborhood in the city were worried about how nearby vacant houses would affect the value of their homes—the single largest asset most of them had. They told me stories about mowing the lawns of the vacant properties or shoveling the sidewalks to eliminate blight, but they could only keep up superficial appearances. They couldn't fix the evidence of rodents moving into the house, the roof leaking, or its use as a drug haven.

Contrary to my assumption, finding out how many properties were vacant was not easy. Every city department had a separate definition of what constituted a vacant property. The code department's list was based on the number of neighbor complaints and some eviction data; the assessment department's list derived from observations assessors made when they were out in the field; the water department's list encompassed properties where the water had been shut off; and the fire department had a list from site checks it made to properties. There were also properties vacant only during certain times of the year, like when the owners went South for the winter or when college students went home in the summer. Figuring out how many vacant properties we had in Syracuse depended on which department you asked on any given day.

We felt we could get close to an answer by ascertaining how many properties had stopped paying property taxes. The reasoning behind that was if you abandoned a property, it's likely you would not pay taxes on it. Once I reviewed the list of the tax-delinquent properties, I understood we had a bigger issue.

That list made it clear there were people who had not paid property taxes on their primary residence for years. So long, in fact, there were several beautiful and occupied homes eligible to be seized by the city. I asked for a number to quantify how much Syracuse was losing because of the properties not paying taxes, and we discovered the city was foregoing almost $11 million a year. How is it possible, I thought, that a city would overlook that revenue stream? The answer was revealing.

Syracuse's primary remedy for failing to pay taxes is to seize the property. A decade earlier, Syracuse had seized tax-delinquent properties and sold them at tax auctions. The auction process was an ineffective political embarrassment. Property owners would arrive at the auction with stories of economic hardship, painting city officials as ruthless landlords throwing families out of their homes. Other delinquent owners would find a third party to purchase the home for them at the auction and have the property transferred back to them after the purchase. Some landlords would create an anonymous shell corporation to buy their delinquent property under a new name at the auction, meaning the same entity operating under a different name would regain control of the property. The property owners would continue to fail to pay taxes, and the same properties would end up on the list repeatedly.

City leaders stopped the auction process and promised to develop an effective and compassionate replacement. City lawyers warned that when the city seized property for failure to pay taxes, it assumed legal liability for the property. In other words, if someone took a fall and was injured outside a property, the city could be sued. Faced with such a predicament, city leaders decided to just ignore unpaid taxes.

While bureaucrats worried about assuming millions in legal liability and politicians worried about political fallout, thousands of property owners simply stopped paying taxes. With rare exceptions, Syracuse had not seized or even threatened to seize properties for almost ten years.

By asking a basic question, I had uncovered a perverse and uncomfortable reality: the neighbors who complained to me were paying their taxes and living with the consequences of a system unable to solve their problem while it allowed other people to take advantage of the situation.

While we pondered these discoveries, Maxwell told me he was thinking we should enter a competition called "IBM Smarter Cities." If successful, he explained, a team of IBM experts would visit Syracuse for three weeks to help us improve public policy, for free. The competition was stiff—just twenty-four cities from around the world would be chosen for the program. I wondered if we were playing out of our league.

Months later, Syracuse was chosen as one of eight cities in the United States designated an IBM Smarter City. We asked IBM to help us with our vacant-housing issue. IBM responded by showing us how we could use data to predict what factors would cause an increase in vacancy in a neighborhood and, importantly, what government interventions could reverse that trend.

The head engineer explained that a city was "a system of systems," akin to a human body. Each of those systems produced data, and the city could use all that information to make better and smarter policy decisions, resulting in an overall healthier body. IBM demonstrated how the administration could transform the anecdotes and loud complaints we'd heard into data, informed insight, and testable, proactive interventions.

The work IBM did with us as part of the Smarter Cities grant laid the groundwork for a new strategy to systematically deal with our vacant properties. Using the data we had, we ascertained that there were approximately eighteen hundred vacant properties in the city.[6] We located those properties and planned interventions to change the dynamic. We were able to answer questions like does a failure to pay a water bill for two quarters indicate a house is abandoned, or is a year of water-payment delinquency more determinative? Is a personal visit from a code officer or strict enforcement of sidewalk regulations more likely to keep a property from becoming tax delinquent? Do certain neighborhoods require intensive interventions such as financial counseling while others just need a property to be quickly cited?

The Smarter Cities work became a catalyst to create a "land bank," formally known as the Greater Syracuse Property Development Corporation. The land bank allowed us to seize tax-delinquent properties and minimize legal liabilities. This led us to launch a successful initiative to recoup millions of dollars in long-owed property taxes[7]—a much-needed infusion of revenue for the city. When we did seize tax-delinquent properties, we transferred them to the land bank, which focused on marketing them to new buyers to fix and pay taxes or demolish them if necessary. The Syracuse land bank became one of the most active in the state and a model for other communities struggling with vacant and abandoned properties.[8]

6. Tim Knauss, "Mayor Stephanie Miner proposed the fees in hopes of motivating the owners of roughly 1,850 vacant structures to either fix them up or sell them," *Post Standard*, April 16, 2013.

7. Tim Knauss, "Syracuse Plans Mass Foreclosures on 3,900 Tax-Delinquent Properties," *Post-Standard*, September 12, 2012; Tim Knauss, "What Mayor Stephanie Miner Has Done about Syracuse's Fiscal Crisis, and What Remains to Be Done," November 3, 2013, Syracuse.com, https://www.syracuse.com/news/2013/11/post_922.html.

8. Tom Magnarelli, "Syracuse Land Bank Once Again a Top Earner of NY Attorney General's Office Grants," WRVO, March 29, 2017.

## My Not Typical Day

My days usually started around six thirty in the morning. with Jack making hard-boiled eggs and toast for breakfast. I ate while I read the newspaper, listened to the radio, and talked with him. At times, the last category did not receive my full attention. One morning he accused me of not listening to him, saying he was asking a simple question about whether I could find out if our garbage pickup was going to be delayed because of a holiday. I snapped that I had a lot of important things to do, and he was an adult who could figure out the answer. "Sorry to have bothered you," he replied. As I rushed out, he held the door open and said sarcastically, "Go slay some dragons."

Later that day, as a meeting was wrapping up, a new staffer walked into my conference room and said she had just had a weird constituent call. These types of calls were always good for a laugh, so as the attendees packed up, I encouraged her to share it with us. "Well, this very nice gentleman, who was very chatty and curious, asked me how I liked my job and how long I had worked for you. He said he wanted to know when his garbage would be picked up and then," the staffer started laughing, "he claimed he was your husband." At this point, the people who knew Jack joined in the laughter. Embarrassed about my morning behavior, I admitted it was likely my husband. When I called him to apologize and with an answer to his question, he asked how many dragons I had slayed.

On Mondays during my tenure, I would arrive at the office between seven and seven thirty, ready to attack the week. At the office I would read the local, state, and national news—the *New York Times*, the *Wall Street Journal*, the *New York Post*, and any other relevant articles. I would put together my weekly to-do list as I answered emails I'd received between midnight and 6 a.m.

At 8:30 a.m., a starter's pistol went off; I went into my senior staff meeting, where the tasks and problems of the week would be discussed and strategies updated. When I walked out of that meeting an hour later, my email inbox would be full and there would be a stack of telephone messages and requests demanding responses. Then the mail would arrive with more requests and information.

There was a constant flow of crises—snowstorms clogging roads, broken water mains leaving neighborhoods without water, or a bank robber running through downtown. Emergencies were ever-present, and I felt responsible for fixing all of them. But I knew if I spent all my time putting out proverbial fires, I would never focus on the bigger goal of making Syracuse a well-run, modernized city. I might feel like a good mayor every night when I put my head on the pillow because I had solved the emergencies, but that wasn't the same as advancing the bigger-picture goals I envisioned.

That's why choosing who to surround myself with was so crucial. While difficult, I learned to defer responding to routine emergencies to my team and assert myself when they asked for my input. In turn, I would focus on the big picture of changing the bureaucracy.

Nevertheless, I worried every day and every night for eight years about the known and unknown. The offshoot of worrying so much was I never panicked. I had gamed out so many scenarios that the ones that came to be were never as bad as the ones I imagined at three in the morning. While that sense of responsibility aged me, the variety and fast pace was energizing and exciting. I would tell people I suffered from "mayoral attention deficit disorder" as an excuse, but the truth was the job let me pass off my bad traits—short-attention span and overthinking—as strengths. I was thankful there was no typical day for me as mayor, even though there were times I yearned for a calm Christmas, July 4, or family birthday.

## Snow Art

One day in between meetings away from city hall, I called my office to get my messages and was told with a strange urgency "the staff" needed me. "The staff" was shorthand for a group of mayor's office employees under thirty years old. I heard the click of being put on speakerphone and then "Mayor, are you there?" I steeled myself for what was to follow. "Yeah, what's up?"

"I got a call this morning from an old lady"—meaning she could have been anywhere between thirty and one hundred years old—"and she wanted to know what you, as the female mayor, were going to do about the penis in front of the house on West Genesee Street." At which point, the entire room started laughing.

Unsure that I heard her correctly, I said, "Wait . . . what?"

"Well," Lindsay Speicher, the head of constituent services, continued over the laughter, "the woman says there is a huge penis made of snow on the front lawn of her neighbor's house and she wants to know what YOU are going to do about it."

"What did you tell her?"

"That you'd get right on it." More laughter, including mine.

When members of the staff went to the offending site, they found a six-foot-tall snow sculpture of a phallus, which included a sprinkling of Skittles for added affect. Moments later, a man got out of a pickup truck, muttering "stupid kids," and threw his body into the sculpture to destroy it, but not before the staff took a picture for posterity.

### Fiscal Crisis: "It Was My Understanding There Would Be No Math"

In February, on the first quiet Sunday afternoon I could remember having in more than a year, I sat down at my dining room table intent on getting a clearer picture of Syracuse's fiscal health. As I looked over budgets, line items, and projections, I felt like Chevy Chase as Gerald Ford in the *Saturday Night Live* skit, saying, "It was my understanding there would be no math."[9] I had no interest in the finer points of municipal budgets, but I needed to know how much money Syracuse had for me to implement my initiatives.

With some basic pencil pushing, I realized city expenditures were dramatically outpacing revenues. This meant the budget would need to be balanced, as legally required, with our fund balance, which is akin to a savings account. For years, the city's fund balance had been regularly used to bridge the gap between revenues and expenses.

I calculated what would happen if the city continued to spend, raise, and use the fund balance the same way over the duration of my term. Those calculations showed that within three years, the fund balance would drop to a level automatically alerting the state comptroller that the city was in distress. When this had happened in other municipalities, the state government appointed a financial control board. This meant that any decision the city made that impacted spending would be subject to permission of the control board. Simply put, it meant the end of self-governance in Syracuse.

Thus, I found Syracuse was on course to face a fiscal crisis that would

9. Dez, *Saturday Night Live*, Vimeo, https://vimeo.com/65921206.

allow a state takeover the year I would be up for reelection. I had been mayor for only six weeks, and it was a job I wanted to keep.

As I tried to find a way out of this impending fiscal calamity, my friend Assemblyman Richard Brodsky suggested I call Richard Ravitch. I knew Ravitch by reputation only as one of the state's most venerable wise men. He had saved New York City and the MTA from financial ruin in the mid-1970s and, most recently, served as lieutenant governor in 2009.[10] Brodsky gave me Ravitch's office phone number. I was facing an emergency and needed help. As far as I was concerned, all I had to lose was Ravitch saying no, so I decided to contact him.

When I called, Ravitch's secretary asked me to hold. Moments later, he got on the phone, and I blurted out a ten-second pitch about Syracuse's problems. He cleared his throat and, after an uncomfortable pause, said, "Who are you again?" When I repeated that I was Syracuse's mayor, he said, "I don't know anything about Syracuse." As a last-ditch effort, I asked him if he would have a cup of coffee with me when I was next in New York. He agreed, but it occurred to me he may have agreed just to get me off the phone.

A week or so later, I was sitting in the grand dining room of the University Club, a prestigious New York institution where the city's elites and power brokers meet, watching the entrance for Ravitch's arrival. I saw a man who resembled him enter the room and immediately engage in a heated exchange with someone. As he approached my table, I stood up to shake his hand and he said, "Goddamn it, it's 1,000 degrees outside and these guys are hassling me." Within seconds, an employee appeared at our table with a navy-blue suit jacket and said, "Here you are, governor."

I couldn't help but laugh at the absurdity of hassling Ravitch while addressing him with the honorific title. He laughed, too. We started talking about municipal finances and the treacherous headwinds that cities and states were facing. I asked questions and he explained relationships between accounting standards, bond ratings, and political posturing. When our meeting finished, he told me I could call him any time. I did, and we began weekly calls discussing financial issues.

During one of these calls, he summed up my choices by saying, "Look,

10. I. J. Liu, "Paterson Appoints Ravitch as Lieutenant Governor," *Times Union*, July 8, 2009.

kid, it's not that hard. You either have to get more money or spend less." But, as he knew full well, that's harder than it sounds.

## Get More Money: Property and Sales Tax?

Syracuse once had big manufacturers located on large tracts of land paying high property taxes that funded the lion's share of the city's expenditures. When these manufacturers left, the region not only lost employers but almost 33 percent of its population.[11] Property values declined 22 percent between 1970 and 2000.[12] But even as the region's growth fell into a downward spiral, property-tax rates were among some of the highest in the nation.

Additionally, almost half of Syracuse's properties, including government offices, hospitals, schools, and churches, weren't generating revenue because of their tax-exempt status.[13] With half of the properties off the tax rolls and the remaining properties already paying record-high rates, property taxes couldn't rescue us from our fiscal predicament.

Sales tax was the city's second-biggest revenue source. Syracuse's sales tax had been regularly and systematically cut by Onondaga County government for forty years. While city leaders fought bitterly[14]—referring to county legislators as "pirates" and "rednecks"—the political reality was that as more people left the city and moved to the suburbs, city residents lost political power. In turn, suburban residents gained clout and representation, resulting in their jurisdictions receiving about one-third of the sales tax revenue collected in the county.

11. Office of the New York State Comptroller, "Local Government Issues in Focus: Populations Trends in New York State's Cities" (December 2004): 1, https://www.osc.state.ny .us/files/local-government/publications/pdf/pop-trends.pdf.

12. Office of the New York State Comptroller, "Local Government Issues in Focus: Populations Trends in New York State's Cities," (December 2004): 10, https://www.osc.state .ny.us/files/local-government/publications/pdf/pop-trends.pdf.

13. The single largest owner of property not paying property taxes was the state by virtue of a state-owned hospital and associated medical education institution (Upstate University), state college (State University of New York College of Environmental Science and Forestry), a mental-health institution (Hutchings Psychiatric Center), and a state office building.

14. Editorial, "Shared vision of Syracuse, Onondaga County leaders bodes well for future," Post-Standard, April 8, 2010.

Sales tax receipts are volatile and mimic economic conditions. We were in the throes of the Great Recession and, consequently, overall sales tax monies were shrinking. We would advocate for, and receive, more sales tax, but it, too, would not be enough to put us on solid financial footing.

## State Aid? (But Unfunded Mandates)

New York State defines its local governments' boundaries, powers, and responsibilities. To offset regulatory burdens, the state gives money to municipalities. The name and structure of the revenue-sharing program with cities had changed throughout the years; in 2010, it was called the Aid and Incentives for Municipalities (AIM) program. AIM was the third-largest source of revenue for Syracuse. Because of the Great Recession, in my first year as mayor, state leaders cut Syracuse's revenues from this program by $7 million from the previous year. The state cut Syracuse's AIM aid again midyear, reducing it by about $1 million.[15]

As problematic as this was, the state's well-established practice of foisting expensive and unreimbursed obligations onto local governments was of equal concern. The state routinely passed laws mandating that a local government provide a service without appropriating the money to pay for it.[16] These actions are called "unfunded mandates" and add to localities' expenses.[17]

These policies are often enacted without consideration of the cost to local governments. Unfunded mandates apply to matters as crucial as staffing requirements and as mundane as equipment. For example, when the state decided it was good public policy to have heart defibrillators available, it passed a law mandating local governments buy expensive defibrillators for its buildings, pay to train personnel to use them, and pay to keep the

15. 2009–2010 budgeted $75 in AIM aid, zero in spin up; 2008–2009 rec'd $76.2 AIM and $5M spin up; and midyear cut was approximately $1M; 2009–2010 received $74.3 M in AIM and zero spin up.

16. Mildred Warner, "Grace Under Pressure: Innovation in a Time of Forced Efficiencies," April 25, 2014. http://mildredwarner.org/www.mildredwarner.org/restructuring/NYS.html.

17. Gail Robinson, "Unfunded Mandates and 'Uncontrollables,'" *Gotham Gazette*, May 30, 2005.

equipment up to date—a burdensome expense when budgets were under extraordinary pressure.

Not only were property, sales tax, and state aid revenues declining, but the state was unilaterally adding expenses to our budget as well.

## Just Cut Expenses!

Another way to balance a budget, of course, is to cut spending. The spending side of a municipal budget is straightforward. Cities are service-delivery organizations and, as such, the single largest cost is wages and benefits. In Syracuse, wages accounted for 39 percent of the budget, so one option was to cut jobs. Except, even if I wanted to, I could not cut wages or positions.

The state's "Triborough Amendment" effectively blocks municipalities' ability to deal with fiscal crises. The amendment guarantees that a public-employee union contract, including provisions for automatic annual pay increases, remains in effect even after the contract expires. Fiscal conditions, emergencies, or changes in local priorities have no impact; the union contract, including automatic raises, stays in place. As such, public employees have an incentive to refuse contract concessions because raises continue automatically, regardless of a contract's status.[18]

When we approached union leaders to discuss concessions, we were told by every union official that the fiscal issues were our problem to solve. Union leadership made the self-interested and calculated decision not to engage in bargaining, and I was powerless to get any concessions.

Most Syracuse government employees are union members who have enhanced workplace protections. If the economic downturn forced layoffs, collective-bargaining agreements dictated an elaborate process involving "bumping rights." This allows more senior employees who are laid off to "bump" workers with less seniority out of other jobs and take those positions, resulting in people taking jobs without having the requisite knowledge or skills. It's a chaotic process that usually leads to a decline in public services.

Layoffs were also organically problematic. Most of the spending on

18. Edmund J. McMahon, "Triborough Trouble: How an Obscure State Law Guarantees Pay Hikes for Government Employees," *Empire Center*, January 11, 2012.

wages goes to personnel that provide fundamental municipal services like public safety—services that are crucial to maintaining stable neighborhoods. The police department accounted for 26 percent of the city's annual spending while the fire department accounted for 18 percent of spending and the public works department 13 percent.

Greater concentrations of poverty in the city required more government support. This was obvious at the neighborhood level: residents plagued by open-air drug markets, streets with old houses susceptible to fire, and infrastructure that needed maintenance. Given these factors, layoffs would hobble our ability to create positive change and would devastate our neighborhoods.

I tried to find creative answers to our predicament, but every time I had an idea, I would find it blocked. We had a working asphalt plant we used for our roads and thought about selling excess asphalt to private contractors, but the state outlawed it.

Institutions like Syracuse University,[19] the State University of New York, and Upstate Hospital relied on our most expensive services. I considered forming service districts to charge nonprofits in the district for the municipal services they used. On a conference call with the state comptroller's office, I was gently but firmly told it had taken the legal position that the city could not charge for core government services. We could form districts to provide auxiliary services like lighting but not districts that charged for public safety or public works, which, of course, were the exact services Syracuse needed money to provide for.

I walked into city hall every morning thinking about Syracuse's impending financial disaster. I could not legally or responsibly raise enough revenue or cut enough spending to rescue us from imminent doom. There was a real possibility I would be Syracuse's last mayor—the person leading Syracuse when the state ended the city government's democracy.

In what would come to be a regular quandary, I faced the question of what to do with difficult information. I was counseled not to be completely transparent with the public, to downplay bad news and engage in some

---

19. Later, I negotiated with Syracuse University to pay a service fee to help offset the costs for services the city provided to the university community. Tim Knauss, "Mayor Stephanie Miner Talks Nonprofit Syracuse University into Making Payments for City Services," Syracuse.com, June 9, 2011, https://www.syracuse.com/news/2011/06/mayor _stephanie_miner_talks_no.html.

legal, but fiscally dubious, decisions like borrow more or sell off city assets and hope to stave off the crisis until the end of my term.

It was politically smart advice and it had always worked. We think we want politicians to be open and honest with us and make us aware of the problems before they become a crisis. But people want politicians to be positive, full of good news and straightforward solutions.

The easiest choice is to ignore a problem by pretending it doesn't exist. People want their services delivered, and they vote for officials who will ensure that gets done. If you can deliver services for that day, week, and month, you're doing your job. If you must make some compromising decisions that may have a detrimental impact in the future, well, to paraphrase the famous economist, in the long run we are all dead.[20]

For me, there were fundamental problems with the strategy of ignoring the problem. I had the romantic view that a leader's tough choices would be recognized and rewarded.[21] I was motivated to become mayor in order to solve problems. Nothing less than Syracuse's self-governance depended on me solving our fiscal crisis.

Our public policy solutions would require explanation, compromise, and, potentially, sacrifice. While it's an untenable combination in our current political environment, without it, problems never get meaningfully addressed. Making a short-term decision in exchange for long-term damage was not something I could do. It was a part of my psyche that put me at odds with the traditional political decision-making process. I was forced to question myself and weigh the benefits and liabilities of governing on a regular basis.

It was also far from certain we could avoid a fiscal crisis for eight years. The noted American financial analyst Meredith Whitney warned that "significant" municipal bond defaults nationwide would be "something to worry about in the next 12 months."[22] Every day I read about American

20. "In the long run we are all dead," John Maynard Keynes (1883–1946), the great British economist, wrote in 1923.

21. I cannot draw a conclusion about how much of this was driven by my gender. Similarly, academics have refused to draw conclusions about gendered policy differences. Mirya Holman, "Women in Local Government: What We Know and Where We Go from Here," *State and Local Government Review* 49, no. 4 (2017): 291.

22. Joe Mysak, "Meredith Whitney Overreaches with Muni Meltdown Call," *Bloomberg*, December 22, 2010.

cities in trouble: Pennsylvania was said to have at least twenty municipalities in a "distressed city" program; Michigan had thirty-seven; New Jersey, seven; and Rhode Island, one.[23] Harrisburg and Scranton, Pennsylvania, were making front-page news with their financial collapse.[24] Even based on short-term political calculus, it was clear Syracuse might not be able to escape the trend enveloping other cities.

I was also learning about a quiet but pernicious danger preceding fiscal insolvency known as "service-delivery insolvency." Before Detroit filed for bankruptcy, it struggled to keep its streetlights on, its buses operating, and its police and fire forces adequately funded. On the road to bankruptcy, Detroit steadily failed to provide essential municipal services. The phenomenon was so destructive, the federal bankruptcy judge Steven Rhodes found Detroit's "service delivery insolvency [to be] the most strikingly disturbing. . . . It is inhumane and intolerable, and it must be fixed."[25]

The possibility of service-delivery insolvency in Syracuse—that we might not be able to fight crime, fires, or blight—haunted me as much as the fiscal crisis it portended.

## Friday Afternoon Calls Are Bad

Late one Friday afternoon in February, having gone through a week of tough financial conversations and even tougher decision-making, I was standing in front of my office window when my cell phone rang. It was O'Connor, the DPW commissioner. "Mayor, we've got a problem," he said. "A big one." He told me that the roof had collapsed on a large, derelict building at 921–925 North State St. The collapse had caused an external wall to split from the roof to the ground, threatening the bordering highway.[26]

23. Mary Williams Walsh, "Cities in Debt Turn to States, Adding Strain," *New York Times*, October 5, 2010, www.nytimes.com/2010/10/05/business05cities.html.

24. "Harrisburg Becomes Pa.'s 20th Financially Distressed City," WHYY-PBS, December 15, 2010, https://whyy.org/articles/15sdact47.

25. Stephen Fehr, "Pennsylvania Struggles to Help Its Weakest Cities," Pew Stateline, July 12, 2012, https://www.pewtrusts.org/en/research-and-analysis/blogs/stateline/2017/02/23/service-delivery-insolvency-is-changing-municipal-bankruptcy.

26. "State Closes I-81 North in Syracuse Due to Building That Could Collapse," Syracuse.com, February 27, 2010, https://www.syracuse.com/news/2010/02/state_closing_i-81_north_in_sy.html.

When I got to the scene, I saw the gaping, fifteen-foot wedge that took up three of the four stories of the building, with hundreds of cars speeding by below on Route 81. My initial reaction was a less-than-mayoral "Shit." O'Connor apologized, and I said, "It's not your fault, but I was looking forward to my beer." He laughed and said he had the same thought, but with this event, he had upgraded to whiskey. When our city engineer arrived on-site, she stepped out of her minivan, reached for her yellow vest, and in a deadpan voice said, "This isn't good."

The circumstances behind the gaping hole in the building were far from unique in Syracuse. At one time, 921–925 North State Street was a big, brick five-story illustration of success. It started as a brewery in late 1888, became a tin products factory, and then was transferred from one owner to another for various uses until 2002, when it was sold to the current owner for $65,000. The city had been trying to force the owner to fix structural problems and other code violations since 2008. Several times, the city had tried to force the owner to remove his belongings from the largely empty building and vacate the premises.

By the beginning of February 2010, the code enforcement department was so concerned, it started proceedings for an emergency demolition order. On February 26, 2010, the heaviest snowfall of the season hit the area, and the building's roof and some of the walls went. After the collapse, the owner said he could not afford the $1,000 it would cost to remove his belongings from the collapsed building.

At my briefing, I was told we were having a hard time getting the state to pay attention to the scene. Only state transportation officials had the authority to close the highway used by about fifty thousand motorists a day. I was dumbfounded as I watched hundreds of cars speed by the splitting building, which could crumble onto the interstate at any moment. I volunteered to call state officials as DPW employees, city engineers, and fire department personnel went to evaluate the scene.

I got into my warm car and was staring at the gaping hole in the building when my phone rang from an unknown number. I answered and a voice said, "Mayor Miner? Please hold for Governor Paterson." David Paterson got on the line and said, "Stephanie, I have decided not to run for governor, and I wanted you to hear it from me." Paterson had been awash in murky ethical allegations and had not cemented a strong election effort, but it was still surprising news because he was an incumbent and had worked hard to achieve and serve as governor.[27] While I was stunned, I was more fixated on the crumbling building and, in what can only be described as a fire hose response, I said, "ThankyouGovernor-I'm-sure-it-was-a-tough-decision-but-one-that-will-be-right-for-you-and-your-family . . . But I need help, David. I'm looking at a building that may collapse onto Route 81, and I can't fix it."

After a split second of confusion, he responded, "Oh, my God, we've got to help you," and then he yelled for his assistant to get me whatever help we needed. I wished him the best of luck. When I got off the phone, the other people in the car were astonished I had taken a moment of great personal disappointment and asked Paterson for money. I was the mayor, and he was the person who could help me solve the issue. At that moment, our friendship was secondary to our professional roles.

Within minutes, I was told the state folks were on their way to determine whether the interstate needed to be closed, which they did immediately upon viewing the scene. State and Syracuse officials started planning the building demolition, and with each observation they made, the amount of money necessary to resolve the situation got bigger: the size and location of the building made the demolition complicated; there would likely be hazardous materials in the building, adding to the expense; and the owner was unlikely to have insurance or to cooperate with us. By the time I left the scene, there was not enough beer in Syracuse to slow down the buzzing in my head.

Had the building collapse not threatened the interstate, it would have been Syracuse's problem alone. Our proposed demolition budget for the 2010–2011 year was exactly $1 million. This money was used to take down buildings destroyed by fires, remove public safety hazards, and address long-vacant eyesores in neighborhoods—necessary municipal services crucial to maintaining residents' quality of life. Syracuse could not responsibly afford to pay for the building demolition, which was estimated to cost at least $1 million.

Although Paterson had pledged to help with the situation, we would need to negotiate the cost-splitting and the liability of demolishing the building. While the state wanted to split the costs, I refused to agree to an unknown figure. The state was not above manipulating numbers, and I wanted an agreement in writing to avoid misinterpretations.

I refused to move from my position that the state should pay the lion's

27. Danny Hakim and Jeremy W. Peters, "Under Fire, Paterson Ends His Campaign for Governor," *New York Times*, February 26, 2010.

share of the expenses. At one point, an exasperated high-ranking Albany official said she did not understand; it was a building in Syracuse's jurisdiction, so we had to pay for it. When I explained that if we did, we would not be able to demolish any other building for the rest of the year, she told me she didn't believe me. I responded by saying our budget decisions weren't made lightly, unlike Albany budgets. The conversation got us no closer to a resolution, but it highlighted how Albany officials viewed budgets—namely, they assumed that there was always money, likely because between untold numbers of budget lines, quasi-governmental agency revenues, and bonding proceeds, there always was in the state's budget. That was in stark contrast to Syracuse's financial position.

The traffic backups caused by the interstate closure were hours long, which was unprecedented in Syracuse. One local entrepreneur walked between the cars selling bread from a neighborhood bakery. The media covered the gridlock every day for almost three weeks. People understandably wanted the problem solved.

Many people were exasperated by my position. A typical letter to the editor stated I was "fail[ing] to serve the best interests of Syracuse" by engaging in legal game-playing and creating an "us against them" campaign instead of having my "sole focus be on find[ing] a practical solution that opens I-81 without further delay."[28] A number of people said I should just "demolish the building and send the bill to its owner,"[29] even though every news story reported the owner had no resources.

Some politicians told me to jump in the seat of a construction crane wearing a hard hat and, with television cameras filming, take a wrecking ball to the building. I knew it would have been viewed as great political showmanship. But where would the politicians be when the city couldn't tear down a house burned in a fire or deal with a vermin-filled building because our budget was exhausted on a single act of grandstanding? They would be invisible. As the mayor, I was responsible to people who did not have the media following their neighborhood blight issues. Political grandstanding was not a constructive strategy for combating governmental "service-delivery insolvency."

28. Dan Guyder, "Spare Us the Legal Posturing and Find Practical Solution," *Post-Standard*, March 7, 2010.

29. Ted Brooks, "City Should Demolish Building and Send Bill to Its Owner," *Post-Standard*, March 7, 2010.

After three weeks of negotiations, during which time thousands of motorists a day were inconvenienced, we finalized an agreement. We agreed to pay $100,000 toward the demolition of the building, which was $80,000 more than Syracuse typically paid for a demolition. When the bills finally came due, the demolition, which included the removal of hazardous material and bringing the building up to code, cost $858,000. The city paid $125,548, which represented 15 percent of the cost.[30]

It was a good deal, some even said a triumph for me, but there was no time to celebrate. At a public safety budget hearing during this period, city councilors asked the police and fire chief what would happen if the budget required laying off uniformed employees. "Chaos. Devastation. Crime will rage on and probably get worse,"[31] the police chief answered. The fire chief added that response times would rise. Service-delivery insolvency.

## New Sheriff Arrives in Albany

At the end of the year, Andrew Cuomo was elected governor in part by promising to turn around upstate's economy. With great fanfare, he announced a blue-ribbon panel of experts called the Mandate Relief Task Force and charged them with reducing state-issued unfunded mandates for local governments. He insisted the state would alleviate the fiscal pressures on citizens and local governments.

Cuomo himself articulated an understanding of the importance of local government. At a meeting with the editorial board of the *Post-Standard*, Cuomo was asked about the predicament of New York's cities. He said they could not be allowed to fail. "If the body is the state, the cities are the organs. There is no future for a state when your cities are going bankrupt."[32]

Heartened by the public pronouncements of the newly elected governor, I believed Cuomo and other state leaders would help address Syracuse's

30. Mike McAndrew, "City's Hard Bargain on Demolition: 85% Off—City Hall's Negotiations Resulted in a Local Share of Just 15 Percent of $858,000," *Post-Standard*, August 23, 2010.

31. Robert A. Baker, "Smaller Forces, Larger Problems, Chiefs Say Budget Cuts Will, In Turn, Diminish Public Safety, Says Syracuse's Fire, Police Leaders," *Post-Standard*, April 30, 2010.

32. Editorial, "A Hand, Not a Handout—That's What Mayors of Cash Strapped Upstate Cities Want from Albany," *Post-Standard*, October 28, 2012.

problems. Confident that the new governor wanted to effect real change, I was thankful for the opportunity to work with him to institute solutions and sound policy. While exciting, it was not surprising the new governor Cuomo was focusing his abundant skills on effectuating constructive change. After all, I heard his father say we worked in this field to do "good work."

I turned hopeful eyes to Albany, blissfully unaware that I was about to learn that "good work" had different connotations for Mario and Andrew Cuomo. For Mario, it meant fighting to make policy to solve problems, and for Andrew it meant making announcements aimed at ensuring election.

# Pensions

## Crossing the Rubicon

Months into becoming mayor, I was sitting at a table in a tony brownstone in Manhattan. The venue was a room in two buildings architecturally combined through the removal of a wall. The setting was filled with exquisite art, regularly rotated I was told, as I was directed to my seat. My feelings of discomfort were sparked by the elegant setting and ignited by the exclusive group of mayors from the cities of Atlanta, Boston, New Orleans, and Philadelphia seated around me. All of them were strangers to me save one. I grabbed a pen and pad to steady my nerves, determined to take notes in an attempt to belong.

The lights dimmed and exploding colors, regression analysis, and heat charts danced on the wall—all accompanied by the McKinsey consulting group explaining the large and growing problem of funding public pensions. When the stunning presentation finished, I turned to my left to the one person I knew in the room, who was also the host. "Mike, what are we going to do about this?"

"Well, Stephanie," he said. "I know what I'm going to do. I'm going to die." And with that, Michael Bloomberg, the man who never saw a problem he did not want to solve, launched me into the thicket of public employee pensions.

I had become aware of the pension issue in a completely different, but altogether Syracuse, way a year earlier. Days before I was to be sworn in, I attended the department of public works Christmas party at the Pastime Club, a beer and bowling establishment. The talk that night was about the arrival of a pending snowstorm. The employees wondered if the storm would force them to work on Christmas.

Hearing this, I suggested the city's contract for weather radar technology should answer that question. The employees responded politely there was more to it than just a machine. "Really, like what?" I asked. An employee motioned toward the window and told me to look out. I moved the window's curtain and saw a wizened employee spit on the sidewalk and look to the sky. Another employee standing next to me said, "Yup, it's coming, and it's going to be a big one." I stared at my newly named public works commissioner, hoping to communicate, "This is our 'famous' snow-fighting technique?"

Just then, my phone rang; it was the city's budget director calling. He told me estimates for the pension bill had been released and asked how I wanted to pay. With money, I thought, but responded, "How do we usually pay?" After pausing, he said, "It's getting tougher and tougher to answer that question."

I was not yet the mayor and I had a man spitting to decide whether to plow and a budget director saying he didn't know how we pay our bills. When I hung up the phone, I asked my new commissioner if the spitting routine was real and he said, "Yup, trust me, they know what they're doing." At least one of us does, I thought.

## New York State's Pension Systems

The state pension plans cover most public employees working in New York State, including local government employees.[1] The terms and conditions of the pensions are determined solely by the state.[2] The benefits are generous and referred to as the "gold standard of pensions."[3] Once benefits are given, they cannot by law be reduced or taken away. Local government's only role

1. Some New York City public employees are not covered.

2. E. J. McMahon and Peter Ferrara, "Report: Defusing the Pension Bomb: How to Curb Public Retirement Costs in New York State," Manhattan Institute, November 2, 2003, https://www.manhattan-institute.org/html/defusing-pension-bomb-how-curb -public-retirement-costs-new-york-state-5821.html.

3. Delen Goldberg, "Public Pensions Sock Taxpayers—As Cost Grow, Some Seek to Rein in N.Y.'s Retirement Benefits," *Post-Standard*, February 15, 2009.

is to pay the bill sent by the state, which is a calculation of the monies owed to fund the pension obligation of that municipality's employees.

Separating the people who give the benefits (state leaders) from those who pay for the benefits (local officials) is problematic. Savvy lobbyists and ambitious state politicians often use the process for mutual gain, leaving local officials feeling abused. Unions commonly lobby state officials from both parties to approve billions of dollars in new pension benefits.[4] In turn, the unions back candidates supporting the enhancement with campaign contributions, endorsements, and grassroots support. New York City mayor Ed Koch once described the process as "outrageous," saying "the municipal unions own the state legislature."[5]

Amid the 2000 stock market windfall, state leaders gave extremely lucrative pension-benefit enhancements to public employees.[6] The benefit enhancements bill received unanimous support in both houses of the legislature.[7] Shortly after the bill was passed, the World Trade Center was attacked, the stock market plummeted, and the economy tanked. Compound interest—interest on both the principal and interest—and permanent benefit enhancements continued unabated.

This resulted in the net assets of the state's retirement plans increasing a miniscule 4 percent while benefit bills doubled between 2000 and 2010.[8]

I took office as the pension fund shortfalls required major infusions of cash from local governments. Syracuse was already burning through our

4. The *New York Times* did an analysis showing Governor George Pataki, a Republican, and the politically divided legislature approved billions of dollars in new pension benefits after lobbying and campaign contributions from unions. Michael Cooper, "City Foots Bill as State Upgrades Pensions," *New York Times*, August 2, 2006.

5. Michael Cooper, "City Foots Bill as State Upgrades Pensions," *New York Times*, August 2, 2006.

6. Eliminated some participants' contributions, added automatic cost of living adjustments, indexed benefits to inflation, and allowed police and firefighter to include windfall overtime in a pension calculation.

7. Chapter 110 (A11531/S8229) and Chapter 126 (A11418/S8142) of the laws of 2000. Votes recorded:

$$A11531/S8229 \text{ Yea/Nay} = A = 142/0 \text{ S} = 59/0$$
$$A11418/S8142 \text{ Yea/Nay} = A = 142/0 \text{ S} = 149/0$$

8. E. J. McMahon, "Report: New York's Exploding Pension Costs," Empire Center, December 7, 2010. https://www.empirecenter.org/publications/new-yorks-exploding-pension-costs/.

savings at a rate that would subject the city to a state takeover if everything stayed the same. But far from staying the same, the pension bill was climbing by the millions. The year before I became mayor, city pension bills totaled $15 million a year. The bill during my first year increased almost 33 percent. The numbers were astronomical and showed no signs of slowing down.

I was desperate for a plan to avert financial and social disaster. A month after I was sworn in, the deadline arrived to pay a pension bill of $20 million. As I contemplated that number, knowing the bill would continue to grow, I asked what our options were. I was told we could pay, or we could "amortize" a portion of the total bill through a new program[9] the New York State comptroller's office offered. The program allowed local governments to spread the pension bills over ten years and pay an interest rate on the amount amortized.

It was putting off paying the bill into the future and, in exchange, increasing the total amount to be paid. I made the decision to amortize $3 million[10] in costs, hoping to buy time to determine how to pay pension bills and other costs in the middle of a financial storm. It was a mistake. It's a cardinal sin of fiscal stewardship to authorize borrowing to pay for a recurring expense.

Yet I committed the sin of fiscal imprudence without any scrutiny, accountability, or consequences. My decision received no attention. The media, which prides itself on holding government leaders accountable, was not interested in the fiscal situation driving my decision or the decision itself. Stories about fiscal problems do not lend themselves to thirty-second video clips or clickbait headlines. The unions representing the people counting on the pensions were silent. Political wisdom seemed to be to let someone else deal with this issue when it became an emergency. But it was an emergency. Syracuse could not pay its operating bills with regular, recurring revenues.

When the entire system supports an action, it effectively means it's not a mistake, just a necessary compromise. It was a glimpse into a system that routinely failed to protect the interests of citizens in favor of vested interests.

Solutions for Syracuse's predicament had to be effectuated in Albany, so

9. Under the "rate mitigation program," the contribution rates for the police and fire retirement system were capped at 17.5 percent for pension fund participants, instead of 18.2 percent. The delayed payments were counted as liabilities and as receivable assets of the pension fund, transferring the liabilities into the future.

10. Ultimately, the amount amortized was $2.3 million.

I started making regular trips to brief state leaders on our issues. I explained to the audience du jour that our precarious financial situation was threatening Syracuse's ability to deliver services to maintain the quality of life in the fifth-largest city in the state, that is, service-delivery insolvency. The impacted people were not just Syracusans but, importantly, New Yorkers.

At one meeting, a state budget official said to me, "I know you don't have a lot left in your rainy-day fund; it's been raining in upstate New York for a long time." One state legislator told me the problem was that I was too good of a mayor: "People don't see the problems yet. You are doing a good job." I was incredulous and asked if that meant I would not see a solution until financial disaster struck Syracuse. He said yes, maybe. The Speaker of the Assembly Sheldon Silver[11] gave me an emblematically inscrutable answer: "I understand, mayor. We're working on it." I asked what that meant but never got an answer.

In one meeting, a high-ranking staffer in the comptroller's office told me he had been a local official and understood our fiscal situation. When I asked him what I could do, he sheepishly said, "You can ask for a financial control board."[12] His suggestion to request the end of Syracuse self-governance and concede failure seemed to be the only solution. Every official understood we were headed toward fiscal ruin through little fault of our own yet offered nothing except sympathy as we sped toward that destination.

I presented my charts and data about Syracuse's predicament to reporters in Albany covering state government. They, too, would agree it was a problem. Joseph Spector, a reporter from *Gannett News*, memorably said to me, "Yeah, these numbers for upstate cities have been a problem for a long time, but no one in Albany seems to want to do anything about it." He shrugged, closed his notebook, and walked away with my charts.

Sitting on a plastic chair under fluorescent lights in a cavernous, empty fast-food restaurant in the basement of the Albany capitol building, I wondered if the collective absence of interest I was facing was a product of the lack of accountability or learned cynicism from years of observing the Albany governing process.

My next step was expanding my advocacy outside of Albany. I traveled

11. Jesse McKinley, Thomas Kaplan, and Susanne Craig, "Sheldon Silver to Be Replaced as Speaker of New York State Assembly," *New York Times*, January 27, 2015.

12. See chapter 3, p. 77.

to other upstate cities where I thought I would find an audience worried about the same trends impacting Syracuse. High on this list was Buffalo. As the second-largest city in the state, it had seen its once prosperous conditions disintegrate. I met with the editorial board of the *Buffalo News* to discuss fiscal pressures on local governments, including the pension crisis. It was a serious paper with thoughtful news coverage, and I felt it would be a helpful partner in demanding the state address the trends impacting local governments.

At the meeting, I ran through my pitch, arguing the state needed to intervene to help solve the underlying causes of the dire fiscal conditions of upstate cities in general, and the pension issue specifically. The editorial board members nodded absently. When I was done, they asked me what office I was running for. I responded I was there to call attention to a public policy issue, not as a political tactic. Politicians only stopped to pitch issues as a tool for higher office, they told me. While I assured them that was not my intention, they were unconvinced.

When the editorial leaders of an important media outlet state categorically that ideas are tools of ambition only, it means constructive public policy advocacy is effectively inconsequential. If an idea is only relevant if the person pushing the idea is a serious contender for office, then anyone not seen as relevant candidate is discounted. In such an environment, only the monied and vested elite get their problems addressed. As the mayor of a struggling city in a part of the state lacking political power, it was disconcerting.

By 2012, Syracuse's pension bills had risen by a shocking 587 percent in ten years. My budget commissioner, Mary Vossler, told me she dreaded opening the emails the state pension system sent her. Vossler was a hardened, experienced CPA. She once told me a contributing factor in our high health-care bills was not enough people were dying. I would jokingly refer to her as the second-most-feared woman in city hall and was frequently told she was the first. When I responded with surprise over her anxiety at the numbers, she said what we all knew: "We are absorbing these costs, and where are you supposed to find the money?"

Shortly after, an answer arrived when Lieutenant Governor Robert Duffy called to say Governor Cuomo was proposing pension-reform legislation designed to help local governments and asked me to help get the proposal passed. I readily agreed and asked some questions about the proposal. Duffy responded he was not sure about the details but would have somebody answer my questions. Shortly after, Cuomo's press office called with a drafted supportive quote about the pension proposal from me:

"The Governor's plan shows a willingness to reform pension and mandate systems that have been driving up costs and leaving cities like Syracuse in crisis. I am thankful the Governor has begun to confront these issues head-on."[13]

I agreed to the quote and asked for details of the legislation. Again, I was told someone would get back to me. When I finally received a copy of the legislation, I learned it did not alleviate any pressure the current pension bills were creating. Instead, it created a new pension tier for newly hired employees that might save local governments money when the employees retired in twenty to thirty years.[14]

The Cuomo administration's press release language had no relationship to the pension legislation's impact. Specifically, the proposal did not show a "willingness to reform pension and mandate systems," nor did it "confront these issues head-on." When I raised this, the governor's aides told me the legislation was just a first step. He had publicly committed to reducing unfunded mandates. But Albany insiders told me to beware because the unions were opposed to any pension reform. In fact, it was whispered that Cuomo had told the unions this would be the only time he would touch pensions to mitigate their opposition.

The fact that local governments were being driven toward bankruptcy was not compelling. Nor was the fact that local governments were cutting important public services to pay the pension bills. Welcome to Albany, the insiders told me, your city's problems have no bearing on us.

But that was not what the governor was saying.

## Governor, not Green Stripe

Many people who worked with me under Mario Cuomo were now working for Andrew. When Andrew became governor, many acted as if my relationship with them was the same as it had been when his father was governor.

13. Teri Weaver, "Cuomo: No New Fees. No New Taxes. No Surprises. Governor's Spending Plan Once Again Puts Unions, Schools under Microscope," *Post-Standard*, January 18, 2012.

14. Chapter 18 of the Laws of 2012.

They called with requests, often posed as demands, wanting me to do something serving their purposes but never my constituents.

The interactions all went something like: "Hey, Stephanie, I need you to do this favor for me." Later, it became, "You need to do this for the governor," and eventually, "The governor wants you to do this!" I refused unless the action benefitted the people of Syracuse. Most of them did not. After a couple of months of these conversations, I got a call from Joe Percoco. He was now the governor's right-hand man. I prepared for him to be the same punky advance guy that years earlier pushed me around.[15] Instead, he was respectful and almost deferential.

"Madam Mayor," he said, "I think we need to find a communication avenue that works between our office and you." I was happy to do that, I said, but his team needed to understand I wanted information when I asked. I would not agree to do things just because they asked and certainly never when threatened.

He said he understood and that I could always reach out to him. He suggested I could work through Duffy, making a point to say Duffy, the former mayor of another upstate city, Rochester, understood my issues. Or I could work with Todd, meaning Todd Howe. When Percoco suggested Howe as a conduit, I readily agreed. Howe was friendly, almost charming. Unlike nearly everyone else associated with Cuomo, he did not yell, scream, or threaten.

A couple of days later, I told an old Albany hand about the conversation. She shook her head and said, "Joe Percoco, the velvet glove. The world is upside-down." She followed up with the prescient question, "What does Todd Howe do anyway?"

In March, the state legislature passed the governor's pension reform bill. It was a great success for the governor. When I was invited to the ceremonial bill signing in Albany, I was ambivalent about attending because the painting of the "Green Stripe," the start of the all-important St. Patrick's Day festivities in Syracuse, was scheduled for the same day.

Hours after the governor's office was told I might not attend, I got a call from Howe. Bluntly, he explained it was an honor to be invited and I could not say no because of a "Green Stripe." I explained it was not my intention to offend, but painting the stripe was a big deal. I committed to attend the

15. See chapter 1.

governor's event even if it required speeding on the Thruway. In a refrain that was to become utterly familiar, Howe said to me, "You know these guys, Mayor. They're tough."

The day of the painting-slash-bill signing arrived. I painted the stripe and jumped into the car. Before I closed my car door, I answered my ringing phone saying, "It's okay, Todd. I'm on my way." Relieved, he said, "On another topic just between us, if the governor were to ask you to become chair of the state party, would you agree?"

When I said I'd never thought about it, he went into sell mode: "Well, you know they [the governor's people] know you are different, and they want to give you something that meets your talents. It's an important election year and it will be great exposure for you. Just think about it, and if he [meaning the governor] says anything to you today about it, just don't say no." I agreed.

I arrived in Albany and got to the holding room on the second floor of the state capitol building with plenty of time. The room was filled with elected officials from different levels of government and various parts of the state. I was directed by a staff person to take a seat. The governor walked in and everyone in the room began vying to get his attention. Elected officials requested selfies or pointed to their phones with complimentary news stories about him: one state legislator even told him he looked like he had lost weight. During this frenzy, I was quiet and tried to discern if this was standard behavior or the composition of the room, or if people in Albany were just different.

A member of the governor's staff entered and, in what was to become a familiar ritual, went through in excruciating detail how the event would proceed. Reading from a white index card with typed text, the staffer recited the order in which we would enter the room, saying we were to walk single file, not two at a time. Then we were told where to stand, making it clear we couldn't choose who to stand next to. Then the staffer ran down the order of speakers, of which I was one. We were told when we should applaud. We were asked if we had a copy of our prepared talking points and were warned not to change them. It was akin to a teacher telling kindergarteners how to proceed to the cafeteria.

When the time came, aides directed us into the ceremonial signing room, and we filed in as told. As the governor walked in, all his aides started clapping, and through the open doorway from which we had just come, I saw secretaries in a separate room stand and applaud. I forced myself to look away because I knew the audience in the press conference would notice the strange look on my face and might misinterpret it as a judgment on the bill.

When my allotted time to speak came, I changed my remarks to fit me. I spoke about the importance of the legislation and referred to the mayor of Albany, Jerry Jennings, as the dean of the mayoral delegation. I knew it would get a laugh because his persona was more Rodney Dangerfield than a staid academic dean. In his comments, the governor laughingly referred to my designation of Jennings. As directed, I stood next to the governor as he signed the bill.[16] The picture would become ubiquitous in the media. The event ended, and as I walked away, Percoco approached me, smiling. Funny remark about Jennings, he said, and added, "Don't ever do that again."

I was more concerned about the remarks made during the event than Percoco's admonition. The Deputy Speaker of the Assembly Earlene Hooper had said with great emotion that the pension vote was the most difficult one she had to make in her twenty-four years of service.[17] If such an essentially meaningless vote was difficult, what I needed in terms of reform was Herculean.

I left Albany fearing I wasn't going to see the type of leadership the governor's administration was publicly promising, much less the leadership I needed. Our pension bill, due in December, was an estimated $30 million, while our entire tax levy was $33 million. The legislation did nothing to mitigate that problem.

A couple of days after I returned to Syracuse, Howe called to ask if I would accept the job as chair of the state Democratic Party. President Barack Obama was going to be running for reelection and the importance of the presidential election meant there would be a lot of activity. As I talked with Jack about it, I was excited by the opportunity to be in the middle of the political scrum in an important year. I told Howe that if offered, I would accept. Like clockwork, twenty-four hours later, I was scheduled to meet with the governor at his second-floor office in the capital.

On the appointed day of my meeting with Cuomo, I was ushered into the same room where I had waited for the governor for the pension bill

16. Skip Dickstein, "Governor Signs Pension Reform Bill," *Times Union*, March 16, 2012.

17. "New York: Pension Reform Signed Into Law," Compensation Management News, April 18, 2012, https://compensation.blr.com/Compensation-news/Benefits-Leave/Employee-Retirement/New-York-Pension-Reforms-Signed-into-Law/.

signing. As I waited, I looked around at the displayed items, hoping I might see some family memento with Mario. I was looking at a piece of pottery when Cuomo walked in. He immediately told me it was something President Clinton had given him. He walked me around the room and excitedly pointed out dozens of things that were related to the Clintons and, disappointingly, nothing related to his father.

Eventually, Cuomo ushered me into a smaller side office with a couch, a desk, and a chair. A leather motorcycle vest with his name and an official seal in huge print on the back hung on the back of the chair. I sat on the end of a couch, and he sat in a nearby chair and asked me how Jack was. I responded he was fine, and he said Jack and his father had been good friends.

While I nodded, I knew it was much more nuanced. Long before Jack became a part of my life, he and Mario Cuomo had been friends, or so Jack thought. They had attended family celebrations and Jack had been Mario's earliest and most prominent supporter in Central New York. When Mario lost the governor's race in 1994, Jack sent him a heartfelt letter and called him several times. He never heard back. After years of silence, Jack wondered if it had been a friendship or just a relationship of convenience to forward Mario Cuomo's ambition.

When Andrew ran for governor in 2002, Jack supported H. Carl McCall. During that campaign, Andrew spoke derisively about Jack to one of his employees and then for good measure added, "Make sure you tell him I said that." When Jack would tell the story, he would shake his head and rhetorically ask, "Why would he do such a stupid thing?"

A few years later, when Andrew ran for attorney general, he went around the state apologizing to people he had offended. It was referred to as the "Andrew 2.0 tour." During this time, Matilda Cuomo, Mario's wife, called Jack. While Jack had not spoken to her in a long time, he had great affection for her. To his surprise, she was calling to apologize for Andrew's behavior and ask him to accept Andrew's call. He agreed.

In many ways, it was a smart move for Andrew to have Matilda call Jack. He would never have refused her call, but Jack found it strange that a grown man had his mother call to make apologies. When Andrew did call, he opened the conversation by obsequiously calling him "Uncle Jack" and walking down memory lane. Apologies were made and accepted, but Jack never forgot the slights and insults or the culture that allowed them to be slung with such impunity. Jack and Mario were friends, but it was complicated.

Andrew asked, "Is there anything Jack wants? Does he want to be on any boards or anything? I'm sure there is something I could do for him." I assured him Jack was not interested in anything, but he would be flattered to know Andrew asked about him. Andrew nodded and the tone of the conversation shifted.

He said he didn't want to say too much because of the nature of the position he wanted me to take. We needed to be careful about discussing politics in a government office. In selling the deal, he leaned in toward me and said, "You are a bright light in an otherwise dim universe, and we could use that." I was immensely flattered.

Much later, I realized it was a compliment wrapped in a denigrating comment about upstate. When he said it, I was too blinded by the flattery to see it for what it was: a cutting remark about the very people who had put me in front of him.

The governor continued, "We'll need to get some details worked out, and I have someone in mind to be a cochair with you." That was the first time I learned it would be a cochair position, not the chair, but, again, I was so flattered, the major change in the position didn't give me pause. Then the governor stood up, shook my hand, told me Percoco would be in touch, and I was escorted out.

Percoco called me the next day and said he understood I had a good meeting and was willing to accept the position. I told him I had three conditions: (1) my expenses needed to be paid by the state committee; (2) the position would not be merely ceremonial; and (3) the governor would headline a fundraiser for me in my reelection effort. He grudgingly agreed to all three, but I suspected my expenses would be paid months, if not years, after they were incurred. I would have to fight to ensure the position had any influence, and it was unlikely the governor would help me raise money for reelection.

Percoco explained the state was so big it needed two chairs and the cochair was likely going to be Harlem assemblyman Keith Wright. Cuomo was putting representatives from two key constituencies—women and African Americans—as head of the committee, and it dawned on me that the optics of the selections may have been more important than the substance of the position.

Wright was a beloved character. I, too, became part of his fan club shortly after introducing myself on the phone. We agreed we didn't know what we were supposed to do, how to do it, or when to do it, but we would try to have fun.

At our first New York City event to announce our leadership of the state party, Percoco cornered me and made sure I knew to follow the talking points as drafted. When I protested that the remarks were terrible, he said he would find someone better to write them the next time. He never did and, in fact, I began to see a pattern I thought had to be by design where the only remarks that came close to being well done were the ones the governor delivered. At every Cuomo event I witnessed, the talking points for the other speakers were barely grammatically coherent and overly fawning about Cuomo. Yet just about every person delivered them as instructed.

Before the main event, there was a small, exclusive gathering I was told to attend. When I walked in, I knew almost no one in the room and there wasn't anyone I could ask to introduce me to the attendees. Before I had time to worry, though, people began coming up to me to introduce themselves and followed with a declaration of the huge contributions they had given, or were about to give, to the state party. One said, "I know you know, but I wanted to put a face with the donation." I had no idea who the donor was or the amount of the donation. It was clear that was top-secret information only select members of the governor's staff knew.

It was almost time for the main event, and Wright and I were directed to a holding area just to the side of the stage. We were in high spirits, laughing about the private gathering and the characters we met. When we walked into the holding room the atmosphere there was so funereal, we stopped talking. No one told us to, but it was obvious that was what we were supposed to do.

Off to the side, surrounded by suited men but otherwise alone, Cuomo stood in stoic silence with his neck craned down and his eyes focused on his feet. It was clear no one was to talk, much less talk to him. The governor was about to give standard comments to an adoring group of party activists, but it felt like he was about to face a firing squad.

When the governor made his remarks, he was, as expected, treated to wild applause and fawning attention. I gave my prepared and blessed remarks. Percoco thanked me for sticking to the script and disappeared. It was over. But unlike every other political event, there was no invitation for a post-event get together. When Jack and I were sitting at dinner later, I remarked on how strange it was to not have an invitation. Jack joked, "Maybe Andrew doesn't like you."

While the comment was prescient, I thought maybe he did not like people or, more precisely, the unpredictable nature of people's reactions. As an introvert myself, I recognized the traits, but Cuomo had taken his ability to control his environment and created a world where unpredictability was to be avoided at all costs.

Later that year, I was at the presidential debate between Obama and his Republican challenger, Mitt Romney, at Hofstra.[18] There was a strict security and television protocol, so everyone in the audience needed to be in a seat early. The group of attendees for each candidate was exceedingly small, enough to fill a couple of bleacher-like benches for each side. Everyone in the Obama section had worked together, knew each other, and was committed to getting their candidate elected. We spent the time laughing and trading gossip. I noticed there were only two seats at the end of a row that remained open. Eventually, the lights went down, and a moderator began reciting instructions to the audience. Out of the corner of my eye, I saw Percoco come into the room, look around, walk out, and return with Andrew. The governor took the last seat in the row and Percoco took the seat next to him, presumably to protect him. From whom I could not imagine.

To me, it seemed Cuomo was missing out on the best part of politics—the people, including their unpredictability. It was an element I saw his father enjoy unabashedly. While Mario had characteristics of an introvert, like his deep thinking and diary writing, I saw him joyfully interact with people behind closed doors and in public. He teased politicians, debated priests, and complimented children with a genuineness that was never forced.

## The Mayor Who Wanted to Know Too Much

My political stops across upstate confirmed that every locality was facing economically turbulent waters. This became widely known at the end of the summer of 2012, when the comptroller issued a statewide report[19] warning

18. Hofstra University presidential debate, October 16, 2012. https://www.hofstra.edu/debate/debate-2012/.

19. Thomas Kaplan, "Local Governments Face Fiscal Peril, State Comptroller Warns," *New York Times*, August 1, 2012.

that local governments were "facing a perfect storm" of fiscal pressures. The report said that more than one hundred local governments had insufficient cash to meet current liabilities, approximately three hundred local governments had deficits during 2010 or 2011 or both, and twenty-seven municipalities had exhausted their reserve funds.

The report indicated that cities faced the most significant risk, but all municipalities were vulnerable. While there were many factors to blame for the poor financial position of local governments, including population loss and a lack of economic growth, in my view, pension payments were the proverbial straw threatening to break the back of these governments.

I hosted a meeting in Syracuse of the mayors of the state's largest cities, including Michael Spano of Yonkers, Thomas Richards of Rochester, and Jerry Jennings of Albany, with the express purpose of sharing our fiscal issues and looking for consensus on potential solutions.[20] The meeting received a surprising amount of media attention.

While the state had never had a city declare bankruptcy, Detroit's bankruptcy made the once unthinkable seem possible. The mayor of Scranton, Pennsylvania, had recently announced[21] he didn't know if he had enough money to pay city employees through the weekend. The story was chilling because Scranton and Syracuse are similar industrial cities situated along Interstate 81.

I wondered what it meant that the Scranton mayor didn't know how much money the city had. Was it a bargaining position? Were people lying to him? Did he not ask the right questions? Could it happen to me? When I had a conversation with Richard Brodsky about it, he volunteered to write a memo outlining the contours of municipal bankruptcy and its history in New York State. As a lawyer and veteran of state politics, he had extensive knowledge on the legal, political, and practical issues cities in fiscal stress faced.

Days later, in a conversation with a reporter from the *Wall Street Journal*, I mentioned I had asked for a legal memo on municipal bankruptcy.[22] My

20. Teri Weaver, "Upstate Mayors Meet to Strategize Ways to Handle Rising Costs to Cities," Syracuse.com, July 17, 2012, https://www.syracuse.com/news/2012/07/upstate_mayors_meet_to_strateg.html.

21. Paul Harris, "Scranton, Pennsylvania: Where Even the Mayor Is on Minimum Wage," *Guardian*, July 14, 2012.

22. Michelle Breidenbach, "Syracuse Mayor Stephanie Miner Brushes Up on

goal was to demonstrate I was being responsible by learning about complex municipal financial issues. I thought it was the right message to send: A smart, thoughtful mayor ensures she understands the issues and ramifications. To the contrary, the comment threatened to upend all the careful financial management we had been doing.

After reading the comment in the *Journal*, two credit-rating agencies issued public reports stating that Syracuse's bond ratings might be negatively impacted,[23] which would be unprecedented in our history with the ratings agencies. When I called our contact at Moody's, he confirmed it was likely that Syracuse's bond rating would be negatively adjusted. He knew about the responsible decisions we were making, our financial position, and that we needed help from Albany. He also agreed that talking about the issue publicly was a way to force the issue before the bankruptcy was imminent.

When I said I was shocked Moody's would downgrade a city because its leader asked to be educated, he responded that I had to understand how his boss would react to the article in the aftermath of the Great Recession and the current skittish state of the stock markets. For the sake of his institution, he seemed to say, it would have been better if I had just ignored Syracuse's burgeoning financial imbalance. Another incentive to keep quiet.

I called Fitch, the other main rating agency and had a much more constructive conversation. After my explanation, the Fitch employee said he understood. He even spoke to the Syracuse newspaper, saying, "We don't anticipate the city being anywhere near bankruptcy at least for a few years at the soonest, and the mayor confirmed that. Bankruptcy is not imminent. The city is doing fine, at the moment, but she wants to be smarter . . . and know how things work and the history of New York State."[24] Fitch's public comments defending my actions were enough to protect me from complete political embarrassment, but I was stung by the reaction to my request for information.

Bankruptcy Law, Just in Case," Syracuse.com, August 10, 2012, https://www.syracuse.com/news/2012/08/post_641.html.

23. Michelle Breidenbach, "Syracuse Mayor Stephanie Miner Brushes Up on Bankruptcy Law, Just in Case," Syracuse.com, August 10, 2012, https://www.syracuse.com/news/2012/08/post_641.html.

24. Michelle Breidenbach, "Syracuse Mayor Stephanie Miner Brushes Up on Bankruptcy Law, Just in Case," Syracuse.com, August 10, 2012, https://www.syracuse.com/news/2012/08/post_641.html.

In the early fall of 2012, I was scheduled to speak at a political rally for Dan Maffei, a Democratic candidate for Congress, in Syracuse. The governor decided to appear at the last minute. While I had seen the governor sporadically over the past year, we had not had any conversations. When I greeted him backstage, he asked me if I knew Mike Spano, the mayor of Yonkers. I said I did.

Cuomo looked visibly angry and, apropos of nothing, began threatening Spano. He said he knew Spano's family, and when he got a hold of him, he was going to make Spano cry and then he'll stop. There was absolutely no context for this adolescent outburst. It was one of the strangest interactions I've had in my life. I was relieved when the event began and put an end to the awkward encounter.

Afterward, I relayed Cuomo's behavior to Brodsky and asked him if I should call Spano. Without missing a beat, Brodsky said to me, "Are you an idiot? He wasn't threatening Spano. He was threatening you. You're the one challenging him." I was organizing mayors to ask Albany for help with our shared existential issues. Was that the challenge? Or was the governor threatened because I was a woman and did not know how to handle that? It was so strange, I didn't think it was worth finding out the answer even if I could. Perhaps I was using my willful denial as a form of self-protection. Regardless, I laughed and told Brodsky I was more familiar with direct threats. "Oh, that will come soon enough," he replied.

## Just Borrow

Finally, at the beginning of 2013, the fiscal issues of the state's cities began to garner public attention. I kept hearing the governor had a plan to help cities that he'd unveil during his budget-proposal announcement. I left multiple messages for Duffy and Percoco to ask about the plan; neither of them called me back. When I asked other state leaders what the idea was, they said the governor's office was leading the charge and nothing else. I told numerous people on the governor's staff that I was already being asked about the plan by the media, implying it would be best if I wasn't surprised.

The day the governor's budget was announced, the media informed me the big idea was allowing cities to borrow money to pay pension bills. Euphemistically called "pension smoothing," the Stable Rate Pension Contribution Option allowed local governments to lock in lower pension contributions for a period of years and presumably pay lower costs in the future based on some convenient assumptions.[25]

The theory was that local governments would see future pension bills slashed because new employees would replace more expensive retiring employees. It ignored the reality that most local governments were shrinking. When employees retired, their positions were likely to be eliminated, not filled. The proposal also assumed the markets would produce a return of 7.5 percent, contradicting the lower rates actuaries suggested for other pension funds.[26]

It was not an idea, it was a gimmick—a tactic that would allow municipalities to underpay current pension contributions based upon the faulty assumption that in the long-term, the government's liabilities would shrink. It did nothing but kick the problem down the road.

Cuomo presented a simple "solution" requiring no sacrifice, which, he said, would solve the problem. Instead, the problem was likely to grow bigger and necessitate tremendous sacrifices in the future to pay the bill. All we had to do was look at Detroit to see how destructive this strategy would be.

All the work I had done to brief, lobby, and explain the dire circumstances of the fiscal condition of Syracuse only to have the governor's office propose the worst type of public policy was a staggering rejection of what I believed leadership should do—solve problems. When the Syracuse media called me about the plan, I said I wanted time to study the idea, but I found the proposal "puzzling, and it raised more questions than answers."[27]

Percoco called immediately after the story was published and disingenuously asked why I hadn't voiced my concerns before going to the press. He knew I had asked several times for a briefing. I was not briefed because they didn't want to give me a chance to marshal my opposition. Given that, I told him saying I was "puzzled" and wanted time to study the plan was gentle. He said he wanted to "calm things down."

25. Rick Karlin, "Pension Option Raises Questions," *Times Union*, January 24, 2012.

26. Martin Z. Braun and Christina Alesci, "NYC Actuary Said to Seek Cut in Pension-Fund Return Rate to 7%," Bloomberg.com, January 11, 2012, https://www.bloomberg.com /news/articles/2012-01-11/nyc-actuary-said-to-seek-lower-pension-fund-rate-of -return-of-7-from-8-.

27. Tim Knauss, "Syracuse Mayor Finds Governor's Pension Proposal 'Puzzling,'" Syra cuse.com, January 22, 2013, https://www.syracuse.com/news/2013/01/syracuse_mayor _finds_governors.html.

When I walked into city hall the next day, I ran into a reporter who told me the lieutenant governor's office unexpectedly asked to speak with the editorial board that day. A couple of hours later, the same reporter called asking for a response to the lieutenant governor's uncharacteristically harsh comments: "I would say to the mayor, if [the pension borrowing proposal] is not sufficient, then I would suggest one viable option she would have is to request a financial control board."[28]

It was stunning. I said the idea was "puzzling," wanted to study it, and Robert Duffy came to Syracuse threatening a state takeover. The message was clear: I was to do the Cuomo administration's bidding or be crushed. While I should have been cautious, I was angry. I got my position because of the people of Syracuse, and I would not cower in the face of threats. Particularly when I knew the public policy at issue was not thought out and would not help the people who trusted me to represent them.

I responded it was a false choice to demand a mayor make an irresponsible fiscal decision or forfeit democratic control of a city. News of the shocking back-and-forth quickly spread. Within hours, I received a phone call from the *New York Times* asking about the pension borrowing plan. I provocatively replied that the proposed idea was "kicking the can down the road" and how "states like Illinois [got] in trouble."[29]

I hung up the phone and drove home. As I walked in the door, Percoco was frantically trying to get ahold of me. Jack asked me how my day was. I shook my head, pointing to my phone ringing incessantly. I then sat at my kitchen table and answered Percoco's call on speaker phone for Jack's benefit. "Madam Mayor," Percoco said, his voice dripping with fury. "I thought we were going to calm things down and you are quoted in the *Times*." I took a deep breath and said, "Hey, Joe, No. 1: When the *New York Times* calls me, I'm always going to take the call. No. 2: If you want to calm things down, having the lieutenant governor come into my town and tell me to stick it up my ass is not how you do it."

As I said it, Jack shook his head, offended by my language, but Percoco was uncharacteristically silent. Eventually he said, "What are you talking

28. Tim Knauss, "Cuomo Says His Pension Proposal Would Save Syracuse $43.5 Million over 5 Years," Syracuse.com, January 25, 2013, https://www.syracuse.com/news/2013/01/cuomo_says_his_pension_proposa.html.

29. Danny Hakim, "Syracuse's Democratic Mayor Gets Under Governor's Skin," *New York Times*, January 23, 2013.

about?" He did not know about Duffy's visit to Syracuse. That meant only one thing: the governor himself told Duffy to do it. Percoco could not get off the phone fast enough.

The next afternoon, Percoco called and told me the administration had not handled the interaction well, but he wanted to calm things down. Never one for subtlety, he asked what I planned to say in my testimony on the governor's proposed budget scheduled for the next week. I assured him I wanted solutions, not a war of words. But we both knew the tenor of the discussion was largely in the hands of the person not on the phone.

Testifying in Albany regarding the governor's proposed budget was an annual event referred to as "tin cup day," with local government officials traveling to Albany with cup in hand, asking for money. Most state legislators did not even pretend to care about municipal issues and skipped attending the local officials' testimony.

The one exception was New York City. The mayor of New York always testified first, presumably because he was the chief executive of the largest local government in the state. State legislators swarmed Michael Bloomberg's testimony, mostly lobbying for their issue of choice, separate from his budget testimony. This appeared to be mainly aimed at getting attention in the media, rather than gaining an understanding of the impact of state decisions on New York City. For the rest of us, the few state legislators who listened to our testimony showed no pretense of being informed or interested in the issues we presented.

I was exhausted from having recently delivered my annual State of the City address. I was also preparing for an annual fundraising event and dealing with the fracas over the pension proposal. For my testimony, I had decided to talk about the risks of borrowing for operating costs, but I hadn't prepared my remarks yet. Three of my staff and I went to Senator Dave Valesky's office to draft my testimony. Every thirty minutes, one of us would receive a call from a different member of the Cuomo administration requesting a copy of my statement.

Bloomberg's testimony was on in the background as I finalized the remarks. I froze when a legislator asked Bloomberg a question about the governor's pension proposal. His response would set the tone for how my comments would be interpreted. If he said the plan was acceptable, my comments would be minimized because the mayor of the largest city in the state was fine with it. If he disagreed with the governor's proposal, he risked adverse consequences by choosing sides in a political fight that did not concern him.

As I held my breath, Bloomberg responded, "As a general policy postponing, down the road, expenses that you are going to have every year is not a good policy."[30] While I felt like he had thrown me a life raft, it was in keeping with who he was. There was a right way and a wrong way to make such decisions, and when asked, he chose the right way, likely without much thought to the political ramifications.

After Bloomberg's remarks, I made my way to the room where testimony was being given. The audience was surprisingly full, and I felt as if all eyes were on me. When it was my turn to give remarks, I passed Onondaga County Executive Joanie Mahoney coming up the stairs as I was headed down. I said hello and she said, "They wanted me to attack you on the pension, but I said I wouldn't." I nodded and thought, *So much for calming it down.*

I delivered placid remarks highlighting challenging fiscal conditions, escalating pension bills, declining revenues, and the need for substantive answers to our problems. It felt exceedingly predictable and boring. As I walked up the stairs to leave, my staffer Elizabeth DeJoseph whispered, "Mayor, apparently some media have been calling the office and want to talk to you." Expecting it would be a couple of reporters from Syracuse, I agreed but told her I needed to go to the bathroom.

When I walked out of the auditorium, I noticed on my left a huge gaggle of reporters, with klieg lights and microphones. As I started toward the bathroom, I wondered if Bloomberg was still around and heard someone yell, "Mayor Miner." I looked up and saw the throng moving toward me. So much for the bathroom.

While I certainly had seen others subjected to it, I had never been the object of such a media gaggle. When I agreed to speak about my testimony, I was instantly at the center of blinding lights, recording television cameras, fuzzy-headed microphones, and a few pens and reporter's notebooks. It was a heady moment. I had an opening to do something, but I wasn't exactly sure what that should be.

One by one, the reporters identified themselves and asked questions about the fiscal conditions and pensions of local governments. They ran the

30. Danny Hakim, "Comptroller Criticizes Cuomo's Plan to Cut Pension Costs," *New York Times,* January 28, 2013.

gamut, from major national outlets to small local papers—the *Associated Press*, the *New York Times*, *Newsday*, NPR affiliates, and cable news stations. A Cuomo staffer was also there recording the event.

The gaggle wrapped up, and I started to leave when a young reporter came running up, breathing heavily, and apologized for being late. He asked if he could interview me. I said only if he let me go to the bathroom first. When I came back, he was looking at his notes and said to me, "Congratulations, most people are afraid to stand up to the governor." As I answered his pension questions, I thought, I'm not most people, but maybe they know something I don't.

## Happy Valentine's Day

I was being credited with forcing the issue of fiscal stewardship and the plight of the state's local governments. It was clear from the media reaction that my argument about the bad policy of shifting expenses into the future had traction. Statewide media was covering the pros and cons of the proposal in depth, and local officials were coming out with their own financial analyses showing the inherent weakness in the idea. The pension funds trustee, Comptroller Thomas DiNapoli, contacted me to talk about the proposal and let me know that he thought my arguments had merit.

I wanted a solution for my city. I thought a discussion of ideas could force the political establishment to create a substantive solution, instead of a press release filled with meaningless talking points. To do so would require me to get in front of a large, important audience and elevate the problem, demand ideas, and inspire a better solution—exactly what I believed leaders were supposed to do. It occurred to me the best venue to do that in was the *New York Times*. I reached out to staff at the paper's editorial board to see if they would be interested in an op-ed about the fiscal plight of New York State's cities. Much to my surprise, they answered they might be.

For the next couple of weeks, I had a series of conversations with Sewell Chan, the deputy editor of the editorial page. Getting an editorial accepted at the paper of record was the definition of hurry up and wait. Chan and I were on completely different schedules. I worked in the early morning until early evening and Chan worked at night. We spoke at night when I was exhausted from the day, and he was exasperated by looming deadlines.

He would ask me to send a draft. I would work on it at night, then again in the morning, and email it to him. I would wait all day to hear from him, and then around eight in the evening he would call and ask for more information, an explanation, or even to say he had not had time to review my most recent draft. There were several drafts, and then, when the op-ed was finalized, there were legal documents to be signed and, finally, it came down to finding the space and time to publish it. It was sidelined by Pope Benedict's retirement announcement and the death of former mayor Ed Koch.

Finally, the night came when Chan said it would be published. Up until that point, I had not shared with my staff that I was writing the editorial. I wanted to give myself room to think about the decision. As the interactions with the *Times* kept getting attenuated, I wasn't sure it would ever happen.

I walked out of my office and went to see who on my staff was still around at seven thirty. My director of administration, Beth Rougeux, and my planning director, Andrew Maxwell, were busy working. I asked them to stop and gave them a copy of the editorial and told them it would be published in the *New York Times* the next day unless I called to stop it in the next thirty minutes. They read it and recognized immediately it would have serious repercussions.

We talked about the rationale and consequences of publishing the editorial. It was the first time I had vocalized my thinking about the political system I was working within. If I didn't discuss the plight of upstate cities and the impact of poor state leadership on the citizens of Syracuse and other New Yorkers, it was unlikely anyone else would. They gave me their blessing, knowing it meant crossing a Rubicon.

I spent enormous amounts of time and energy working through the accepted political channels with no tangible benefits for my constituents. While it was unlikely the op-ed by itself would change the political dynamic, it would be a call for substantive leadership to address the state's civic ills. I would rather be known for standing up for something that mattered than for capitulating to the status quo.

I let the half hour pass and called Percoco to tell him about the piece. I thought the right thing to do was to give him notice. Not surprisingly, he was furious and started screaming at me. After berating me for what seemed like several minutes, he screamed, "Who put you up to this?" and immediately followed up with, "What do you want!" I repeated what I'd been saying over and over. I wanted the administration to pay attention to Syracuse's problems. He blurted out, "Yeah, Stephanie, like anyone in Syracuse reads the *New York Times*!"

There it was. What he, Cuomo, and his administration thought of me, Syracuse, and my constituents. We were illiterate rubes who should be thankful for any attention we got from the governor's office and never question them or their policies. I was so offended by his comment that I glossed over the implications of his first remarks, which implied I did not have the agency, intelligence, or skill to execute a political strategy on my own. Any misgivings about writing the piece vanished. I was disgusted and curtly responded, "Joe, I'm getting off the phone now." I put on my coat and walked to my car.

As I started the car, my phone rang. It was Chan. My heart sank because I thought the *Times* had pulled it. I answered and Chan said, "Mayor Miner, can you tell me how the Cuomo administration knows about your piece? They have been calling and screaming at people here about it and my shop certainly didn't say anything." I said, "I told them. I thought it was the right thing to do." After a beat, he said, "Okay, good luck, mayor," and hung up.

I walked in the house to find a Valentine's Day card on the kitchen table. I had forgotten the next day was February 14. The card was sentimental, and Jack had written in it how proud he was of me and how much he loved me. I climbed the stairs to our bedroom, exhausted. When he heard me, he yelled that the piece was online and said, "Oh my God, I'm so glad your last name isn't Mannion." I laughed and went to bed feeling good about my decision.

## Political or Pyrrhic Victory

The repercussions of the *Times* piece were immediate and long-lasting.[31] It elevated my profile, with many observers calling me "courageous" and a "truth-teller,"[32] and others saying I was disloyal and foolhardy. A couple of

31. Stephanie A. Miner, "Cuomo to Cities: Just Borrow," *New York Times*, February 13, 2013, https://www.nytimes.com/2013/02/14/opinion/new-york-states-cities-cant-borrow-their-way-to-solvency.html.

32. Tim Knauss, "Syracuse Mayor Stephanie Miner Picked for 'Trailblazing Women in Public Finance' Award," Syracuse.com, November 26, 2012, https://www.syracuse.com/news/2013/11/syracuse_mayor_stephanie_miner_picked_for_trailblazing_women_in_public_finance_a.html.

weeks after my op-ed was published, the comptroller and the governor's office announced a pension compromise called the New Alternative Contribution Stabilization Plan.[33] It allowed localities to engage in more borrowing than they had previously been allowed for a longer period. It was viewed as a less risky plan than the governor's original proposal. It was seen as a compromise.

All the arguments about the inherent risk and irresponsibility of borrowing to pay for operating expenses evaporated with the discussion of the compromise. Instead, the stories were about how the state was offering local governments a solution to the problem. I was told the Cuomo administration pressured the largest municipalities to enroll to undercut the argument that the contribution stabilization plan was a bad policy. Several leaders were told a failure to enroll would mean the administration would not be receptive to helping them on any issue. One by one, local governments, a total of twenty-nine, took advantage of the plan and pushed off the inevitable day of reckoning.[34] I refused to have Syracuse participate and force future mayors to bear the consequences of the risky policy.

I was congratulated and recognized for engaging in a worthy political fight and winning by forcing a compromise. It turned out it wasn't just the Cuomo administration that was uninterested in a serious policy solution; the state's civic culture wasn't either. Editorial boards and think tanks that had been vocally opposed to borrowing to pay pension bills stopped talking about the issue once the compromise was announced. It was as if the pension problem had been solved.

I wrestled with my purpose in politics. If it was simply for the sake of ambition, I should've felt good, because the whole affair had elevated my profile considerably. But I did not feel good; I felt ineffective. All my advocacy and political risk-taking had transformed a short-term, irresponsible policy into a compromise mitigating fiscal damage but still deferring a substantive public policy solution. Here I was being congratulated for being politically astute, but my advocacy had not made things better for my city, just for my reputation. Such was the working definition of being a successful politician.

33. Office of the New York State Comptroller, Alternate Contribution Stabilization Program, Overview, https://www.osc.state.ny.us/retirement/employers/alternate-contribution-stabilization-program.

34. The number provided by the New York State comptroller's office.

The Cuomo administration was convinced I was a puppet for someone else, and the speculation landed on Bloomberg. When that theory was debunked, I was told the governor thought Jack had "put me up to it." When one of the members of the Albany establishment shared the administration's speculation, I repeated what I had been saying all along: I wanted a serious discussion and policy solution for Syracuse's fiscal problems. "Well, that's the problem," he said. "They don't think that way, so they can't imagine anyone else thinking that way." While I assumed regional bias or sexism was underlying the Cuomo's administration conjecture, I didn't spend much time examining it, because it was secondary to a more profound issue.

Cuomo and I had distinct views on what our jobs entailed. Cuomo's philosophy seemed to be that successful governing was about winning and generating the right buzzwords, like "leadership," "head-on," and "reform." Difficult problems requiring honest analysis and potential confrontations were to be avoided. He was able do this, I realized, because there was no accountability for his lack of constructive solutions. The state did not run out of money. State services continued unabated, even if poorly delivered, and problems just festered.

I, on the other hand, had an excess of responsibility. Syracuse was on track to run out of money. Every day and every night, I worried about the impact of a city without the finances to replace police officers, provide code inspections, or in the worst-case scenario, make its own decisions. Our problems would smolder and then explode with real consequences. When they did, people would look to me for a solution.

After all, I was Mayor Miner. I was accountable, professionally and morally, for solutions every day when I walked out my door and saw my neighbors. Ideas and substance were the only effective way I knew to institute solid public policy. Ultimately, that cemented my determination in how I would govern, even if it caused painful consequences. The perversity, of course, is that by choosing substance over style, I was governing in a manner closer to Mario than Andrew.

## Postscript

Syracuse's pension costs grew an estimated 76 percent in the years I was in office. We paid the bills in full and on time. We strictly managed our spending, negotiated a beneficial change in the sales tax formula, created a system to improve property-tax collection, and decreased borrowing to lower our debt service. While difficult and requiring sacrifice, we were responsible fiscal stewards.

The refusal to participate in the "pension smoothing" plan saved Syracuse about $124 million over twenty-five years. The assumptions used to justify the benefits of Cuomo's plan failed to materialize. S&P Global Ratings considers the "pension smoothing program/contribution stabilization plan" a deferral of annual operating expenses. It stated that "a government's regular use of the program" is an "indication of a structural imbalance," which could lead to closer review and negative ratings.[35]

Across the country, localities' debt levels are at all-time highs and their debts related to pensions have grown significantly. Far from having disappeared, the risk of insolvency for large cities is now higher than at any point since the federal government first passed a municipal bankruptcy law in the 1930s.[36] As the *Economist* pointed out, "The pensions crisis has been rumbling on for years, but some states and cities will soon enter a downward spiral, in which pension costs lead to bad public services or tax rises, in turn encouraging workers and firms to move out, which then shrinks the tax base, making promises even less affordable."[37]

---

35. "Assessing Local Governments' Use of New York's Pension Smoothing Program," S&P Global Reports, January 11, 2018.

36. Daniel DiSalvo and Stephen Eide, "When Cities Are at the Financial Brink: The Case for 'Intervention Bankruptcy,'" Manhattan Institute, January 12, 2017, https://www .manhattan-institute.org/html/when-cities-are-financial-brink-case-intervention-bank ruptcy-9894.html.

37. *Economist*, "Pensions Are Woefully Underfunded," Economist.com, November 16, 2019. https://www.economist.com/leaders/2019/11/16/public-pensions-are-woefully -underfunded.

# Infrastructure

## Make It Work

It was a beautiful spring day, and the sidewalk was filled with smiling, laughing people enjoying the weather. As I whisked by in a car, I, too, reveled in the sunshine and my whimsical decision to wear new open-toed shoes—shoes no other Syracuse mayor had ever worn, I thought with amusement. Suddenly, the car jolted to a stop in several inches of water gushing around us and down the city street.

With the car at a standstill, I opened the door and stood on the doorjamb inspecting the rushing river beneath my feet. A man in front of an Army Navy store yelled, "Hey, Mayor!" When I turned, he said, "Like your shoes," and with a laugh, pointed toward his store. "There's some boots inside I can sell you." Others standing on the dry sidewalk joined in the laughter. I looked down at my new shoes and the gallons of water coursing beneath me. So much for trying to separate myself from other mayors. I called the probable water-main break into the city's dispatch office and then called Deborah Somers, the water commissioner.

Somers answered saying she and a crew were on their way. The water department had an ancient but working system continuously measuring water pressure. A significant decline indicated a potential water-main break. Based on what I saw, there was no doubt it was a break. Rivers do not flow through city streets.

Within moments, the commissioner arrived. She waded over to my car, holding up a long, flowing skirt that exposed industrial knee-high black rubber boots. "Do you want to have one of my guys carry you?" she asked provocatively. "No, I'm fine," I said and stepped into water above my ankles.

Laughing, she asked my shoe size and told me she would get me a pair of "stylish" rubber boots to keep in my car like she did.

We watched the workers scurry to contain the flooding, and the commissioner explained the break was relatively small and would be fixed quickly. No one would lose access to water for longer than a couple of hours. "The guys," by which Somers meant the long-term water department employees, "tell me we used to have breaks like this only in the winter, but now they're happening all the time."

As I listened, I was hit by a lightning-bolt realization that residents could have their access to all-important potable water interrupted at any time. Really, I thought, Syracuse is at risk "all the time" of not having clean and essential water? Sensing my anxiety, the commissioner said, "The guys are good. They'll fix it." I watched the workers and wondered what other secrets were buried beneath the pavement.

When I started digging a little deeper, it became evident all the city's infrastructure systems were in various states of disrepair. Local governments are responsible for operating systems directly serving the public—water, roads, bridges, and sewer systems. At its most basic, a city is a collection of infrastructure systems. A mayor's daily, fundamental challenge is to ensure the systems operate so the city can function.

City workers were hiding the deterioration by executing fast, reliable repairs, but we were facing the wholesale decline of many of those systems. Syracuse's water mains were breaking year-round, and we were on track in 2010 to set a record. Our sewer system was so fragile, staff quietly suggested turning the system over to Onondaga County before an inevitable disaster struck.

The buildings housing our police and fire departments had outdated electrical systems, unreliable elevators—sometimes resulting in police officers and accused criminals getting stuck together in uncomfortably close quarters—malfunctioning computer systems, and crumbling sections of buildings that needed to be roped off to protect the public. Police cars had street signs welded to the floor to cover holes, snowplows constantly needed servicing, and some city workers were driving twenty-nine-year-old Chrysler K cars.

During a routine meeting in February, the budget director told me we might not be able to open our pools in the summer. "Come again?" I asked, wondering why the budget director was talking about swimming pools in the winter. The parks department, she explained, said it was worried about the operation of a thirty-year-old water pump for one of the city's eleven public pools.

The department submitted an estimated price for a replacement part and an estimated price for a new pump. Neither option provided any real solution; the part was difficult to find because the pump was so old, a new pump was cost prohibitive, and several other pools were using the same vintage pump. The result was we might be forced to close one or more of the pool facilities used by thousands of children. "We've been using chewing gum for a long time. I don't know how much longer it can last," the budget director said pointing to a growing trend among all city departments: more and more money was being budgeted for emergency repairs.

## The Water Is Running . . . Not Resources

Syracuse's increasingly precarious infrastructure system wasn't simply suffering from regular wear and tear. Infrastructure in the United States had traditionally been paid for by a partnership between the federal, state, and local governments. In the 1970s and into the 1980s, the federal government paid for 75 percent of wastewater infrastructure, the state matched the investment with 12.5 percent of the cost, and Syracuse paid the remaining 12.5 percent with mostly in-kind contributions.[1]

Starting in 1956 with the passage of the Federal-Aid Highway Act, the federal government started expanding its infrastructure spending. In 1956, the percentage of federal spending on transportation and water infrastructure was 15 percent. It rose in 1960 to 31 percent, and between 1959 and 1975, the federal share of infrastructure spending averaged 30 percent. Spending increased to 38 percent until 1981 when it started to decrease with the advent of Reaganomics.[2]

Public spending on infrastructure has been falling ever since, and in 2014, it was at 23 percent.[3] Once, when speaking with a policy expert in DC,

1. "Wastewater Infrastructure Needs of New York State," New York State Department of Environmental Conservation (March 2008): 15, 16.

2. Hunter Blair, "What Is the Ideal Mix of Federal, State, and Local Government Investment in Infrastructure?" *Economic Policy Institute*, September 11, 2017.

3. Blair, "What Is the Ideal Mix of Federal, State, and Local Government Investment in Infrastructure?" 4, Figure A.

I said federal lawmakers would not be able to avoid addressing infrastructure when Americans started dying because of the state of disrepair. He despondently said that had already happened and they were still ignoring it.

Similarly, state funds allocated to wastewater, drinking water, and transportation infrastructure has also declined.[4] With little public attention, federal and state governments dramatically cut the amount of money they made available for local governments to maintain infrastructure.[5] This put the funding responsibility for these large, crucial—but easily ignored—systems squarely on Syracuse's overburdened shoulders.

Consequently, Syracuse repaired fewer miles of roads, water mains, and sewer pipes. The department of public works (DPW) employees started referring to work on roads as "painting it black"—that is, just laying on a top layer of asphalt instead of making an actual repair. The city bought fewer or skipped replacing snowplows, police cars, and fire trucks. This, in turn, led to even faster deterioration of the existing vehicles. Syracuse's routine deferral of maintenance to fund daily services meant most equipment was in wholesale decline and exorbitantly expensive to fix.

Syracuse was no outlier. The state comptroller estimated that state and local governments' infrastructure needs for water, sewer, and transportation alone were underfunded by approximately $89 billion. The comptroller said in a 2012 report that such shortfalls could cause "devastating potential results [leaving] future New Yorkers with crumbling roads and bridges and failing water and sewer systems."[6]

Yet the issue did not garner much public attention because our infrastructure—water mains, sewers, bridges, and roads—was functioning, albeit unpredictably. Early in my term, a newspaper editor casually asked me

4. "Wastewater Infrastructure Needs of New York State," New York State Department of Environmental Conservation (November 2008): 16–17; "Drinking Water Infrastructure Needs of New York State," New York State Department of Health (November 2008): 3, 9, 17.

5. Federal aid for capital projects increased in 2009 and 2010 because of the stimulus package known as the American Recovery and Reinvestment Act. That funding ended in 2011. From 2002 to 2010, when adjusted for inflation, state aid fell. "Growing Cracks in the Foundation," Office of the State Comptroller (December 2012): 13. https://www.osc.state.ny.us/files/local-government/publications/pdf/infrastructure2014.pdf.

6. "Growing Cracks in the Foundation," Office of the State Comptroller (December 2012): 2. https://www.osc.state.ny.us/files/local-government/publications/pdf/infrastructure2014.pdf.

what kept me up at night. Without hesitation, I said failing infrastructure. Clearly surprised, he said, "I guess that's what a mayor should say—the stuff that none of us ever think about."

## My Mother's Storm

Late in the afternoon of April 26, 2011, I stood looking out my office windows preparing to call and wish my mother a happy birthday. As I was about to hit the call button, the sky changed from blue to gray to black before my eyes. Along with the sudden darkness came deafening thunderclaps, giant bolts of lightning, large hail, and then a deluge of rain. The hail dented the cars parked below and blocked out sound until loud crashes of thunder and streaks of bright lightning drowned out the hail's impact. I stood with the phone in my hand, enthralled by nature's show of force, until I remembered I was the mayor.

"This probably is not good," I said aloud. My cell phone rang over the tremendous background noise of thunder, flashing lightning, and crashing hail. It was my security officer, calling to say there was chaos on the streets; then my secretary appeared telling me the police chief was on one phone line and the fire chief was on another. When I got on the line with both, they calmly reported there was already widespread damage.

Hundreds of motorists were stranded on flooded roads. One motorist was driving under a small bridge when the storm hit and was instantly stranded. The water rose so quickly she had to crawl onto the roof of her car to be rescued by a fire truck that lifted her to safety. She was lucky to have been able to climb out of her car in time to be rescued. The elevated highway passing through the middle of Syracuse, route I-81, was shut down because of the water. Storm covers were exploding because of the water pressure underneath the roads in the mains. A burst rainwater pipe forced Upstate University Hospital to close its lobby. Power was out throughout the city and region.[7]

My secretary told me a long-term public works employee was demanding to talk to me. "Right now? I'm on the phone with the chiefs." She said he insisted it was important. I told the chiefs to hold on and got on another line with the public works employee with a clipped, "What's up?"

7. "Sudden Deluge Overwhelms Central New York," *Post-Standard*, April 27, 2011.

"Yeah, Mayor? Tell them to open the valves and gates, it will drain the water." I had no idea what he was saying, but he was insistent. "Who should open them up?" I asked.

"The fire department, DPW, anyone. Just tell them," the long-term public works employee pleaded with me.

I got back on the phone with the chiefs and told them to work with the public works department to make sure the gates and valves were opened. An hour or so later, when the acute emergency had passed, the fire chief and I drove around inspecting various sites. He told me he had never experienced such a fast-moving and damaging storm. We stopped in front of firefighters hunched over water rushing around their knees. When I asked him what they were doing, he told me they were trying to open the valves and gates.

I learned the valves were part of the water system that, when closed, isolated areas of the system and, when opened, let water flow. The gates controlled the amount of water flowing to its eventual destination, Onondaga Lake. The problem, he told me, was the valves and gates were old and seldom used, so they broke easily and took a great deal of manual labor to open. In a fast-moving storm, it's questionable whether that's the best use of workers' time. Yet the ability of the valves and gates to control water levels could be the difference between life and death.

Later, we were told the storm was likely a "microburst," a localized column of sinking air within a thunderstorm that causes high winds, driving rain, and hail. They often cause severe damage and can be life-threatening. In our case, no one died, but several sinkholes opened underneath the roads, including one that was twenty feet deep and cost $90,000 to repair.[8]

Microbursts are traditionally common in the summer in the southeastern United States. Now these storms were happening in Syracuse, the heart of the Northeast, with unprecedented regularity. In addition to paying for short-term repairs, we also had to prepare for major reconstruction of infrastructure systems to survive climate change in what came to be known as "the new normal."

8. Charley Hannagan, "Syracuse Officials Fear April Storm Created More Sinkholes," Syracuse.com, May 12, 2011. https://www.syracuse.com/news/2011/05/syracuse_officials _fear_april.html.
The National Weather Service reported the storm dumped a startling 1.79 inches of rain in a short period of time and brought golf-ball-sized hail and damaging winds of more than sixty miles per hour.

## "Fix Your Own Pipes"

By 2013, Syracuse was on pace to set a record for broken water pipes. Water crews had been doing emergency repairs every night for three weeks; we estimated it would cost $2 million to replace one-hundred-year-old mains; we needed $5 million for road construction, but we could afford to bond for only $2.5 million; $500,000 to fix the parks department's collapsing roof; $1.5 million to replace a soon-to-be-obsolete refrigerant allowing Meacham ice rink to function; and a host of other infrastructure needs.[9]

I decided to use every water main break, road-condition complaint, and sewer backup as an opportunity to talk about the state of our infrastructure to get federal and state officials to help fund much-needed repairs. We started a Twitter hashtag #FixOurPipes,[10] where we posted photos and video of every damaging infrastructure collapse across the country. We used it to show what could happen in Syracuse without this investment.

There wasn't a speech, address, or public comment I made without mentioning our crumbling infrastructure. It became so tiresome to the local media, they rolled their eyes when I would start talking about it and say, "Yeah, yeah, we get it." The strategy was not without political risk: I was warning about systems collapsing under my watch and essentially pointing out problems I couldn't fix. Yet, I could tell I was gaining traction. Constituents frequently told me they agreed that infrastructure should be a priority.

State officials began warning me that the governor and state leaders were interested in economic development, not infrastructure: "You're the mayor, it's your problem to make things work. Do your job and stop blaming us." Members of the state assembly and senate repeatedly told me it wasn't possible to get money for infrastructure and then ask about economic-development projects that could be funded with state money. At the same time, they regularly sent me letters from their constituents demanding I fix potholes, malfunctioning water systems, and deteriorating roads.

9. Michelle Breidenbach, "Miner's Wish List for Cuomo = $16.4 Million," *Post-Standard*, January 12, 2014.

10. Tim Knauss, "Higher Sewer Fees, More Cops, Flat Taxes in Proposed Onondaga County Budget," Syracuse.com, September 14, 2018, https://www.syracuse.com/news/20 18/09/higher_sewer_fees_more_cops_flat_taxes_in_proposed_onondaga_county_bud get.html.

When I called Assemblyman William Magnarelli's attention to the duplicity of sending such letters but not supporting increased state spending
for infrastructure, he memorably replied, "You can't cut a ribbon on pipes."
In other words, they wouldn't get attention for bringing resources to old
systems the public took for granted. Their unquenchable thirst for positive
headlines overtook any desire to do the grinding and boring work that is
actual governing.

Cuomo's priority of economic development over infrastructure investment became clear in a Syracuse newspapers' editorial board meeting.
He started the conversation by asking: "How about economic development? Anything happening?" As Cuomo explained his plans for spending
$50 million on the state fair, an editor asked: "There's been a suggestion that
$50 million would go a long way toward fixing a lot of water mains in Syra-
cuse. Why do we need $50 million for the fair?"

Cuomo responded, "Because you're going bankrupt. You are unsus-
tainable. That's why." When asked if that meant let water mains break, the
governor answered, "No. You need jobs. You need an economy. You need
business. You need a viable economy. That's what you need. . . . The upstate
cities have to be stronger economically. They have to do better. . . . Show us
how you become economically stronger, and you create jobs." Adding, "And
then, you fix your own pipes."[11]

Cuomo's comments were a mischaracterization and, at worst, ignorant.
If he had brushed up on his history, he would have learned the state wholly
funded the infrastructure project that put Syracuse and the rest of upstate
New York on the map: the Erie Canal. Construction and operation of the
canal was authorized, funded, and managed by the state. The $7.1 million
project, opened eight years after the start of construction, fortified the position of New York City as our country's preeminent commercial center and
helped the state become an acknowledged leader in population, industry,
and economic strength—the "Empire State."[12]

11. Teri Weaver, "Cuomo to Syracuse: 'You Are Not Sustainable. You Need Jobs, an
Economy, Business,'" Syracuse.com, February 4, 2014, https://www.syracuse.com/polit
ics/2015/02/cuomo_to_syracuse_bring_a_job_to_attract_jobs_then_fix_your_own
_pipes.html.

12. "Fast Facts," Erie Canalway National Heritage Corridor, https://eriecanalway.org
/learn/history-culture/fast-facts; "Building a Nation," Erie Canalway National Heritage
Corridor, https://eriecanalway.org/learn/history-culture/build-nation.

Moreover, the state had never allowed the economic conditions of a municipality to determine whether its citizens had access to water. New Yorkers in the most rural reaches of the Adirondacks had the same rights to clean water as millionaires in Manhattan. "Fix your own pipes" was a statement made by a person who either did not understand or assumed he would not be challenged.

The important and immutable truth was that the governor of New York, who led the state's entire policy and spending agenda, said economic-development projects would save upstate New York. And I was the mayor of a city on track for 372 water main breaks in a year, with no hope on the horizon of receiving any state or federal help.

One answer to Syracuse's infrastructure problem, I was told was a public-private partnership, known as a "P3." Starting in the 1990s, many government-reform advocates argued that contracts between governments and the private sector could bring efficiency and much-needed capital to municipal services.[13] The theory was that through innovative, long-term public-private partnerships, cash-strapped local governments could save money by applying private-sector discipline to the delivery of public services. Services would be better, and taxes would stay level, according to many government services experts.[14] It was the perfect "win-win" scenario for any mayor.

In my case, I was advised to enter a public-private partnership in which Syracuse's water system would be sold or leased to a private entity that could bring it up to a state of good repair and end the thorny and expensive responsibility of a hundred-year system breaking down on my watch. I started investigating it and held meetings with two different Wall Street firms. Each firm sent a team of well-heeled salespeople to my office to pitch me on selling our water system to them through a P3, touting the arrangement with PowerPoint charts, graphs, and spreadsheets. Syracuse would get a "major" injection of cash to help with our budget problems, they promised, and our infrastructure headaches would be cured.

Sounded good, but then I asked: Would they promise not to raise

13. Mildred E. Warner, "Local Government Infrastructure and the False Promise of Privatization," In the Public Interest, September 1, 2008, https://inthepublicinterest.org /local-government-infrastructure-and-the-false-promise-of-privatization/.

14. Patricia Bloomfield, "The Challenge of Long-Term Public-Private Partnerships: Reflections on Local Experience," Public Administration Review 66, no. 3 (2006): 400.

rates, so water remained affordable for the city's residents? No. Would they commit to having someone answer complaints about the water system twenty-four hours a day? No. Would they commit to immediately fixing a break, even if it was two in the morning and fifteen degrees below zero? No. If the water was turned off, would they commit to getting it turned back on within twenty-four hours, as was our goal? No. I never had another meeting regarding the potential arrangement.

Throughout my tenure, I was told countless times that public-private partnerships were the antidote to local government's problems. At meetings with mayors from around the country, I saw a trend of private corporations seeking to replace key parts of local government's job. At one meeting, a presenter discussed how "innovative" it was when the New Balance Corporation offered to build a commuter train station in Boston. When I asked about the neighborhoods that did not have an affluent corporation to build a station, there was sheepish silence. At another meeting, an official from a Western state excitedly told me he thought his city hall could be housed within the Zappos complex.

At another meeting of mayors, a wealthy businessman addressed our group, earnestly asking us about potential public-private partnerships for service delivery and pointedly saying taxes were not the answer. I raised my hand and said I appreciated his comments, but "someone has to pay for police and firefighters and clean water. That's what taxes do." There was stunned silence in the room, but the mayors nodded and later thanked me for making the point.

I rarely witnessed anyone raise the point that government is not a for-profit entity for a reason. Americans believe the funding for some services should be shared so they can be delivered equitably for everyone in a community, not just the lucky few who can pay for it. Mayors are usually among the lone voices making the point that if the federal and state government gave resources to infrastructure, municipalities would be able to meet the mission of providing key services. Instead, federal and state government officials market public-private partnerships as a new and easy way to solve problems that their lack of financial support created in the first place.

Public-private partnerships may be useful tools for certain situations, but they cannot be a replacement for a functioning government to provide services for everyone.[15] One person who explicitly recognized this was a certified titan of the private sector.

In October 2009, I was scheduled to attend a political luncheon in New York City. I invited Terri Bright, my friend, and Ashley Sulewski, my fundraiser, to accompany me to the event. I also invited my cousin Kate, who worked on Wall Street, to join us. After the luncheon ended, I asked Kate the best way to get to the Upper East Side of Manhattan, one of the swankiest neighborhoods in New York City. When Kate asked where we were going, I told her "Gracie Mansion." Stunned that I would casually say we were headed to such an august destination, she asked, "Why?" I answered, "That's where our next meeting is, with Mike Bloomberg."

Days before the luncheon, Kevin Sheekey, a representative for Bloomberg, reached out to my campaign to see if I was interested in meeting the New York City mayor. I had never met Bloomberg and my impression of him was limited to what I had read about him. He was rich, not a typical politician, and, my personal favorite, short. I agreed to the meeting without a thought about why I was invited, what I might get out of it, or who I could bring.

Kate seemed floored. "We can't go with you to meet Mike Bloomberg!" she said. "Why don't you tell me these things? We can't go." Terri and Ashley, convinced by Kate's forceful position that the three of them had no business going there, joined Kate in insisting it should be a private meeting. After all, one of them was "just" out of college, one was "just" my friend, and the other was "just" my cousin. I dismissed their concerns by giving the distinct misimpression I had cleared it with Bloomberg's staff.

When we got out of the taxi and walked across a park to the mansion, Terri asked again if it was appropriate for them to come. I responded, "It's not a big deal; it'll be fine." Kate said, "He's the billionaire mayor of New York City. It is a big deal." Everyone quieted down as we approached the outdoor security station, and I gave my name. The security guards looked at the four of us and motioned us to pass without going through the metal detector or having our bags inspected. "See," I said. "We don't even need security." Kate replied that the security machine's belt was broken.

15. Successful public-private partnerships have objective market-driven competition, risk-sharing, and transparency. Patricia Bloomfield, "The Challenge of Long-Term Public-Private Partnerships: Reflections on Local Experience," *Public Administration Review* 66, no. 3 (2006): 400–411.

We were greeted by a mayoral staffer at the mansion's steps who ushered into a side room on the first floor. The room had two chairs and two couches surrounding a coffee table set with cookies, fruit, coffee, and tea in a formal silver setting. The mansion seemed strangely quiet. I was shocked when Sheekey came in with Bloomberg exactly on time. He introduced Bloomberg to me and left. Bloomberg looked at me and my guests and grinned from ear to ear. "So, you all are from Syracuse?" he asked.

As he sat down in one of the chairs, I sat on the couch next to him and said, "Thank you, Mayor Bloomberg, for agreeing to meet." He put his feet up on the coffee table and said, "Call me Mike." Looking at the silver tea set, he asked us, "Do you want something stronger to drink? We have other stuff if you want it." We all demurred.

He then turned to me and said, "So how can I help you?" I realized I needed to make the most of this opportunity, and I started throwing questions at him. Should mayors take over school systems? "Of course. It's the only way to get accountability." What about dealing with public safety, fiscal issues, public health, young people—I asked anything and everything I could think of.

After some time, I suggested he must have had other pressing engagements as a polite way to end the discussion. He said no, and we kept talking. I peppered him with questions, and he shared his distinct points of view on cities, governing, and public policy. A staffer interrupted us once, announcing that Senator Charles Schumer was on the phone, saying he needed to speak with the mayor. Bloomberg declined the call and said to us, "That means he's done something he shouldn't have."[16]

Bloomberg cautioned me that as a mayor you can work hard, make beneficial changes, and people may still not be satisfied. It was clear he was thinking about the outcome of his reelection. The news was filled with stories about the contradiction between how well voters thought Bloomberg was doing as mayor and his tight race with the New York City comptroller Bill Thompson.

At one point, Terri stood across from us and took our picture with a disposable camera. Bloomberg looked at her and she immediately apologized, asking if it was something she was not supposed to do. He laughed and said, "You know we have professionals who do that," meaning people who

---

16. The next morning as we sped up the Westside Highway back to Syracuse, we learned from the radio that Schumer had endorsed Bill Thompson for mayor the previous day.

take photos with real cameras. I took the opportunity to introduce him to everyone: Terri, my friend; Ashley, my campaign fundraiser; and my cousin Kate, who worked on Wall Street. He laughed and said I had good taste and spoke with each of them individually.

When I took office in 2010, I received an invitation to join the Bloomberg Philanthropies Mayors Project, which was billed as a government innovation program. I was excited to be part of it and believed Bloomberg was actively engaged in wanting to make constructive change.

I was told the Mayors Project had two goals: increase innovation capacity within municipal government and disseminate effective programs and policies across cities. Bloomberg believed mayors were uniquely positioned to tackle the most pressing civic challenges and, as a result, focused part of his philanthropic empire on those goals.

When Andrew Maxwell and I arrived for my first Mayors Project meeting, we were greeted on the street and escorted into the Bloomberg Philanthropies building. We were shown into a side room awash in outside light with a full breakfast buffet and several small tables set up. We sat down adjacent to Thomas Menino, then the mayor of Boston. As we drank our coffee, we overheard him say, "Parked a car in Harvard Yard," and we struggled to keep from laughing over the preeminent Boston politician repeating the accent joke.

In short order, we watched a handful of prominent American mayors arrive from Miami, Atlanta, Newark, Houston, and New Orleans. I asked Maxwell if he remembered that children's game of "one of these things doesn't belong" and said I was feeling like it might be Syracuse. When there were about ten of us, along with ten staffers, we were escorted into a small, elegant interior conference room. The staff sat along the wall and the mayors sat around a table in prearranged seats.

As I sat down, I looked to my left and saw Bloomberg's name card. He walked in shortly after and greeted everyone by name and asked me how I was. I answered warmly but was feeling decidedly uneasy in the new setting. Thankfully, as I was reaching for something other than "fine" to say to Bloomberg, Katie Couric came into the room and greeted him. I gathered she had been brought in to open the session with an icebreaker. Yup, I thought, this is totally normal. She made a remark about me being the only female mayor in the group. I smiled at the comment as I looked at the big city mayors all supremely comfortably chatting with each other around the table and thought, "Honey, that's the least of the things that makes me different right now."

After Couric left, there was an informal discussion between the mayors about public education systems and reforms, public safety, gun laws, and a host of other issues. Not wanting to call attention to my ignorance, I took notes surreptitiously. A consultant from the McKinsey group, one of the top consultancy firms in the country, then gave a presentation on pensions. After some discussion about the issue, there was a break. When I went to get a drink, Newark mayor Cory Booker, by way of introduction, said to me, "The snacks are always bad at these because Mike's on a healthy-eating kick." He was right. In comparison to the breakfast and dinner offerings, the snacks of nuts, berries, and naked popcorn were underwhelming.

We sat down for the next presentation on something called "social im-pact bonds," which were being heralded as an innovative new financing tool for social programs. It amounted to a government setting an outcome it wanted to accomplish and agreeing to pay a private organization a sum of money if the outcome was achieved.[17] The approach is different from nor-mal arrangements in which funding is committed to a program regardless of the outcome. This was one of an array of tools being introduced under the category of public-private partnerships.

The SIB presenter was a woman who had worked at Google and was now working for the White House. She gave an in-depth presentation about the United Kingdom's success with using the bonds to reduce recidivism in the prison population. She went through charts and graphs and excitedly talked about the potential this new system presented for solving public chal-lenges in the United States. It was a dense and esoteric presentation. One or two of the mayors asked polite questions.

As the session was about to end, Bloomberg cleared his throat and, in a matter-of-fact manner, said to the presenter, "I have a question." He contin-ued, "I think I can speak for all the mayors here in saying I have no fucking idea what you are talking about." At this point, Bloomberg's staff of around twenty, seated along a side wall, all jumped to their feet. Bloomberg con-tinued, "I mean, I don't know why you just don't give cities the money. We know how to solve these problems. We don't need this stuff."

---

17. Social Impact Bond (SIB) Financing: Investing in positive outcomes. (n.d.). https://socialfinance.org/social-impact-bonds/.

The presenter looked as if she had seen a ghost. Her jaw clenched and she seemed to be gasping for a reply she could not quite muster. As I told myself not to burst out laughing, I imagined that as a former Google executive and current White House official, she had not been the focus of such a such a pointed comment in a long time. A Bloomberg staffer named Jim Andersen inserted himself and said in a loud voice, "Thank you. I think it's time we took a break." The discomfort in the room was palpable. Bloomberg turned to me and said, "I'm right, right?" I said yes because he was, and I thoroughly enjoyed him speaking the truth.

The truth that Bloomberg pointed out so directly was if the federal government gave cities resources to help solve problems, the cities could, by and large, do it themselves. Local governments exist to solve problems and can do so if supported and allowed to be creative. If the federal government wanted, for example, to cut the recidivism of former prisoners, it could work with local governments to fund the programs to accomplish this goal.

Bloomberg had voiced a frustration common to local leaders: rather than trying to be a partner, the federal government was marketing a new tool to solve a problem that could have been solved by city governments themselves. Indeed, federal officials would herald supposed new civic approaches that, to many local officials, seemed to be superficial talking points or, at worst, a way to siphon much needed revenue away from government to the private sector. There was no need to invent a new model to fix something local governments were experiencing, thinking about, and had the know-how to tackle if given a willing collaborator. The cycle was all too common—starve a municipality of resources, attack it for not solving problems, and then give money to the private sector, assuring people a for-profit entity was sure to do a better job than the unsupported, half-starved local leaders they'd elected.

As I spent more time watching Bloomberg, I understood why he was successful. He was whip-smart—a human computer. He seemed to enjoy solving problems for the satisfaction of solving the problem. He wanted to be surrounded by the smartest and most talented people to help solve those problems, and he didn't feel upstaged when people demonstrated their talents. His staff and administration were filled with brilliant, skilled professionals who were encouraged to do innovative work.

Perversely, I thought this was his fatal flaw as a politician. He lacked the sense of insecurity that made him want people to like him—he didn't seem to care if they did or not. Being a billionaire probably helped, but every politician I've known has a need—and in some cases a pathological desire—for people to like them. Not Mike Bloomberg, or at least that's how it seemed to me. He was too outspoken and too sure of himself.

It was this unusual political trait that made him a good mayor. It allowed him to question orthodoxy, make hard decisions, and directly confront uncomfortable realities. He was not a perfect mayor and New York was not a perfect city, but I admired him for using both his strengths and weaknesses to be the best mayor he could and then sharing the fruits of that labor with others.

A couple of months after the Mayors Project initial meeting, Jim Andersen made a trip to Syracuse to see what we were doing and how well we were doing it. At the end of his trip, he sat in my office and extolled the excellent work of Syracuse's city workers. As he left, he told me to contact him if there was anything I needed. I was struck because I could tell he meant it, and there was so much I needed as mayor.

## My Nerds

In working with the Mayors Project, we were able to apply for a lucrative Bloomberg Philanthropies grant to modernize our approach to civic problem-solving. The program's explicit goal was to increase the capacity of local governments to improve the lives of citizens by designing and implementing new governing approaches. Syracuse was one of fourteen cities in the world selected to participate in the so-called Innovation Team program, which resulted in the city receiving funds of approximately $1.3 million over three years to create an innovation team, or "i-team."[18] Bloomberg Philanthropies committed to training the i-teams how to function as in-house innovation consultants, and the mayors committed to ensuring city staff worked in tandem with them.

The grant allowed us to create positions requiring advanced skills not traditionally associated with civil servants. This primarily meant people who were comfortable and experienced working with big data and the

18. Office of the Mayor, "Miner Announces Syracuse Awarded Bloomberg Philanthropies Innovation Team Grant," Office of the Mayor, December 15, 2014, http://www .syrgov.net/uploadedFiles/City_Hall/Mayors_Office/Content/Press_Releases/2014-12 -15%20Office%20of%20Innovation.pdf.

burgeoning world of information technology. When we advertised for the positions, we were flooded with interested people saying they were intrigued by the idea of doing "good public policy."

Maxwell became the director of the office of innovation and culled through hundreds of applicants. He chose four outstanding individuals who each brought a unique skill set to city hall. They had experience in science, data, analytics, geography, and visual arts. When they were assembled, someone joked, they looked like a group of students on a college admissions brochure. I called them, with great affection, "my nerds."

The first challenge I asked the i-team to tackle was "innovative ideas and imaginative models for advancing Syracuse's infrastructure." They were talented and enthusiastic, yet I worried that they might not be able to rise to the task. But I was out of other options.

While Syracuse had reams of data, it lacked the tools to use it in an effective way. We hoped the i-team could change that. They were already part of the data revolution—a revolution already disrupting every sector of society. Syracuse would benefit if we could integrate the nerds and "muddy guys," as many of the infrastructure workers were known, to blend their unique skills into actual solutions.

Data was just one part of solving a civic problem. In one of our regular meetings, the team asked me why we split the city into quadrants and rotated the roads we repaired by quadrant every year. Instead, why not just fix the worst roads in the city that year? I explained that might lead to neighborhoods suspecting political favoritism if one neighborhood constantly received all the road reconstruction. There were necessary adjustments because we were a government beholden to citizens' impressions.

A key factor for the project to work was acceptance of the i-team by the institutional bureaucracy. One afternoon, after a mind-numbing meeting with the i-team about data, Sam Edelstein, the chief data officer, told me that Adria Finch, the twenty-nine-year-old i-team project manager, had gone into the field to "exercise" valves. Edelstein pulled out his phone and showed me pictures of Finch in protective gear standing across from a "muddy guy." In the picture both looked like a modern-day Archimedes. They had their hands on either end of a long metal pole, which was perpendicular to a pole attached to a valve in the ground. Each stood with an opposite end of the pole in their hands and using manual labor pushed to rotate the pole, which would turn the rod attached to a valve and would cause the valve to open or close, that is, "exercise." Finch, who was present, laughed and told me it was demanding work, and then volunteered she was going to learn how to "hot patch" a pothole after the "guys" had asked her if she was interested. It was evidence the crucial integration was happening.

It became routine for i-team members to swap out ties and dress clothes for protective gear, show up at work sites to learn the ropes, and return to the office repeating stories they'd heard or skills they'd picked up from long-time city employees. The i-team went through the painstaking process of building rapport with the muddy guys, the clerks, and everyone they encountered. The old-timers started telling me they thought the i-team "were good kids."

After spending time in the field, questioning and listening to workers, the i-team unveiled some low-cost, data-driven solutions to help fix our infrastructure crisis.[19] They implemented the use of a GPS tracking system already attached to public works trucks to collect and transmit data on potholes. This data was used to update a map, inform public works operations if roads in certain neighborhoods were predisposed to forming potholes, and create a visual tool to ensure equity across neighborhoods.

The i-team learned about and obtained a tool called a street quality identification device, which was basically a low-cost camera and accelerator apparatus that could be attached to a vehicle. It measured the bumpiness of the roads, took pictures, and transmitted the information, allowing objective evidence to identify which roads were in the worst shape.

They used water-main data that showed break hot spots were prevalent and especially inconvenient in the central business district. The breaks forced the city to close streets, which resulted in restaurants, coffee shops, and other small businesses shutting down because of a lack of water and customer access. The city incurred the cost of overtime pay for workers making emergency repairs on off-hours.

The i-team developed a program to test water mains by dropping sensors into the mains. The sensors emitted acoustic waves that could detect and identify leaks before they became debilitating breaks. This information allowed the water department to plan to repair leaks during off-peak hours and allowed small businesses to function, minimizing costly interruptions. We used technology to allow people to both report and track infrastructure

19. Innovation Team: Our Impact: Meaningful Results for Residents (n.d.), Syracuse i-team website, http://www.innovatesyracuse.com/our-impact.

issues on the city website, as well as use data technology to help provide widespread notice of public construction projects. All of this was affordable and efficient and had a positive impact on the citizens of Syracuse.

At one of my meetings with the i-team, I was greeted by some unfamiliar faces. The i-team members introduced a stranger sitting to my right as a project manager with the Eric and Wendy Schmidt Data Science for Social Good (DSSG) at the University of Chicago. The program places aspiring data scientists from around the world with governments and nonprofits to tackle problems. All the new people in the room were scientists associated with some of the world's most prestigious institutions who'd been brought together to determine the primary causes of Syracuse's water-main failures: Was it age alone, or would the data show other factors at play, such as soil content, pipe material, or weather? Or was there some combination more likely to lead to a break?

The DSSG team built an early-warning system for water infrastructure problems.[20] It was a predictive model incorporating various pieces of data to identify specific water mains at the highest risk of rupturing. The tool would allow us to make decisions to repair and replace mains based on where they were located and who they served. Were the mains with the highest risk serving a dense area, hospitals, or schools? Or were they in an industrial area with few users?

We could use the information to plan, schedule maintenance, and efficiently budget for repairs, instead of using estimates and facing emergency repairs. It was a major cost-savings and planning tool using data Syracuse had been gathering for a hundred years—and an illustration of how the data revolution could positively impact governing.

All this infrastructure work was garnering a great deal of attention in public policy circles, and I was frequently asked to speak about it. At one forum, Flint, Michigan, mayor Karen Weaver and I headlined a session on municipal infrastructure. We joked that "we were making infrastructure sexy." Flint was suffering from a horrendous man-made crisis of lead in its water. After the session, Weaver asked me if I could send her information on the work we had done, and I told her I would send her the information and the i-team itself.

20. Data Science for Social Good partnership on water system predictive model (2016). https://www.dssgfellowship.org/project/early-warning-system-for-water-infrastructure -problems/.

It was the type of interaction Bloomberg Philanthropies had hoped for when the innovation team program was designed—improving the lives of citizens by designing creative governing approaches that could be replicated across cities. It was a welcome departure from the typical system in which politicians were more interested in taking credit than in solving a problem.

While I was running around the country talking about infrastructure and headlining press conferences on the issue, the real impacts to my constituents were never far. On one spring Sunday night, I was at home with the rare sensation of no obligations. I heard the phone ring and Jack answered it. Moments later, he bellowed for me saying, "You need to talk to this woman." I got on the phone to hear a panicked female voice. "Mayor, I'm so sorry to call you at home," she said. "I didn't know what else to do. Your husband was very nice and said you would talk to me." She continued, "It's raining here really hard. My basement is flooding. The water is coming up to the first floor and my 85-year-old mother-in-law is bed-ridden on oxygen on the first floor, and I can't get her up the stairs."

Her voice was tense with anxiety. As she spoke, I looked out my window and saw a light rain falling. Her house was, at most, a five-minute drive from mine, but there was no question she felt she was in danger. I told her I would make a call and call her right back. A firefighter on duty confirmed that a flash flood only in my caller's neighborhood was overwhelming the sewer system. When I called back, the woman, obviously relieved, said she was watching firefighters move her mother-in-law up the stairs.

The next day, as we cleaned up the aftermath of the flood, we assessed the infrastructure impact and discussed the unprecedented nature of the event—a narrow geographic area with a large volume of water falling in record time. The sewer department employees told me it was a one-hundred-year storm, and the system was not designed to handle such storms. Relieved, I thought it would not be my problem in the next century. Two weeks later, the same thing happened—two microbursts in two weeks in the same small neighborhood.[21] Welcome to the new normal.

After these storms, I received a message that Assemblyman Magnarelli wanted to speak with me. Magnarelli had continued to tout economic

21. Tim Knauss, "Sewage Floods in Basements Have Residents Howling in Syracuse Neighborhood," Syracuse.com, August 8, 2015, https://www.syracuse.com/news/2015/08/sewage_floods_in_basements_have_residents_howling_in_syracuse_neighborhood.html.

development programs while refusing my entreaties for infrastructure help. I felt like he was a walking illustration of what was wrong with state government and its priorities. I made a few half-hearted and unsuccessful attempts to contact him. Finally, I suggested he talk to Beth Rougeux, my director of administration.

Shortly after, my director of administration told me she had just spoken with the assemblyman, and he had been uncharacteristically short with her, saying he needed to talk to me, not her. "I guess I have to take my medicine," I said as I dialed him on my cell phone from her office. He picked up right away and was clearly irritated. In an exasperated tone, he said he had been trying to talk to me and he did not understand why I was dodging his calls. In a moment of complete candor, I told him I was frustrated by the near collapse of our infrastructure systems and his misplaced priority on specious economic-development projects.

After I finished, he said, "Well, that's why I have been calling you." He explained he had secured $10 million from a pot of money available to assemblymembers known as the State and Municipal Facilities Program to enable Syracuse to start fixing our crumbling water and road systems. I thanked him, but he chastised me, saying I should return his calls promptly in the future. I agreed, but before we got off the phone, he told me it was extremely important that no one find out about this news until he and I announced it together. His concern about the optics of the announcement made me feel less guilty about dodging his calls.

Two months later, we made the big announcement, surrounded by water trucks and road crews.[22] We packed the event with visuals that made the assemblyman look good. We participated in an editorial board meeting in which I thanked Magnarelli profusely and said he was showing the kind of leadership we needed in Albany. Magnarelli was asked by the editorial board if the award ran counter to the governor's comments "challenging Syracuse to grow its local economy to fix its own pipes." Magnarelli responded that it did not "contradict" the governor and the money was just a "start."

I tasked the i-team and other city officials with coming up with a plan to link projects across jurisdictions so we could do multiple jobs all at once by cross-referencing faulty water mains with private utility work, road

22. Teri Weaver, "NY Assembly Delivers $10 Million Gift for Syracuse's Water Pipes, Roads," Syracuse.com, July 22, 2015, https://www.syracuse.com/news/2015/07/ny_assembly_delivers_10_million_gift_for_syracuses_water_pipes_roads.html.

reconstruction, and building projects. In doing so, we could fix the faulty water mains and utility lines, install fiber for broadband, and, finally, repair the road—minimizing the amount of money spent and maximizing the amount of infrastructure repairs. We developed and rolled out this "Dig Once Policy" and made it a regular element of the permitting process.

We also investigated using the money to qualify for any other federal, state, or even private sector programs available for water and road projects. We researched the idea of using those resources as a basis to launch an aggressive infrastructure-renovation bonding plan through Wall Street. While it wasn't enough to fix everything, $10 million well-spent would build a firm foundation for a modern, resilient infrastructure system.

A few months later, as we were putting together a plan for how to spend the $10 million, I got a call from a high-level staffer from Assembly Speaker Sheldon Silver's office. He said Governor Cuomo told Silver the $10 million would never be released to Syracuse while I was mayor. I didn't ask why because it didn't matter. Was it animosity over my *New York Times* pension editorial? Would putting money in infrastructure undercut the governor's preference for economic development projects, or was he being vindictive simply because he could? When I asked the staffer if Magnarelli was aware of the governor's comments, he said yes.

I met with Magnarelli a couple of days later and asked him if the governor would withhold the money while I was mayor. He shifted in his seat and told me he thought the governor was doing a good job. When I asked again, he said he didn't know, but he would ask and let me know. I never got an answer to that question.

Eventually, Syracuse did receive the $10 million, but only after I had left office.[23]

## Postscript

While there could have been more progress, our infrastructure work was not erased and continued to provide guidance for Syracuse and others.

---

23. In 2020, my successor's administration received the money. Chris Baker, "How Should Syracuse Improve Traffic at Butternut Circle?," Syracuse.com, February 12, 2020. https://www.syracuse.com/news/2020/02/how-should-syracuse-improve-traffic-at-butternut-circle.html.

Cuomo's economic development programs were documented failures.[24] In 2021, the federal government passed the Bipartisan Infrastructure Law, which allocated $1.2 trillion for infrastructure projects around the country, including roads and water systems.[25]

24. Starting in 2010, state spending on economic development—in direct expenditures and forgone tax revenue—rose 57 percent, reaching $4.4 billion in 2018. According to the Federal Reserve Bank of New York, all upstate regions saw declines in the labor force following the 2008 recession and its economic recovery was among the weakest of any region in the country. Some upstate regions never recovered; "Report: Economic Development. Raising the REDC Bar," Citizen's Budget Commission (December 17, 2019): 2; Jaison R. Abel, Jason Bram, Richard Deitz, and Jonathan Hastings, "Growth Has Slowed Across the Region," Liberty Street Economics, Federal Reserve Bank of New York, December 17, 2019, https://libertystreeteconomics.newyorkfed.org/2019/12/growth-has-sl owed-across-the-region/.

25. Betsy Klein and Kate Sullivan, "Biden Signs Infrastructure Bill into Law at Rare Bipartisan Gathering," *CNN*, November 15, 2021, https://www.cnn.com/2021/11/15/poli tics/biden-signing-ceremony-infrastructure-bill-white-house/index.html.

My frequent visits to my grandparents were idyllic. Whether I was in Syracuse with my maternal grandmother, Betty Cooney, or in Binghamton with my paternal grandmother, Genevieve Miner, all activity stopped to read the morning and afternoon newspapers cover to cover. As soon as I was able, I started reading the newspaper to be like them. *Left to Right*: Betty Cooney, author (on lap), Bud Cooney, Mary Margaret O'Hearn, Ralph Miner, Genevieve Miner, Christian Miner (on lap) in 1975. Courtesy of Stephanie A. Miner from her personal collection.

Author and Governor Mario Cuomo discussing remarks at a fundraiser in Syracuse in October 1994. Mario Cuomo made me believe that politics was a higher calling, grounded in ideals and marked by inspiring battles. Courtesy of Stephanie A. Miner from her personal collection.

Elect a *Real* Fighter
to the Common Council.

Stephanie
**MINER**
Democrat for Councilor at Large

Vote Democrat on November 6th.    Paid for by Friends of Miner.

In 2001, my advertising firm, Romanelli Communication, suggested buying billboard space to improve my name recognition. In one day, multiple billboards with a five-foot-high cropped headshot of me next to the slogan "Elect a Real Fighter to the Common Council" went up across Syracuse garnering a lot of attention. Courtesy of Stephanie A. Miner from her personal collection.

I won the 2009 mayoral race by a margin of 50.1 percent to 39.2 percent. I was to become "Madam Mayor," a role that would challenge everything I knew about myself and the world around me. Syracuse general election, November 3, 2009. *Left to Right*: Jack Mannion, author, former mayor Tom Young, Kate Faraday, Luke Mannion, and Nicholas Mannion (partial). Courtesy of Stephanie A. Miner from her personal collection.

"I'm proud of the positive campaign we've run, and I'm convinced that with a fresh approach—and with your help—we can move Syracuse in a new direction."

−Stephanie Miner

MINER
FOR MAYOR

PRIMARY
Vote Tuesday, September 15
Polls are open from NOON–9P.M.

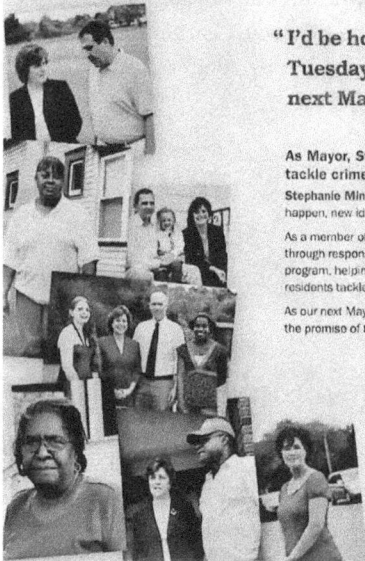

"I'd be honored to have your vote on Tuesday and I promise you that, as your next Mayor, I will make you proud for casting it."
−Stephanie Miner

As Mayor, Stephanie Miner will create jobs, improve our schools, tackle crime and continue her work to renew the promise of Syracuse.

Stephanie Miner doesn't just see problems in Syracuse, she sees solutions waiting to happen, new ideas ready to be implemented and a city full of people ready for change.

As a member of the Common Council, Stephanie has led the fight to create jobs, through responsible economic development. She championed our Say Yes to Education program, helping more of our youth get the chance to go to college. And she has helped residents tackle problems that other politicians just ignored.

As our next Mayor, Stephanie will use her new ideas and fresh approach to renew the promise of the city we're all proud to call home. www.minerformayor.com

MINER
FOR MAYOR

For all the right reasons

Endorsed by the Syracuse Democratic Committee and the Working Families Party

My 2009 mayoral campaign sent people likely to vote in the primary five direct-mail pieces, one piece for each of the five weeks leading up to the election. The strategy was to communicate directly with voters that I would be a strong mayor implementing needed change. The final direct-mail piece in the primary, shown here, combined the messages and images of the previous pieces. Courtesy of Stephanie A. Miner from her personal collection.

Author addressing a public meeting at Lincoln Park on August 16, 2011.
My first name, "Stephanie," disappeared the night I was elected, replaced
immediately by "Mayor." People acted as if the title bestowed the superpower
of giving them a shot at a better life. After all, I was mayor of the city that was
the economic, cultural, and intellectual hub of the central part of New York
State. Photo by Joel Rinne. Courtesy of City of Syracuse.

People expected City Hall would solve their problems. One constituent called
wanting to know what I, as the female mayor, was going to do about the snow
penis sculpture in front of her neighbor's house. Courtesy of Stephanie A.
Miner from her personal collection.

Image of the State of the City, January 28, 2010, at the SUNY College of Environmental Science and Forestry's Marshall Hall. In my first State of the City address, twenty-seven days after I took office, I shared that Syracuse was using antiquated systems and its expenditures were dramatically outpacing revenues. Photo by Joel Rinne. Courtesy of City of Syracuse.

Image of the demolition of 921 North State Street, March 17, 2010. On February 26, 2010, the roof and a wall of a building located at 921–925 North State St. collapsed. The estimated cost to demolish the building would have exhausted Syracuse's entire annual demolition budget. Photo by Joel Rinne. Courtesy of City of Syracuse.

At my first meeting with Mayor Michael Bloomberg, shown here, I peppered him with questions about cities, governing, and public policy. Bloomberg cautioned me that as a mayor you can work hard, make beneficial changes, and people may still not be satisfied. Photo by Terri Bright. Courtesy of Stephanie A. Miner from her personal collection.

Syracuse workers reconstruct a road. Federal and state governments cut the amount of money they made available for local governments to maintain infrastructure. This put the funding responsibility for these large, crucial systems squarely on Syracuse's overburdened shoulders. Photo by Addison Spears. Courtesy of Addison Spears.

Syracuse water department workers working on a water main on August 15, 2016. Syracuse was annually setting records for broken pipes. In one period during 2013, water crews had been doing emergency repairs every night for three weeks. Photo by Joel Rinne. Courtesy of City of Syracuse.

Image of author listening to kindergartners on first day of school, September 2, 2014. Syracuse voters made it clear with their questions, opinions, and poll results that they expected the mayor to address the schools' unacceptable performance. Photo by Alexander Marion. Courtesy of City of Syracuse.

*Opposite:* Image of Café Kubal owner Matt Godard and author speaking about the economic importance of accessible water on September 15, 2016. I used every opportunity to talk about the state of our infrastructure to get federal and state officials to help fund much-needed repairs. This included events like "Imagine a Day without Water" during which customers at Café Kubal coffee shops received cups with the message of "No Water, No Coffee" and directed them to a website with information about the city's water infrastructure. Photo by Joel Rinne. Courtesy of City of Syracuse.

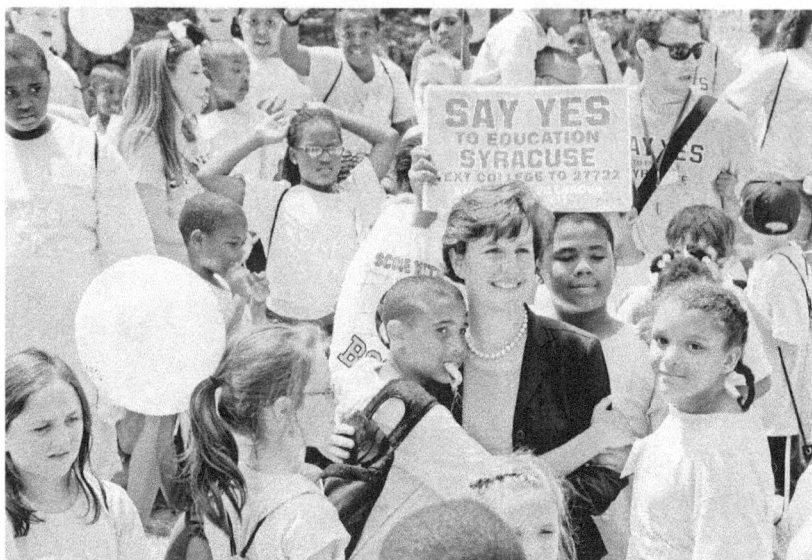

Image of author and Syracuse students at Say Yes festival on July 27, 2011, celebrating Say Yes summer camps. Say Yes to Education, a nonprofit formed to close the achievement gap between urban and suburban districts, was part of a movement of wealthy capitalists proposing and funding dramatic changes in public schools' orthodoxy nationwide. Syracuse partnered with Say Yes to implement its educational turnaround strategies. Photo by Joel Rinne. Courtesy of City of Syracuse.

Chief Frank Fowler and author speaking to Black Lives Matter protestors in front of city hall on July 18, 2016. Photo by Joel Rinne. Courtesy of City of Syracuse.

The police were citizens' first call to nearly every problem that arose from living in dense neighborhoods—to stop people from selling drugs on a street corner, of course, but to get rid of the homeless addict and stop children from swearing on a basketball court, too. Once named chief of police, Frank Fowler became omnipresent—appearing at all serious crime scenes, speaking to leaders and neighbors at churches, parks, and sports events. His work ethic and availability endeared him to rank-and-file officers and residents alike. Photo by Joel Rinne. Courtesy of City of Syracuse.

COR quickly became the recipient of generous state funding for major projects, including Syracuse's Inner Harbor. *Left to Right*: Cor's Steve Aiello, Robert Simpson (background), author, Governor Andrew Cuomo, State Senator John DeFrancisco, and County Executive Joanie Mahoney looking at a model of COR's planned development of the Inner Harbor on October 2, 2012. Photo by Joel Rinne. Courtesy of City of Syracuse.

**Jimmy Vielkind**
@JimmyVielkind

A perfect boondoggle: New York taxpayers spent $15 million to build it. It created no jobs, @NYGovCuomo's promises notwithstanding. The contractors face bid-rigging charges. Now, a SUNY Poly arm is selling the CNY Film Hub to Onondaga County for ... $1!

syracuse.com

3:44 PM · Jun 1, 2018

**119** Reposts   **23** Quotes   **125** Likes   **2** Bookmarks

Image of Tweet by Jimmy Vielkind, June 1, 2018. Despite the governor's much ballyhooed economic development announcement, Hollywood never did come to Onondaga. The CNY Film Hub remained empty and was eventually sold to Onondaga County for $1. Soraa, the California-based LED lightbulb manufacturer, never came to the region. The Buffalo Billion program, in addition to being mired in a federal corruption trial, was a substantive failure. Courtesy of Jimmy Vielkind.

---

*Opposite:* Image from Start-Up New York Announcement at SUNY Upstate, May 22, 2013. I did not find Andrew Cuomo's kisses any more objectionable than the other ways he bullied me. It was part of the rules of engagement as a politician. I chose to be in the arena, and his kisses were the least of his control tactics. Courtesy of New York State Governor's Office.

To: The Honorable Stephanie Miner

Best Wishes, Mayor Richard M Daley

Chicago mayor Richard M. Daley told me being mayor would be the best job I would ever have. "That's why we don't ever do anything else." Courtesy of Stephanie A. Miner from her personal collection.

Being with Jack was the craziest thing I ever contemplated, but the alternative, being without him, was inconceivable. While I knew it was never going to be easy, there simply could be no me without him. Courtesy of Stephanie A. Miner from her personal collection.

*Opposite:* Image of author and Michael Volpe being interviewed on a Manhattan street, September 14, 2018. The political system is designed by the winners and vested interests who use their power to narrow, almost to the point of exclusion, challenges. To contest the status quo is to toil in ignominy, and it is by design. Photo by Michael Wilner. Courtesy of Stephanie A. Miner from her personal collection.

Jack bridged my cynicism with an inherent faith in the system. He was my sounding board, therapist, and champion. *Left to Right*: Caroline McDonald, Tim McDonald, Jack, and Kevin Grossman. Courtesy of Stephanie A. Miner from her personal collection.

1 - IF EVER I WOULD LEAVE YOU
2 - I COULD HAVE TOLD YOU
3 - THESE FOOLISH THINGS
4 - MY FUNNY VALENTINE
5 - THESE FOOLISH THINGS
6 - MY FOOLISH HEART
7 - AGAIN
8 - I'VE GROWN ACCUSTOMED TO HER FACE
9 - AND I LOVE HER SO
10 - YOU ARE SO BEAUTIFUL
11 - BEWITCHED
12 - NEARNESS OF YOU
13 - YOU'RE JUST IN LOVE
14 - BABY, ITS COLD OUTSIDE
15 - SWEET GEORGIA BROWN
16 - TEACH ME TONITE
17 - BECAUSE OF YOU
18 - GEORGIA ON MY MIND
19 - BESAME MUCHO
20 - JUST ONE OF THOSE THINGS
21 - TENDERLY
22 - HEY THERE
23 - OUR LOVE IS HERE TO STAY
24 - MEMORIES
25 - ONCE IN A WHILE
26 - WHAT I DID 4 LOVE

Jack's 2019 playlist. Courtesy of Stephanie A. Miner from her personal
collection.

# Education

## Sisyphus in the Rye

Like a buoy in a sea of blue-suited men, I took my spot in the ornate, packed State Assembly chamber at the 2010 State of the State address. I was feeling out of place until I saw that Rochester's mayor, Bob Duffy, was seated next to me. Located seventy miles to the west, Rochester is a sister city of Syracuse and shares similar characteristics. Duffy was a well-respected two-term mayor and a member of the political establishment. Even though he was wearing the standard blue uniform, his discomfort was obvious as he attempted to fit his six-foot, five-inch frame into his allotted space. I introduced myself and joked that fitting into a cramped seat was the one mayoral issue we did not share.

One of the most worrisome issues Rochester and Syracuse did share was the dismal performance of our schools, with each system regularly producing some of the state's worst educational scores. As Duffy fidgeted, I told him I heard he was planning to challenge the state's entrenched educational system. He stopped moving to tell me Rochester's underperforming school system was the city's death knell. He was committed to improving the schools by gaining control of them as mayor.[1] "Stephanie, this is a hill I am willing to die on," he said earnestly.

I had already decided to try to fix my city's schools, embarking on a major reform effort initially as a city councilor and, with the input of voters, resolving to grow that initiative as mayor. Duffy's comments reinforced my belief I wouldn't be alone in my quest to fix urban schools. But I was to learn

1. Nate Dougherty, "Duffy Releases Draft of Mayoral Control Report," *Rochester Business Journal*, January 29, 2010, https://rbj.net/2010/01/29/duffy-releases-draft-of-mayoral-control-report/.

that the fight to reform urban education is a lonely hill on which the mayor often does die.

## The Syracuse Challenge

The year I ran for mayor, the Syracuse school district had approximately twenty-one thousand students; 53 percent identified as Black or African American, 11 percent as Hispanic, 5 percent as Asian, and 29 percent as white. Many of these students faced significant challenges: More than 75 percent of all students qualified for free or reduced-price lunches, about 10 percent of students had limited English proficiency, and four thousand qualified for special education.[2] Syracuse's high school graduation rate was 45.2 percent, 27 percent of students dropped out of school after ninth grade, and only 30 percent of eighth graders passed standardize tests in reading and math.[3]

Syracuse's performance was not an outlier. Many of the nation's urban school districts have a graduation rate of less than 60 percent; fourth graders from large cities score an average of 15 points lower on the National Assessment of Educational Progress in reading than their nonurban peers, and data shows urban minority and poor students lagging behind their suburban peers.[4] While the abysmally low achievement levels for urban schools have been a national concern for decades,[5] public education is almost entirely within the jurisdiction of states.[6]

2. The New York State District Report Card Accountability and Overview Report 2010–2011, the University of the State of New York and the State Education Department, April 20, 2012. https://data.nysed.gov/files/reportcards/archive/2010-11/AOR-2011-42 1800010000.pdf; Glenn Coin, "Syracuse University Professor Asks: Should We Tear Down the Walls Between School Districts?" Syracuse.com, December 14, 2009, https://www.syracuse.com/news/2009/12/syracuse_university_professor_2.html.

3. Maureen Nolan, "CNY High School Graduation Rates: How Did Your School Do?" *Post-Standard*, March 10, 2009; Coin, "Syracuse University Professor Asks."

4. Andrew J. Rotherham and Sara Mead, "A New Deal for Urban Public Schools," *Harvard Law & Policy Review*, https://journals.law.harvard.edu/lpr/online-articles/a-new -deal-for-urban-public-schools/.

5. "Why Big Bets on Educational Reform Haven't Fixed the US School System," *Conversation*, March 8, 2018, https://theconversation.com/why-big-bets-on-educational-re form-havent-fixed-the-us-school-system-92327.

6. Todd Donovan, et al., *State and Local Politics: Institutions and Reform* (Stamford, CT: Cengage Learning, 2014), chapter 15, 531.

The state constitution promises free schools "wherein all the children of this state may be educated." While the state consistently spends more per pupil on education than every other state,[7] the largesse does not translate into statewide achievement. Instead, the educational outcome of the state's schools illustrates there are two distinct school systems: one is suburban, wealthy, and overwhelmingly white. Some of the nations' greatest schools are in places like Westchester County, Long Island, and wealthy suburbs around upstate cities.[8] The other system is urban, poor, and composed mostly of children of color. The second state education system encompasses the state's five biggest cities, including Syracuse, and serves more than 40 percent of the state's students.[9] This system routinely has substandard educational outcomes. The two systems often share a man-made border: on one side is wealth and great schools, and on the other, a concentration of poor people of color with significant challenges and a poorly performing school system.

This dual education system is a result of the state's historic, legal, and regulatory practices.[10] These practices, sometimes seemingly race-neutral, were discriminatory in impact and often in intent: suburban zoning practices blocking the development of affordable housing and public transit; redlining practices keeping minorities from obtaining mortgages, effectively blocking the accretion and transfer of wealth in families; and urban-renewal plans destroying Black neighborhoods and separating minority city neighborhoods from white suburbs.[11]

7. "Elementary and Secondary Education, 2019," Financial Condition Report, New York State Office of the Comptroller, 2019, https://www.osc.state.ny.us/reports/finance /2019-fcr/elementary-and-secondary-education; Olivia Hoffmann, Elizabeth Chi, and Raquel Blandon, "Analyzing Funding and Achievement Gaps in New York State Education Using GIS," *Cornell Policy Review*, https://www.cornellpolicyreview.com/GIS-Special-Edition/article.php?id=2.

8. New York's Top School Districts, Background Checks.org, (n.d.), https://background checks.org/top-school-districts-in-new-york.html.

9. "Financing Education in New York's 'Big 5' Cities," Local Government Issues in Focus, Office of the New York State Comptroller, May 2005, https://www.osc.state.ny.us /files/local-government/publications/pdf/financingeducation.pdf.

10. John Kucsera, "New York State's Extreme School Segregation: Inequality, Inaction and a Damaged Future," Civil Rights Project at UCLA, March 26, 2014, 13–26.

11. Noah Kazis, "Ending Exclusionary Zoning in New York City's Suburbs," Furman Center, November 9, 2020, https://furmancenter.org/files/Ending_Exclusionary_Zon

The state has the highest concentration of segregated public schools in the nation,[12] and its urban schools, composed largely of children of color, have some of the worst educational results in the country.[13] Syracuse fell squarely into this category.

In 1993, a group of New York City parents and education-reform advocates, calling themselves the Campaign for Fiscal Equity (CFE), decided to address the state's urban education performance through the court system. In a suit against the state, the CFE claimed New York City children were not being provided the opportunity to receive an adequate education as mandated by the state's constitution.[14] The lawsuit wound its way through the state court system for thirteen years, and in 2006, the state's highest court ruled in CFE's favor.

The court found the state was violating New York City students' constitutional right to a "sound and basic education" by failing to provide the necessary funding to the school system.[15] While the ruling addressed only New York City, the reasoning was applicable to upstate urban schools, and the Syracuse schools became entitled to a windfall of state education funding.

## Deciding to Say Yes

In early 2007, Jack told me he had gotten a call from someone connected with the former governor Hugh Carey looking to meet me. It was common for people to call Jack to request an introduction to me. Initially, it irritated me because I felt the callers thought I had no agency apart from my

ing_in_New_York_Citys_Suburbs.pdf; Noah Kazis, "New York's Ideas for Zoning Reform Offer Many Paths for Tackling the Housing Crisis," Brookings Institution, January 31, 2022, https://www.brookings.edu/blog/the-avenue/2022/01/31/new-yorks-ideas-for-zoning-reform-offer-many-paths-to-tackling-the-housing-crisis/.

12. There is a striking relationship between segregated schools and unequal school success, along with a plethora of research demonstrating that racially and socioeconomically isolated schools limit educational opportunities and outcomes. John Kucsera, "New York State's Extreme School Segregation: Inequality, Inaction, and a Damaged Future," Civil Rights Project at UCLA, March 26, 2014.

13. Kucsera, "New York State's Extreme School Segregation," 27–31.

14. Norm Fruchter and Christina Mokhtar-Ross, "Historic Steps Towards Funding Equity for NYC's Students," New York University Steinhardt. https://steinhardt.nyu.edu/metrocenter/historic-steps-towards-funding-equity-nycs-students.

15. *CFE v. State of New York*, 8 NY3d 14, November 20, 2006.

relationship with Jack. For his part, Jack would shrug his shoulders at my irritation and say, "What do you want me to do, not talk to people who call me?" That was akin to stopping the snow in Syracuse. My irritation wore off when I realized the callers were not giving Jack instructions for me. Or, if they did, he never relayed that. Jack was well-known, he was friendly, and it was an easy way for people to get my attention.

Soon after Jack's "heads-up," I received a request for a meeting with someone named Mary Anne Schmitt-Carey. Schmitt-Carey asked to meet with me and Bill Ryan, the common council majority leader, to talk about an idea for the Syracuse school system. At the initial meeting, Schmitt-Carey was elegant in her presentation and obviously used to being in boardrooms in Manhattan and Washington, DC.

She explained she was the new president of a nonprofit called Say Yes to Education, which was formed to close the achievement gap between urban and suburban districts. She wanted to partner with Syracuse to bring Say Yes's expertise in raising urban educational achievement to our city. Say Yes presented itself as an experienced savior where others—government specifically—had failed. She used a lot of terms that I was to become familiar with—"collective governance structure," "mapping resources," "pathway metrics," "higher education compact"—but I had no real idea what they meant at that meeting.

She said if Syracuse partnered with her organization, Say Yes would pay for graduating seniors to go to college. She continued that Syracuse, with its entitlement to CFE monies, was positioned to be able to partner with Say Yes to implement its educational turnaround strategies. All I heard was an organization with deep pockets wanted to help students in Syracuse go to college for free and thought, "Where do I sign?"

I was nominally aware of a recent movement of wealthy capitalists from Wall Street to Silicon Valley, dubbed "venture philanthropists," proposing and funding dramatic changes in public schools' orthodoxy nationwide, including Bill Gates, Michael Dell, and Eli Broad, a California magnate. They were seeking sweeping changes to public schools with a stated focus on children, even if it challenged school system employees.[16] The Say Yes organization was a part of this movement.

---

16. Dale Russakoff, *The Prize: Who's in Charge of America's Schools?* (Boston: Houghton Mifflin Harcourt, 2015), 8–9.

Founded by George Weiss, a multimillionaire hedge fund manager, Say Yes to Education started as a promise to pay college tuition for 112 fifth graders from West Philadelphia if they graduated from high school. Weiss's initial promise evolved into a program to provide college scholarships and safety-net services to urban students to increase high school and college graduation rates.[17]

In 2007, Say Yes was looking to expand its program to an entire urban school system. Believing the CFE money could create an opportunity to do that, Say Yes sent a letter to several state school districts pledging to pay for college tuition scholarships for five years, if the school district committed to meeting a goal of postsecondary completion; partnered with higher education, government, and the private sector; used data to assess success; and committed its own revenues to fully fund the Say Yes program by the sixth year of the partnership. The goals were audacious—to improve graduation rates from below 50 percent to 95 percent and improve performance at every grade level.[18]

The Syracuse school district had already agreed to the terms. The district had a long history of failed education-reform efforts, including years of state-sponsored programs to enhance early reading.[19] All of them had negligible impact. I faced the classic local government quandary: take the cynical position formed by experience and do nothing or take a risk on an unproven program that might fail. The gamble was to spend money to improve the lives of children and families we represented, the people I saw every morning on my way to work who stood outside, often in the freezing cold, waiting and watching as their children got on the school bus.

On the plus side of my analysis, Syracuse University's chancellor was a full partner in the program. As I listened in the meeting, I thought Syracuse's chance to be part of a movement to help children succeed had arrived. Perhaps too enthusiastically, I agreed to support the program.

17. Richard V. Reeves, Katherine Guyot, and Edward Rodrigue, "Gown Towns: A Case Study of Say Yes to Education," Brookings Institution, June 2018, 8, https://www.brookings.edu/research/gown-towns-a-case-study-of-say-yes-to-education/.

18. Op-ed, "Say Yes Verdict Not In Yet: Syracuse Schools Showing Small Gains, but Coming Year Is Crucial," Syracuse.com, June 3, 2012, https://www.syracuse.com/opinion/2012/06/say_yes_verdict_not_yet_in_syr.html.

19. Gene Maeroff, Reforming a School System, Reviving a City: The Promise of Say Yes to Education in Syracuse (New York: Palgrave Macmillan, 2013), 39.

Together with Ryan, I lobbied members of the common council to give $1 million of Syracuse's fund balance to the Say Yes foundation to support its efforts. It was a huge risk with the city's precious savings account money, but it was a chance to improve the lives of children and families in our community. My Democratic and Republican colleagues on the city council felt the same and all of them voted for the legislation.[20] I chose to take the risk and become a Say Yes advocate because I believed progress was not made by cynics.

## Mooting Mayoral Control

At the beginning of the 2008–2009 school year, Say Yes announced it would pay for college scholarships for students graduating that year and would start implementing its program for students in the first of the district's four quarters.[21] The services would be expanded to each quadrant annually, so by the beginning of 2011, all quadrants would be offering the Say Yes program benefits to all students and their families. The announcement and work I had done to advocate for Say Yes allowed me to point to a legislative accomplishment that would benefit many people in Syracuse. Changing the educational system through Say Yes became a cornerstone of my mayoral campaign.

Syracuse voters made it clear with their questions, opinions, and poll results they expected the mayor to address the schools' unacceptable performance. It was widely agreed that the school system's performance foreshadowed a bleak future for both Syracuse and its children. One evening during the campaign, I knocked on a voter's door and was greeted by an owlish-looking man. He volunteered that he was despondent over the state of the city's schools. When I told him the Say Yes program would change things, he shook his head and said he admired my spirit, but he had heard too many promises to believe anything could change. He said, "Without good schools, we're done," and closed the door.

I thought often about that voter's desire for change and his sense that government could not deliver what he thought was desperately needed. I

20. Meghan Rubado, "Council to Add to City School Budget—Amendment Will Give $1M to the Say Yes to Education," *Post-Standard*, May 5, 2008.

21. Say Yes to Education Syracuse. https://sayyessyracuse.org/about/history/.

wondered if an inevitable part of getting older is getting cynical about the ability to create positive change. Or was it a reasonable feeling, given government's chronic inability to solve problems? Much later, I wondered if I added to his sentiment by promoting change but failing to deliver. Is the role of a leader to promise too much simply to be able to deliver a modest result? Does that, in and of itself, create cynicism about government?

Despite its importance to the city, the mayor of Syracuse has little control over the schools. State law dictated the school system be governed by an elected board of education.[22] As evidenced by my conversation with Duffy, my lack of mayoral control over Syracuse's school district was not an anomaly. Governance by a school board, instead of a mayor, was historically seen as the best way to insulate public education from political interference.[23] This governance structure became codified under law and required state approval to change.

In the 1990s, the chronic education failings in urban areas led many to argue that the decentralized governing structure of school boards was failing children of color. These reformers suggested a centralized system wherein mayoral authority over schools would be better, assuming that a unified leadership structure with accountability would focus the bureaucracy on achieving better educational results.[24]

This debate became relevant in the state in 2001 during the New York City mayoral campaign, when candidate Michael Bloomberg pledged to take control of the school system if he became mayor. He promised voters they could hold him accountable for achieving better educational results. After his election, Bloomberg successfully lobbied the state to give him

22. The Board of Education in Syracuse, Buffalo, and Rochester have almost exclusive governing authority but do not have independent taxing authority. This relationship is legally characterized as a city with a "dependent" school district; "Financing Education in New York's 'Big Five' Cities," Local Government Issues in Focus, Office of the New York State Comptroller, May 2005. https://www.osc.state.ny.us/files/local-government /publications/pdf/financingeducation.pdf.

23. Jeffrey R. Henig and Walter C. Rich, *Mayors in the Middle: Politics, Race, and Mayoral Control of Urban Schools* (Princeton: Princeton University Press, 2004); Deborah Land, "Local School Boards Under Review: Their Role and Effectiveness in Relation to Students' Academic Achievement," *Review of Educational Research* 72, no. 2 (2002).

24. Kenneth K. Wong and Francis X. Shen, "Mayoral Governance and Student Achievement: How Mayor-Led Districts Are Improving School and Student Performance," American Progress, March 22, 2013, https://www.americanprogress.org/article /mayoral-governance-and-student-achievement/.

mayoral control over the school system. Under the mayoral control system, New York City's school system increased test scores and graduation rates. Bloomberg was able to use the impressive data to successfully renew mayoral control seven years later.[25]

After my discussion with Duffy at the 2010 State of the State, I thought mayoral control of schools would become a statewide issue. I started making and fielding phone calls to generate support for the idea. Accountable, centralized leadership, I argued, would allow us to be nimble and make change. This was especially important considering all the transformational work Say Yes was promising to do.

Supporters were excited by the idea of implementing a change that could positively impact something as important as education. Citing the results Mayor Bloomberg had achieved, supporters of the idea would discuss it as both a moral issue and something crucial to the strength of our democracy. The primary opponent was the teachers union. I had a long-standing good relationship with the members of Syracuse's teachers union and had had difficult but overwhelmingly positive discussions about the issue. The leadership shared they were worried about what would happen to the schools after my tenure as mayor. Would a mayor be able to raid the schools' budget to pay for pet projects or engage in something equally irresponsible?

During these discussions, gubernatorial candidate Andrew Cuomo announced Bob Duffy would become his running mate as lieutenant governor. I saw it as another positive sign that mayoral control would become a hot political issue. It had been only four months since Duffy had told me that this issue was a hill he was willing to die on. He was going to be in a position of statewide influence where he could advocate for the change.

When I said as much to Assemblyman Richard Brodsky, a state political soothsayer, he characteristically upbraided me: "It's never going to happen, kid." I explained that Duffy said he was willing to "die" over it. Brodsky cynically laughed saying it did not matter what Duffy said. The state teachers union was opposed to it. Cuomo wanted the union's support, so there would be no discussion of mayoral control. Sure enough, in short order, Rochester's effort to obtain mayoral control collapsed. Duffy stopped advocating for it and all discussion of it ceased.

25. "Seven Years of Mayoral Control, Gotham Gazette," (n.d.). https://www.gothamga zette.com/index.php/archives/377-seven-years-of-mayoral-control.

I was disillusioned because I'd thought Duffy was a leader to be emulated. Instead, he had seemingly chosen ambition over a self-declared priority. Could it be worth subjugating an important position to become lieutenant governor? While not the proverbial warm bucket of spit, the role was close. Yet the ability to quietly walk away from an important belief might be the most relevant measure of success for Duffy.

A year into my term, the incumbent superintendent of the Syracuse school system, Daniel Lowengard, announced he would be leaving. The departure created an opportunity to hire a reformer as the new superintendent. As evidence of its important role, the school board hired Say Yes to run the search process. With no mayoral control, I had no formal role in the selection, but the position was integral to the success of my education initiatives and the success of Syracuse, so I followed the proceedings carefully.

When a woman named Sharon Contreras, the chief academic officer for the Providence school system, became the front-runner, I called the former mayor of Providence, Rhode Island, David Cicilline. While Cicilline and I did not know each other, I hoped he would talk to me as a matter of professional courtesy. When I reached him by phone, I asked his view of Contreras and he answered with the equivalent of "she's a good person, I like her." A classic politician nonanswer.

I told him I was asking as a fellow mayor if she would be a good superintendent. He told me Contreras was smart but tough and aggressive. "If you don't like that type of personality, she might not be for you." I laughed thinking the same could be said of me and responded those were the traits I wanted. Shortly after, Contreras was announced as the new superintendent.

On my way to our first joint appearance, an event to highlight summer school programming, I skimmed Contreras's biography: forty-one years old, a native New Yorker, raised on Long Island, a classic overachiever who had graduated high school early, and a woman of color. We pulled into the event, and I saw throngs of media, teachers, administrators, and parents gathered for the event. I was getting out of my car when a breathless school administrator ran to me and whispered, "The new superintendent has hearing aids. She's not ignoring you—I don't know how much she can hear." I nodded and felt like it was something I should have known before our first event.

When I reached the new superintendent, she was in the eye of the media storm. I watched and was struck that she looked to be around forty years old. I was so used to being surrounded by older, mostly white men, it came as a surprise to see a woman my age in a position of power. When I shook her hand, the cameras were flashing and there was a lot of background noise. I said, "Welcome to Syracuse," but I couldn't tell if she could hear me. We were given a tour around the Hillside Work-Scholarship program facility, where I was able to discreetly look and see hearing aids in both ears partially hidden by her long hair. We stopped at the end of the tour to take media questions and all I could think to do was to nonchalantly repeat the question as a support. When the event ended, she smiled and thanked me, and I realized that was the only time we had talked in our time together. When I got in the car, I asked my staff if they had noticed anything unusual about the event. None did.

Days later, she came to my office for our first private meeting. She said she could turn the schools around, saying "poverty is not an excuse for failure." The teachers were doing the best job they could, she said, but they did not have the right tools. She was committed to putting the elements in place—a rigorous curriculum, better professional development, appropriate instruction tools, comprehensive assessment, and an intervention program. Once the academic piece was better designed and implemented, she promised, the results would improve.

We agreed we would focus on the mission of improving outcomes, support each other, and have regularly scheduled meetings. She said our initial event was terrible because she had trouble hearing over the noise and thanked me for repeating the questions. When I told her my crack staff, including a police officer, had not noticed anything unusual, she laughed out loud.

Almost immediately after assuming office, Contreras was thrown into a hurricane when the state released academic assessment results showing Syracuse was, once again, at the bottom. At one of her first school board meetings, she called the dismal student achievement numbers unacceptable. In a departure from blaming another entity for the poor results, she said it was the district's responsibility to produce better outcomes.

Months later, in November 2011, the state education department identified every one of Syracuse's public schools as among the lowest-performing schools in the state.[26] Because of this, the state said the schools needed to be

26. Maureen Nolan, "Syracuse Students Score Lowest in State's Big Cities," *Post-Standard*, August 9, 2011; "SCSD High Schools Show Progress," The New York State District Report

restructured or closed. Contreras skillfully negotiated an agreement with the teachers union to extend student learning time as well as the number of school days by 180 hours a year, enabling students to have more "time on task," which had been shown to improve educational outcomes. She established an "Innovation Zone" to enable flexibility in identifying different techniques for success. By implementing these plans, the community was spared the painful process of closing schools.

I made regular visits to classrooms as part of my schedule. The visits were intended to show my support and the fact I was prioritizing education. Once I arrived in the classrooms, I would answer questions. The youngest students' queries were full of refreshing honesty and unpredictability: Do you have a limousine? Do you live in a mansion? What's your favorite color? Do you like dogs? The young children treated me as if I was a superhero and always would ask me to return.

After a few visits, I leveraged my status by challenging students to read. I would return to the class and autograph a bookmark if a student had read ten books. If a student had read twenty books, he or she would receive a both an autographed bookmark and a T-shirt, sunglasses, or backpack emblazoned with a graphic of city hall and the words "Mayor Miner's All-Star Team." If each student in the class had read thirty books, they would receive all the gifts, as well as a pizza party and cake, with me in attendance. It amazed me that a couple of hundred dollars of our the mayor's office budget every year could encourage so many children to read books and fill them with pride when handed the well-earned gifts.[27] For years, I would run into students who proudly told me they had participated and met the challenge.

These visits made the reality of students' lives inescapable. Many were poorly nourished, moved frequently because they didn't have permanent homes, or routinely witnessed violence. Many students were unkempt, not dressed for the weather, did not live with either parent, or had attended

Card, New York State Education Department, 2009–2010 report, https://data.nysed.gov/files/reportcards/archive/2009-10/AOR-2010-421800010000.pdf.

27. The bookmarks were made in the mayor's office printed with a different quote highlighting the importance of education every year. A local merchant gave the other products to us at cost. At the end of my tenure, I started seeing children wear the T-shirts in classes I had yet to issue in the challenge. When I asked them how they got the shirt, they told me it belonged to an older sibling, but they wore it because I was scheduled to visit the class that day.

several different schools in the past year. Their lives were chaotic and filled with obstacles to learning.

Teachers and administrators were facing enormous pressure to hit academic benchmarks and were clearly anxious. Almost every student talked to me about taking and preparing for tests. Once when in the office of a newly installed high school vice principal, I noticed a list of names and symbols tacked to back of his door under where his coat was hanging. When I asked about it, he explained it was a list of students who were in danger of not graduating. The symbols represented challenges: homeless, parent in jail, or just the inability to focus, often because of the chaos they faced daily in their home lives. The vice principal was both worried about and intent on getting the students to cross the stage on graduation day.

I was committed to showing my support in any way I could, including shaking the hand of every high school graduate who crossed the stage. My determination to be present led to a hectic schedule. In June 2013, after a grueling day, I was checking into a hotel in New York City. As I signed my name in triplicate, I asked the lone hotel clerk without looking up when coffee would be available in the lobby. The clerk answered, "Four a.m." I said "perfect" and heard her typing stop. When I looked up, I saw the clock behind her show it was after one in the morning. My eyes met hers and she asked me how long I planned to be in the hotel. When I answered three hours, her face contorted, and I realized she was probably wondering if I was trying to fit in a quickie. I explained, "It's not what you think. I'm a mayor and I have to get back to attend high school graduations." She laughed and promised the coffee would be ready at four.

## Fixing the Buildings

One area I did control as mayor was the renovation of school buildings, because they were owned by the city. Most of the buildings had serious structural issues, so were an impediment to learning, teaching, and safety. While the state reimbursed Syracuse for a percentage of the maintenance and upkeep costs, the funds took decades to materialize. In the intervening time, the old buildings deteriorated at a rate outpacing Syracuse's financial ability to repair or upgrade them.

A solution to this problem was announced before my tenure, in 2003, when the state created a new entity known as the Joint School Construction

Board (JSCB). It was charged with establishing a school-renovation plan and issuing debt to pay for the renovations.[28] With great fanfare, my predecessor and the then superintendent announced that every school building would be renovated and upgraded over a ten-year period for under $1 billion.[29] Yet, six years later, the JSCB program had completed only two school roof projects.[30]

The legislation actually provided $140 million for phase one, not the announced $900 million, and the schools were in much worse shape than anticipated. There were multimillion-dollar financing gaps and the project had become mired in finger-pointing. Parents, teachers, and residents were deflated by the results.

As mayor, I became head of the JSCB, which I described as "a morass" and an "embarrassment to the community."[31] During my first year as mayor, I focused on renovating schools to restore faith that city government could accomplish things.[32] It became a crusade to get construction projects off the drawing board and on the ground. I demanded a master plan from district staff, engineering professionals, and construction experts detailing project costs, a timetable, and hard figures for each project. I negotiated a cut in the project's fee of $600,000 and another $400,000 if the contractor failed to complete major renovations at four schools. I had regular meetings with the general contractor and engineering staff for status updates.

This process was completely contrary to the district's experience with school renovations. In the district's traditional method, budget estimates were a floor, and if a project became more expensive, the state would routinely work with a school district to pay for cost overruns, which would be reimbursed over years. Consequently, traditional renovation budgets had

28. The City of Syracuse, Joint Schools Construction Board, https://beta.syrgov.net/Boards-and-Commissions/JSCB.

29. Frederic Pierce, "Syracuse Wants to Spend $600M to Fix Every School—Officials: Creative Financing Using Bonds, Savings from Renovations Means No Tax Increase Needed," *Post-Standard*, August 17, 2003; M. Nolan and E. Kriss, "Pataki Approves $900 M for City School Projects—to Begin in the Fall," *Post-Standard*, April 13, 2006.

30. Meghan Rubado, "Next Mayor on City Schools—Where Candidates Stand on Key Issues Facing Syracuse District," *Post-Standard*, October 28, 2009.

31. Meghan Nolan, "City Cuts Fee for School Renovation Firm—a 'Scathing' Job Review for Gilbane," *Post-Standard*, June 25, 2010.

32. Meghan Rubado, "Get Schools Renovated Quickly," *Post-Standard*, January 28, 2010.

flexible numbers. In contrast, the JSCB process budget had a hard ceiling with a maximum number. If projects surpassed that amount, then another project would have to be scaled back or skipped.

This new process required the district to work closely with us instead of operating independently. When district staff believed the recommended construction contingency amount was too large, we insisted on it. They thought the state would help us pay for items, while we insisted on a budget that did not rely on additional help. When they thought the construction budget estimates would be less when construction started, we refused to be flexible. When they wanted to tell people a school would be renovated, we would commit only to schools that were part of an approved budget.

The district had an inherent aversion to making decisions and operated by making promises and hoping things would work. They usually didn't, and it led to paralysis. Forcing decisions meant there was always someone who was convinced the decisions were wrong: parents of children at schools that were not being renovated; parents of children at schools that were going to be renovated, requiring their children to be moved during construction; and people who did not understand how construction of four schools could cost $140 million. I managed the process by presenting numbers and listening to the heated views at regular public meetings.

After a year, we had a master plan and budget for completely renovating four schools to a LEED silver standard and a date for the start of construction. Choosing to have the work speak for itself, I refused to hold a groundbreaking ceremony to celebrate.

As we started making progress with first-phase renovations, we were ready to ask the state for permission for a second-phase of JSCB to continue fixing the buildings. As we were planning for this request, I received a call from Judy Rapfogel, a top aid to the Assembly Speaker Sheldon "Shelly" Silver. Rapfogel and I were friendly and had a professional relationship.

Assuming she was calling about the second-phase legislation, I was caught short when she said Shelly asked her to call to see if the schools had asbestos issues. I said I wasn't sure what she meant, and she slowly repeated the same thing she just said. Then I remembered Silver worked for a law firm in New York City specializing in asbestos work. I surmised I was being asked if there was any work I could refer to the speaker. Relieved, I answered that the work was already being done. She thanked me and said she told

Shelly that would be the case, but she wanted to make sure. It was not to be the last time I spoke with Rapfogel about JSCB.

The whole interaction felt uncomfortable, but, as I understood it, it was not illegal. Legislators are allowed to have second jobs. The fact that this legislator had a great deal of power over the legislation moving forward and was asking about work tangentially related to the legislation was troubling. The work and the legislation's passage were not linked, and the rules of the system allowed it. But it was a gray area, and it made me deeply uncomfortable.

To highlight our school-renovation progress, I told the audience in my 2013 State of the City address that Syracuse's delegation would introduce legislation allowing us to move forward with a second phase of JSCB. I said it was "an important step in providing the children of the Syracuse City School District safe and productive learning environments; a core responsibility of each and every one of us." The state delegation moved the bill, and it passed both houses of the state legislature in May.

When it was scheduled to be advanced to the governor's office, I was told there was a problem, which strangely could not be identified. Soon after, I received a call from Todd Howe, a close confidant of Governor Cuomo's. Howe said forebodingly, "You know how these guys are." He said he knew JSCB was a priority of mine and his voice faded into silence. After a pregnant pause, he continued, "The governor wants what he wants, and he is tough"—obliquely indicating the governor wanted something from me, but the timing could not be linked.

I understood immediately. Howe had been tasked with communicating to me that the governor would not sign the second-phase legislation unless I agreed to resign as cochair of the State Democratic Party, and there could be no evidence of a connection between the two. I was filled with revulsion for Howe, the governor, and the entire political process. After an intentionally long pause, I said, "Yeah, I get it. I will resign quietly." Relieved, Howe thanked me and hung up.

Months later, on the evening of Good Friday, I had an email sent out to the state press corps announcing my resignation as cochair of the State Democratic Party. The following Monday, Rapfogel called to tell me she and Shelly believed the governor refused to sign the school reconstruction legislation until I had agreed to resign. When I said they were right, she said they thought it was a terrible thing to do. It was, but she and Shelly failed to offer to do anything to stop it.

Perhaps they couldn't because it was in the governor's power to refuse to sign legislation, but I felt their silence in the face of such an act was complicity. Was I naive to believe that the state's leadership would prevent the governor from stopping legislation intended to help poor, needy children? The answer, I realized as I hung up the phone, was yes. With transactional politics, power beats policy interests, even when those involve children.

I agreed to the governor's subterfuge, hiding his real purpose of removing me from Democratic Party leadership, because I cared more about fixing the schools than the political position. I was shocked Cuomo used schools for some of the poorest children in the state as a bargaining chip. It seemed to me immoral and counter to his professed values.

On reflection, it was a minimally politically risky thing for him to do. The media does not pay attention to the minutiae of such policies and, even if they did, he had a defensible pretext for the objection. Moreover, if threatened by me with political embarrassment, he could permanently refuse to sign it.

The state legislature and I met Cuomo's public demands to "remedy" the legislation's flaws by accepting: (1) three, not two as originally proposed, additional members to serve on the board; (2) a listing of all eligible schools to be renovated instead of the originally proposed language of "locations to be determined by the city school district and approved by the JSC board," and (3) a seventh member of the JSCB, not employed by the city or the school district, to be jointly designated by the mayor and the superintendent.[33] Despite my acquiescence, the governor withheld signing the legislation, delaying much-needed renovations.

## Asking Everyone to Say Yes

Say Yes's provision of college-tuition benefits for high school seniors graduating in 2009, which was before its programs were implemented, engendered a huge amount of goodwill. But the public clearly didn't understand what Say Yes actually *was*, and the organization was never able to give a succinct answer. Instead, it reinforced the mystery with a mission statement

33. JSCB Chapter Amendment 2014. A08226/S06127.

that included opaque jargon such as: "a theory of action bringing together stakeholders under a collaborative governance structure to improve college readiness through services and then align resources based on transparent data."[34]

I heard that answer hundreds of times and saw confusion cloud the listeners' faces every time. At which point, if I could, I would say it was a program aimed at ensuring students got the support they needed to make education a priority. It was better but not great. The danger was that by not defining its mission clearly, Say Yes created an obstacle to the community taking ownership of the program. People are not going to prioritize something they do not understand, even if they are receiving a benefit like college tuition.

The confusion over Say Yes's mission led many people to believe that it was a Syracuse University program, not a community program. Syracuse University chancellor Nancy Cantor had been the first to recognize the Say Yes opportunity and pushed to bring it to Syracuse.[35] Cantor authorized university faculty and employees to staff the Say Yes programs; the site directors, while paid by Say Yes, were on the university payroll; and the local offices of Say Yes were housed in university buildings. While critical to the implementation of the program, the university was the eight-hundred-pound gorilla of the community. It made key decisions, and its views were sought after and deferred to. While the community was asked to participate, it was under the rules promulgated by Say Yes with the backing and approval of Syracuse University. Consequently, the university was viewed as "owning" the program.

Onondaga County repurposed state funds to hire more social workers for the school system. As the main provider of safety-net programs for city students, the county agreed to help the Say Yes efforts. When Say Yes found a significant number of students did not have health insurance or access to care for other reasons, the county worked with school and city officials to design a process to ensure eligible students were enrolled in subsidized

34. Richard V. Reeves, Katherine Guyot, Edward Rodrigue, "Gown Towns: A Case Study of Say Yes to Education," Brookings Institution, June, 2018, 10, https://www.brook ings.edu/research/gown-towns-a-case-study-of-say-yes-to-education/.

35. Glenn Coin, "Chancellor Nancy Cantor linked SU scholarship to Syracuse in ways not envisioned before," Syracuse.com, October 13, 2012, https://www.syracuse.com/news /2012/10/chancellor_nancy_cantor_legacy.html.

health insurance plans. Initially, the collaboration resulted in 91 percent of eligible students at sixteen schools getting services through either school- or community-based clinics. Say Yes and the county also worked together to ensure students could access mental health care by aligning counselors' schedules with the school calendar and allowing counselors to be supervised by school principals.

Lawyers, higher education experts, arts organizations, and the business community were asked by me, the university, and the school district to provide an array of support for the program. Every student and family was eligible to participate in the Say Yes program offerings. This included students and families receiving one-on-one help with college applications and the financial-aid process. As part of the school programing, students were afforded tutoring, extended learning time, and enriched educational experiences. Say Yes families were also offered legal representation in certain cases, such as securing unemployment benefits. These services allowed teachers to focus on academics and freed up resources to meet other needs.

In addition to delivering more social workers, tutoring, and after-school programming, Say Yes appointed a site director to each elementary school. The site directors were by and large young and energetic. While they were enthusiastic, most lacked solid education experience. The site director was paid by Say Yes to oversee the program's operations in the building. They were responsible for reaching out to students' families, assessing the social and emotional health and the academic needs of children and families, and planning and implementing support to the families. Residents were thrilled to see twenty-somethings in a Say Yes shirt walking through neighborhoods, knocking on doors, and asking why a child was missing from school.

The efforts were implemented in real time. Coordinating separate entities—a national nonprofit, a semiautonomous school district, city and county agencies, and the private sector—and asking them to work together in a new way was a bumpy process. It required a sustained effort to manage, but I felt our united goal of improving education was enough to overcome any issues.

The Great Recession gave rise to Say Yes's first existential crisis. Say Yes and the district estimated the CFE decision would provide Syracuse with an additional $75 million, an extra $3,500 per student over four years. Say Yes projected its programming would provide about the same amount. In 2010, the program's second year, the state announced that instead of an anticipated increase in education funding, it was freezing foundation aid at 2008–2009 levels and imposing a long-term cap on aid increases.[36] The assumptions that Say Yes, the city, and the district made were eviscerated. I held my breath and prepared for Say Yes to announce it was putting its plans on hold until the funding environment changed.

To my surprise, Say Yes and the school district leadership announced they would continue to implement the Say Yes program and instructional improvements. As part of this process, Say Yes hired an outside firm, Education Resource Strategies (ERS), to analyze school spending and resources to assess if the district's spending money aligned with education goals.

While this type of involvement in the budget was a major departure from the normal process, the district's leadership agreed and cooperated with the analysis. The ERS report found areas of overspending and over-staffing and recommended cutting 425 jobs, including 140 teachers, to help close a projected $47 million gap for the following fiscal year. It was at this point that I found myself in the middle of the issue.

Say Yes characterized the ERS process as collaborative, but teachers, district staff, and the union told me it was a setup to justify cuts. Teachers were outraged that an outside group would get involved in such a delicate manner. They reacted bitterly to the intrusion by Say Yes. Teachers and other community stakeholders were clear in communicating ERS's analysis was about pushing Say Yes's agenda, not the needs of the locals.

I shared my concern over the animosity with Schmitt-Carey. She acknowledged the process had been bungled. She apologized to me and others, promising Say Yes would hire another consultant to oversee a process that would be much more amendable to the stakeholders. Contreras took over and was able to manage the loss in revenue without cutting instructional staff or closing schools and, in doing so, succeeded in mending the breach.

Yet, importantly, Say Yes had failed to address the issues of the people who did the daily work to meet the educational challenges. Teachers were a key constituency for implementing the Say Yes program and our educational goals. Their voices were hugely influential to parents, another important constituency. Say Yes made teachers and others feel like they were

36. Gene Maeroff, *Reforming a School System, Reviving a City: The Promise of Say Yes to Education in Syracuse* (London: Palgrave Macmillan, 2013), 150.

subjects in an experiment, not equals. In the eyes of many locals, everyone in Syracuse became "us," and Say Yes was "them."

Say Yes leadership went to great lengths to say community "collaboration" was a cornerstone of the program. But it seemed it was only a talking point. When almost all the Syracuse schools were in danger of being closed due to poor results at the end of 2011, Say Yes demanded the district make a major investment in its information technology capacity. Data, Say Yes said, was a foundational element of the program.

The community priority was to deal with the fate of the schools in danger of falling into receivership, not to spend vital resources on information technology upgrades. The district questioned whether it could legally share protected data with Say Yes. Neither side seemed interested in finding a resolution.

I now heard over coffee, the telephone, and neighborhood events that Say Yes was causing problems. Say Yes staff were muddying the lines of authority in school buildings, causing tension and anger over whether the principal and teachers or the Say Yes director have ultimate control in the building. School personnel complained Say Yes services were nothing more than "glorified babysitting."

When Say Yes retained community-based organizations to run afterschool programming, some complained their organizations were unfairly being forced to compete for funding or unfairly terminated. Many noted that the more than $40 million in cash and in-kind services Say Yes said it leveraged for the community was spent on outside consultants hired to fly in and tell Syracuse what it was doing wrong, collect a fat paycheck, and leave.

By 2012, its four-year anniversary in Syracuse, Say Yes said hundreds of high school students had been prepped for college, thousands of elementary students were tutored, and 2,200 pupils were scheduled to attend summer classes. The actual data showed modest improvement: a rise in the four-year high school graduation rate from 45 percent in 2009 to 48 percent in 2011, an increase in ninth graders passing the Regents algebra exam, and a drop in the number of ninth graders leaving school. It was far from our goal of raising high school graduation rates to 95 percent and improving performance at every grade level.[37]

---

37. Op-ed, "Say Yes Verdict Not In Yet: Syracuse Schools Showing Small Gains, but Coming Year Is Crucial," Syracuse.com, June 3, 2012, https://www.syracuse.com/opinion/2012/06/say_yes_verdict_not_yet_in_syr.html.

Even when Say Yes celebrated the work done in Syracuse, it became problematic. Say Yes officials frequently touted the results from of one Regents exam in Syracuse that showed a 30 percent increase in the number of ninth graders passing the algebra exam. But the biggest increase in the ninth-grade algebra passing rate was only a one-year increase of 10.3 percentage points. Say Yes reported on its website that "the number of county children in foster care has decreased by 45 percent since 2005," which was accurate, but the numbers were countywide, not just Syracuse, and Say Yes did not begin providing services until 2008. Its website boasted Say Yes had increased home values in Syracuse by 3.5 percent since 2009. But housing prices in Rochester, which did not have Say Yes, had also increased.[38]

It was hard to avoid the feeling that Say Yes was taking exclusive credit for the hard work our community had done. The marketing efforts of Say Yes seemed to "brand" the community's good work as a Say Yes accomplishment and quietly blame the community for not making more progress. When Cantor, Say Yes's original champion, announced she was leaving the university, a major constructive force was removed from the team. People openly wondered if the program would be sustainable without Cantor's participation.

I continued to advocate for Say Yes, believing it offered our best chance at positive change, but other local proponents quietly disappeared. More people began to openly wonder if the organization was genuinely interested in making change or interested in promoting itself. I had begun to wonder that, too.

## The Heavy Toll of Justice

By 2013, two years into Contreras's tenure, the district was continuing to show improvement. High school graduation rates had inched above 50 percent, and by August 2014, the rate had reached 56 percent; the dropout rate decreased to 16.5 percent, representing the fourth consecutive decrease.[39] It was modest success built on the focus and hard work of a coalition of stakeholders.

38. Mary B. Pasciak, "Say Yes Too Good to Be True?" *Buffalo News*, November 18, 2012.

39. Dave Tobin, "Graduation Rates Improve for Syracuse City School District," Syracuse.com, December 18, 2014, https://www.syracuse.com/news/2014/12/graduation_rate_improves_for_syracuse_city_school_district.html.

At one of our regular meetings, Contreras sat down and uncharacteristically let out a frustrated sigh. Clearly troubled, she said, "They have been throwing students out of school without any basis." I gave her a quizzical look, and she continued, "They have been throwing Black boys out of school." All I could muster was, "What do you mean?"

She explained that the state attorney general's office had started an investigation of the district after receiving multiple complaints from parents, advocates, and community members about disciplinary practices. She said that Black students were routinely removed from class and effectively given permanent out-of-school suspensions. A teacher would throw a student out of class and the school's administration would issue a suspension and not let the student back into school unless a parent came to a meeting. Sometimes the parents were not officially told of a meeting; sometimes they could not, or would not, attend a meeting. Consequently, the student would be out of school indefinitely.

I thought there had to be some reasonable explanation. People don't become teachers to throw students out of class. Exasperated, Contreras said they were regularly suspending and expelling five-year-old Black boys from kindergarten. I thought about my own five-year-old nephew and understood how absurd that was.

Contreras told me the data showed a systematic violation of students' civil rights. The attorney general believed the teachers' behavior was illegal and was going to sue the district. She faced a choice of how to proceed: she could spend vast amounts of money on lawyers and data experts in an eternal fight over the legal interpretation of the data. By doing so, she would ensure the status quo and allow the teachers' disciplinary practices and routines to continue, or she could face the consequences of poking the entrenched stakeholders for the sake of justice.

It wasn't a question of which decision Contreras would make, but she was asking whether I would stand with her or take the politically convenient tack of separating myself from the issue. When she asked for my opinion, it was my turn to emit a big sigh. I told her I would help. I said the matter should be settled as quickly as possible so we could start fixing the problem. I volunteered to call Attorney General Eric Schneiderman. In the confines of that room, it seemed like the obvious choice—fix the problem. It became a decision that exposed a shocking and ugly reality.

When I placed the call, I expected Schneiderman to be an agreeable partner. I liked him, but we were not close. In my view, he was a creature of an ultrawealthy, ultraliberal Manhattan crowd, and he was aware he did not fit in upstate. He always seemed uncomfortable during his frequent appearances in Syracuse for press conferences bolstering the narrative that he cared about upstate issues.

He unintentionally highlighted his differences in his talking points, saying he was a sheriff in Massachusetts for a time while attempting to find a career. It always fell flat because most upstate people do not have the option of drifting in and out of careers, looking to find themselves. He did not look like a sheriff, especially in his elegant bespoke suits. It was obvious to even the most casual observer he wore eyeliner. I thought he was uncomfortable in our part of the state because it was different from New York City. Much later, I was to learn Schneiderman had deep-seated disturbing issues that I could not have imagined when he resigned in 2018 after allegations of physical and sexual abuse.[40]

When Schneiderman got on the phone, he was friendly, but his tone changed when I told him I wanted to discuss the district's disciplinary issues. He said he couldn't talk, parroting well-worn excuses about potential litigation and concluding he had not been briefed on the topic. I said I understood but asked him to listen to what I had to say as a vested observer. I told him that Contreras and I wanted to settle the matter quickly to focus on fixing the problem, not litigation. He was silent for a few moments and his tone changed again. "Really? That's different." He said he would get the settlement process started, and we hung up.

Contreras immediately restricted the use of suspensions to only serious offenses. She directed the staff to implement "restorative justice" techniques, a concept where students and staff learn constructive ways to address fear, anger, and anxiety.[41] The blowback was immediate and fell into two camps: Those who concluded that unruly students should face the consequences of their behavior, and those who felt it was a teacher's job to maintain discipline without resorting to expelling students.

40. Danny Hakim and Vivian Wang, "Eric Schneiderman Resigns as New York Attorney General Amid Assault Claims by 4 Women," *New York Times*, May 7, 2018.

41. Patricia Leigh Brown, "Opening Up, Students Transform a Vicious Circle," *New York Times*, April 3, 2013.

Everywhere I went, I heard from mostly white teachers and district personnel telling me in no uncertain terms that the superintendent and her staff had no idea what it was like to teach in a district with so many challenged students. I would hear things like: "Students don't listen. What am I supposed to do if a student stands up and says, 'Fuck you' to my face when I ask him to quiet down?" The examples always involved students being wildly disrespectful, with an undercurrent of physical violence.

Teachers of color told me they rarely had issues maintaining classroom discipline. They made it clear they thought this was an issue with older, white female teachers who could control their classes only by kicking out students.

The practices Contreras was changing—namely, routinely kicking students out of class and school—were not only illegal, but research indicated they were harmful to learning environments. Suspensions, especially for minor misconduct, stunt student progress and damage the school climate for all students.[42] Data showed frequent use of suspensions did not reduce unwanted behavior, nor did it improve learning conditions. In fact, the data indicated that schools in the district with the lowest suspension rates were also the highest performing.[43]

Say Yes was conspicuously silent on the destructive discipline practices. The organization had led the process of choosing Contreras, but it didn't stand by her when controversy arose or publicly support the decisions she made.

## The Ugly Data

The attorney general's office interviewed multiple parents, student advocates, and other witnesses; analyzed reams of data regarding discipline practices; and thoroughly reviewed more than a million pages of documents. By the time the findings were made public, almost everyone seemed to know someone who had been interviewed or involved with the matter.

The findings[44] the attorney general's office released were shocking:

42. Daniel J. Losen, "Getting Back on Track: Final Report on Syracuse," July 2014, 4, https://docshare.tips/syracuse-city-schools-discipline-report_5784a83db6d87f4b2b8b4 5a0.html.

43. Losen, "Getting Back on Track."

44. Attorney General Assurance of Discontinuance, AOD No. 14–159, July 10, 2014.

- The district's suspension rate was one of the highest in the nation.
- More than one-third of all students in the district were removed from class and sent to the principal to be disciplined. In middle-school grades, more than half of all students received at least one teacher referral for discipline.
- Nearly one-fifth of all students in the district had received out-of-school suspensions at least once, and more than one-third of middle school students had received an out-of-school suspension.

The high rates of discipline were also rife with racial bias:

- Almost 44 percent of Black students received at least one teacher referral, while the figure for white students was 26 percent; nearly 27 percent of Black students received at least one in-school suspension, compared to 15 percent of white students; and 25 percent of Black students had been given out-of-school suspensions, compared to 12 percent of white students.
- For Black students in middle school grades, 62 percent received at least one teacher referral, 44 percent received at least one in-school suspension, and 42 percent received at least one out-of-school suspension, compared to 41 percent, 26 percent, and 28 percent for white students, respectively.
- The long-term-suspension process was started for Black students at twice the rate of white students.

The city was inflamed by the findings. People of color told me they had long suspected discrimination in the system. White people openly questioned how such discrimination could exist in Syracuse.

While overwhelmingly white, the teachers union had been a fierce advocate for students of color, who constituted a majority of their pupils. They had forcefully and repeatedly argued the state was shortchanging such students by failing to increase aid to the district.[45] After some therapeutic venting, I believed, the teachers would grudgingly admit change was necessary. I was wrong. The teachers union dug in and decided to blame and argue,

45. Kevin Ahern, "School Problems—Fix It Plan Doesn't Address Real Issue: Poverty," *Post-Standard*, December 16, 2010; Chris Bolt, "Syracuse Teachers, Parents, School Officials Feeling 'The Blues' Over Education Funding, Reform," WAER.org, December 9, 2013.

steadfastly refusing my pleas to accept the inevitable and move forward to change the discipline system.

The union fought and repeatedly said school environments deteriorated because Contreras changed the discipline process, all the while explicitly ignoring the issue of justice as well as the attorney general's findings. It was a departure from the organization that had I had witnessed steadfastly advocate for funding for their students.

At one public meeting, a group of teachers and the union president told the school board that "student behavior has come to such a point where it is difficult to maintain order, let alone teach effectively." They continued, "There were too many reports of students receiving few consequences for their behavior." Finally, they called on "administrators, the school board, elected officials, community leaders" to come together with teachers to "ensure our schools are safe."[46]

In contrast to the union's public statements, analysis of the discipline indicated most suspensions did not fall into the category of a serious offense, such as students possessing weapons or drugs or displaying violence. The overwhelming number of suspensions were for minor offenses, defiance, disruption, or disobedience, which were filed under the category of "other disruptive incidents," and the data showed staff used this to routinely refer and suspend Black students.

The investigation found the "other disruptive incidents" category was overly broad and poorly defined. These offenses were nonviolent, highly subjective, and almost always resulted in out-of-school suspension. Some teachers may have viewed a comment as disrespectful where another one viewed it as a joke. The racial disparity jumped off the page in this category: Black students were nearly twenty-five times as likely to be suspended for subjectively judged minor offenses.

Revealingly, there was almost no racial gap for serious offenses.

## The Uglier Reaction

A vocal group of teachers and parents banded together to form a group called "Be the Change" and argued that the real problem was that school officials were too tolerant of student misbehavior. The group blamed the

---

46. Paul Riede, "Teachers, PTO Leader Speak Out on Discipline to Syracuse School Board," Syracuse.com, December 11, 2013. https://www.syracuse.com/news/2013/12/post_961.html.

district's poor academic performance on lax discipline and a failure to suspend and expel students more often.[47] The group seemed to say schools should only teach the well-behaved.

Be the Change used traditional media outlets and social media to spread allegations of violence and danger in classrooms. When the district tried to correct the facts about an accusation, the media was already chasing another claim of violence. Social media was rife with unproved stories. Be the Change's advocacy gave off a noxious whiff of racism.

The data showing that most of suspensions were the result of nonviolent behavior did not clarify problems or lead to fruitful discussions. One group of people thought the data confirmed long-suspected racial discrimination. The other group refused to recognize the data's validity and allowed racist notions to proliferate. Following a media story on the efforts to reduce suspensions in the school, online commenters posted:[48]

"My daughter-in-law teaches [at a city high school] and until the administration faces these challenges head-on and admits there needs to be a better solution, we will continue to raise a new generation of animals and eventually revert back to the cave man."

"When these kids are being raised by people who only had them to obtain a free living . . . are we really surprised with their behavior? It would be cheaper if we just paid them NOT to have kids."

"Teachers must have teachable pupils and be provided an environment where teaching can be performed. My best guess is that one-third to one-half of pupils before our teachers in SCSD aren't capable of being taught the specific material presented. Those pupils must be placed in an environment commensurate with their aptitudes."

The teachers union announced it was going to hold a vote of confidence on Contreras and the results would be announced at a community meeting at Dr. King Elementary School. It was certain to be a public bloodletting. Contreras had been superintendent for just over three years.

---

47. Paul Riede, "How Can the Syracuse Schools Be Too Tough and Too Lax? What Both Sides Can Agree on About Discipline," Syracuse.com, July 15, 2014, https://www.syracuse.com/news/2014/07/how_can_the_syracuse_schools_be_too_tough_and_too_lax_what_both_sides_can_agree.html.

48. Daniel J. Losen, "Getting Back on Track: Final Report on Syracuse," July 2014, 53, https://docshare.tips/syracuse-city-schools-discipline-report_5784a83db6d87f4b2b8b45a0.html.

That same day, I received a phone call from a senior Black minister. He was raised in the South and was old-school in his approach to religion—conservative with a touch of fire and brimstone in his sermons. While we had a good relationship, he viewed politicians with inherent cynicism and, given his history, it made sense.

When I got on the phone, he said he wanted to hear what I had to say about the teachers union and "Sharon." His tone was both challenging and strangely hopeful. I answered directly that I was on Contreras's side and thought the union's actions were wrong. I heard him exhale, and he told me he was worried Contreras was going to be run over by white teachers and community leaders. I assured him I would do what I could to stop that.

On the day the results of the confidence vote were to be announced, about six hundred teachers, parents, and community members crammed into a school gym to hear the results. Contreras sat at a table and faced the judgment. Kevin Ahern, the union president, announced 95 percent of teachers had no confidence in Contreras and asked the school board to terminate her. When he finished, the teachers in attendance, almost exclusively white, gave Ahern a standing ovation. The teachers, clapping in unison, marched out of the auditorium. As they left, the remaining attendees, largely Black, shouted "shame" and "no justice, no peace."[49] The message was clear: The teachers wanted her gone and did not care what anyone else thought. It was dramatic and destructive.

Following the walkout, parents, students, and community members took to the microphone to have their say for two and a half hours. With most of the teachers gone, the remaining attendees largely praised Contreras. One said, "Tragically, this is hugely about race. . . . It is hugely about seeing particularly young men of color in a different way. We have to stop denying that. . . . The superintendent walked into a district that has been ignoring this issue for decades."[50]

49. Paul Riede, "Syracuse Teachers Association: 95 Percent of Members Lack Confidence in Superintendent Sharon Contreras," Syracuse.com, June 11, 2014, https://www.syracuse.com/news/2014/06/syracuse_teachers_association_—_percent_of_members_lack_confidence_in_superinte.html.

50. Paul Riede, "Syracuse Superintendent Contreras Professes 100 Percent Confidence in Teachers After Union's No Confidence Vote," Syracuse.com, June 12, 2014, https://www.syracuse.com/news/2014/06/syracuse_superintendent_contreras_professes_100_percent_confidence_in_teachers_a.html.

After the meeting, I met regularly with the union president and Contreras in an attempt to bridge the divide. The union president started every meeting with a description of an event at a school implying violence or a physical threat. Contreras would respond by explaining how it had been dealt with and corrected his mischaracterizations. After which, the union president would usually grudgingly concede she was right. After several meetings, it became obvious the union's grievances boiled down to one: it wanted teachers to be able to continue to suspend students at will.

The union was willfully unconcerned about the harm it was inflicting on the community and ignored the criticism of many local community leaders. In one particularly ugly incident, a teacher showed up to a rally to protest Contreras's contract wearing a black mask,[51] which wasn't that far from showing up in actual Blackface. Many community members were shocked that such an overt symbol of racism would appear in Syracuse. Rally organizers said the mask was a symbol of a fear about the ability to speak openly against the district's revised disciplinary policies.

I struggled for an acceptable explanation for the union's behavior. Too slowly, I recognized the union and teachers were allowing race to be used as a weapon. People of color openly shared with me the ugly reality that racial bias was always a part of our system. If not, they pointedly asked me, why did teachers oppose fixing the obvious racial injustice?

The issues of race, discipline, and classroom culture made for a volatile mix. It had been present long before the attorney general's findings. I thought teachers and their union would share their frustrations, talk about accountability, and accept strategies to constructively address issues. But, to do this, they needed to admit the disciplinary practices were wrong and agree to change them. Had teachers reached their breaking point implementing so many changed practices for state standards, preventing school closures, Say Yes initiatives, and then disciplinary practices? Was it easier to fight than admit systemic racism exists and have the difficult conversations that were necessary to address it?

I kept waiting to hear from state leaders who might help heal the wounds. When I received a lunch invitation to meet the new state education

51. Julie McMahon, "Race, Safety Fuel Tension at Syracuse Rally over Extending Superintendent's Contract," Syracuse.com, December 8, 2015, https://www.syracuse.com/schools/2015/12/superintendent_sharon_contreras_school_board_vote_contract_renewal_protest.html.

commissioner, MaryEllen Elia, I thought the opportunity had arrived. Elia was a newcomer to state politics, having previously worked in Florida. To earn her appointment as commissioner, she mustered the support of the state legislature, which was widely known to be influenced by the state teachers union.[52]

During lunch in Syracuse, Elia pointedly asked me if I thought the current superintendent was up to the challenge. When I answered yes, Elia responded she was not sure. Her comments signaled to me that the state education department leadership was going to use its considerable powers of influence to move against Contreras. While I was trying to mend relationships and meet education goals, the state had clearly decided to remove Contreras. Perversely, after my lunch with Elia, the state announced the district had achieved its highest graduation rate in eight years in the 2014–2015 school year, just three years after Contreras had taken the helm.[53]

A couple of months later, Contreras announced she was leaving to become the superintendent of North Carolina's Guilford County School District, a system larger than Syracuse's. Contreras left of her own accord, understanding that in the face of such opposition and vitriol, she'd lost the power to push for anything constructive. While the academic and discipline reforms Contreras started were not stopped, the opposition slowed them down and exacted a heavy toll on the community.

## The Quiet Goodbye

As the city was embroiled in the discipline issues, I learned from news accounts that Say Yes was expanding to Buffalo. I was stunned Schmitt-Carey had not given me advance notice of the development. When I questioned her about it, she apologized. By this time, Say Yes's preferred method of communication was to make the decisions it wanted without consultation and to later apologize. I learned Say Yes was actively looking to expand to other cities only through fielding phone calls from mayors from those cities

52. Kate Taylor, "Cuomo's Education Agenda Sets Battle Lines with Teachers' Union," *New York Times*, January 20, 2015.

53. Julie McMahon, "Syracuse Graduation Rate Reaches 55 Percent for 1st Time in 8 Years," Syracuse.com, January 11, 2016, https://www.syracuse.com/schools/2016/01/syra cuse_graduation_rate_reaches_55_percent_highest_in_8_years.html.

asking about my experience.[54] I shared with the mayors that modest gains had been made but not the promised transformation.

It became clear that despite Say Yes's affirmations of support, its attention had moved away from Syracuse. It began turning its programs over to local partners in 2015. Eventually, its local staff was cut in half and only a couple scholarship coordinators remained to work with students on financial aid. Apart from the scholarships, Say Yes's other programs—including the legal clinics, after-school programing, and mental health services—and their costs were absorbed by the district, the city, and the county.[55]

If questioned about the group's diminished role, Schmitt-Carey would cite the millions Say Yes had invested, remind me that Say Yes's commitment was for five years only, and say the school district had not met its commitment to upgrade its data provisions. For the most part, what Schmitt-Carey said was accurate: Say Yes had stayed when the promised CFE money evaporated. It had made a college education an attainable reality for thousands of Syracuse students and tried to make children's futures better. Despite all of this, our professed joint goal of transformative change was far from realized when Say Yes moved its focus.

Perhaps it was hubris that made me think I could reform the education system and make transformational gains as mayor. I wanted to believe Say Yes was the solution for urban children. It was a cliché that state and federal government were failing to meet the educational challenge because they worried about political constituencies, not children's education. After all, the reasoning went, if the private sector had a product with the same failure rate of the urban schools, consumers would not tolerate it.

But education is not a product. It is the oxygen of a community—parents, teachers, homeowners, business owners, and, of course, children all need it to function well. As such, everyone's voices needed to be heard, and that is ideally what governments should do: listen and take action based on

54. Say Yes has initiatives in Buffalo; Guilford County, North Carolina (the partnership predates Contreras becoming superintendent); and is interested in expanding. Richard V. Reeves, Katherine Guyot, and Edward Rodrigue, "Gown Towns: A Case Study of Say Yes to Education," Brookings Institution, June 2018, https://www.brookings.edu/resear ch/gown-towns-a-case-study-of-say-yes-to-education/.

55. Julie McMahon, "What's left of Say Yes to Education in Syracuse?" Syracuse.com, April 28, 2017, https://www.syracuse.com/schools/2017/04/whats_left_of_say_yes_to _education_in_syracuse.html.

that. The process is antithetical to the private sector's focus on efficiency and decisiveness.

The mission of improving educational outcomes for challenged students requires a never-ending commitment from every part of the community. Say Yes either did not agree with that assessment or was not interested in the kind of commitment that was necessary. I suppose the same accusation could be hurled at me. I was, after all, only going to be mayor for eight years.

Around the country, I saw the same process unfold, with the private sector heralding itself as the savior in the face of government's failure and presenting audacious initiatives—some funded by billionaires—to change education performance. But down the road, most of the initiatives spectacularly failed to meet their professed goals. The Gates Foundation spent $2 billion in an unsuccessful attempt to improve education outcomes by funding smaller schools and then $700 million upgrading teacher-evaluation systems before quietly pulling the plug. Facebook founder Mark Zuckerberg and his wife, Priscilla Chan, spent $100 million of their own money to improve the Newark, New Jersey, school system in a highly publicized but ultimately failed effort.[56] Solutions presented with the promise of private-sector efficiency, no matter how many billions of dollars were behind the efforts, all failed. My aspiration that the private sector be the catcher in the rye of urban education never materialized.

## The $20 Million Boulder

Say Yes had set a daunting goal to raise $20 million to endow college scholarships in Syracuse. The university pledged resources to help, as did most community leaders, but it was a formidable challenge we struggled to meet. By 2012, after significant efforts, only $7 million was raised, and $5 million of that came from one gift contributed by the Scientific Research

56. Dale Russakoff, "Schooled," New Yorker, May 12, 2014; Jeremy Berke, "A $1 Billion Gates Foundation Backed Education Initiative Failed to Help Students, According to a New Report—Here's What Happened," BusinessInsider.com, June 27, 2018; Jack Schneider and David Menefee-Libey, "Why Big Bets on Educational Reform Haven't Fixed the US School System," Conversation, March 8, 2018, https://theconversation.com/why-big-bets-on-educational-reform-havent-fixed-the-us-school-system-92327.

Corporation.[57] Funding the endowment goal of college-tuition scholarships remained a priority for me.

In retrospect, it was clear the community lacked the philanthropic muscle to raise that kind of money and needed resources to address the basics before focusing on college scholarships. It was another consequence of the changed upstate economy. Where once manufacturing and industry flourished, so, too, did philanthropy. As industry waned, so did charitable giving.

By this time, Say Yes had shifted its attention to Buffalo, telling us it had done everything it reasonably could to fund this effort, and now it was up to the community. If the college-tuition promise collapsed, it would be another example of the government overpromising and underdelivering. While I spearheaded many fundraising efforts to raise endowment funds, including an annual back-to-school fundraising gala, they were the financial equivalent of bake sales when we needed a gold mine.

The only entity that could provide the resources we needed was the state. The state's fixation on economic development became an opportunity when Governor Cuomo's Upstate Revitalization Initiative competition was announced. The region's leadership, led by Syracuse University chancellor Kent Syverud and Robert Simpson, president of the business advocacy group CenterState CEO, rallied to put a submission together. I promised to refrain from criticizing the economic development competition if the leadership included funding the scholarship endowment in the submission. They willingly agreed.

When the Central New York region, which included Onondaga, Cayuga, Cortland, Madison, and Oswego Counties, won the competition, I held my breath about the endowment funding. The region's proposal was getting lots of positive attention, and it would be politically risky for the governor to have to explain why a key part of the proposal to help urban children was not being funded. But he had not been reticent to threaten the renovations of our schools under the JSCB program.

After a few months of silence, I got a call from Simpson telling me the governor's office informed him the county executive was announcing the Say Yes endowment funding later that afternoon. The governor's office

57. James T. Mulder, "SRC Gift of $5 Million to 'Say Yes' Program Will Help Syracuse City School Graduates Go to College," Syracuse.com, January 22, 2011, https://www.syracuse.com/news/2011/01/src_gift_of_5_million_to_say_y.html.

insisted I not be part of the announcement. It was, of course, a petty political move by Cuomo. He'd get to take credit for a popular program I was associated with while cutting me out of the spotlight.

I was irritated and asked Simpson what he was hoping I'd say. He responded that he thought I'd want to know about the news. He was right, but it stung to not be part of the announcement. As I ended the call, I thought about why I took the risk to support Say Yes: to help the children who got out of bed early in the morning to walk to school, the parents who watched their children get on the school bus, and the young people who had the opportunity to get a college degree. The tuition endowment would be funded. Untold numbers of Syracuse students would be able pursue a higher education. That was the point. The rest was just politics.

## Postscript

While thousands of Syracuse students have used Say Yes benefits to attend college[58] and the renovations of Syracuse school buildings continue, educational failures are still an existential concern for Syracuse and its children. According to the 2020 Census, Syracuse has the highest rate of child poverty in the nation among cities with at least one hundred thousand people,[59] and Syracuse students continue to lag far behind their wealthy suburban neighbors in education outcomes.[60]

58. Say Yes to Education Syracuse, https://sayyessyracuse.org/about/our-impact/

59. Kevin Tampone, "Syracuse Leads the U.S. with Worst Child Poverty Among Bigger Cities, Census Says," Syracuse.com, March 17, 2022, https://www.syracuse.com/data/2022/03/syracuse-leads-the-us-with-worst-child-poverty-among-bigger-cities-census-says.html (Buffalo and Rochester are also among the top 10 cities with the highest rates child poverty).

60. "Syracuse City School District," Public School Review, https://www.publicschoolreview.com/new-york/syracuse-city-school-district/3628590-school-district; Kevin Tampone, "New York School Districts Ranked from 1 to 670 Based on Graduation Rates," Syracuse.com, February 15, 2023, https://www.syracuse.com/hslife/2023/02/ny-school-districts-ranked-from-1-to-670-based-on-2022-graduation-rates.html.

# Police

## Reckonings

Standing with the police chief and my security officer, I rang a doorbell on a well-kept single-family home in a working-class neighborhood bordering Kirk Park—one of the city's biggest and most utilized recreational facilities. There had been a homicide in the park, and we were asking residents to share any information they had. When a young Black man answered the door, he recognized me and the chief and greeted us warmly. He thanked us for our efforts and, expressing sadness over the death, promised to share anything he learned. As the chief handed him his card, I saw a reflection in a mirror behind the young man and quickly turned my head to hide my reaction.

A safe distance away, I asked my compatriots if they had noticed anything unusual about our interaction. As they looked at me quizzically, I told them the back of the man's shirt read "FUCK the POLICE." We laughed at the juxtaposition of our gracious welcome with the T-shirt's message, but it illustrated our conundrum. We needed residents' help to keep our city safe, but many of them felt the police were part of the problem.

## Saviors from the Outside

Like most places in the United States, police had an exalted status in Syracuse. The police were citizens' first call to nearly every problem that arose from living in dense neighborhoods—to stop people from selling drugs on a street corner, of course, but to get rid of the homeless addict and stop

children from swearing on a basketball court, too. The ease of calling the
police to respond to every issue was a civic drug.

Residents' reflex to have the police respond to an array of problems was
not just about efficiency but also fundamentally about fear—fear of impending urban chaos. Everyone knew about strong, vital neighborhoods
that had become transitory and dangerous. The descent was usually marked
by crumbling and abandoned properties, overt drug use, and violence. Because police could deal with the consequences of these issues, many citizens
viewed them as the instant solution to protecting their quality of life.

Police, too, brought a sense of fear to the job. As the illicit drug trade
continued to grow, so did violence. Guns flooded the streets. Police saw
victims and shooters getting younger every year. Their training was based
on the key precept that the officer must always have the upper hand because
danger was ever-present. "Officer Friendly" was replaced by Robocop.

The police might be considered saviors to some, but to many others,
they were outsiders. The department was predominately made up of white,
well-paid officers who lived in the suburbs surrounding Syracuse. Along
with these demographic differences, their behavior bolstered their outsider
status.

When I was a city councilor, I walked with Helen Hudson, the head of
Mothers Against Gun Violence, through her largely minority neighborhood
one sweltering summer evening. We chatted with people sitting outside on
porches and lawn chairs attempting to cool off. I was laughing at her stern
warning to children playing with hoses not to get her hair wet when we saw
several police cars and sirens.

We walked to the periphery of the scene and Hudson approached a police officer. She introduced herself, asked what was going on, and put out
her hand. The police officer summarily dismissed her and refused to shake
her hand, saying he was a "germaphobe." I was shocked, but Hudson said it
was commonplace.

A particularly searing incident from several years earlier was still fresh
in the minds of many residents. Police responding to an emergency call
from two fellow officers at a domestic dispute had arrived at a home and
ordered family members to disperse. One of the responding officers struck
a twelve-year-old girl, who had been attempting to help the officers, several times with his nightstick. The police arrested three people, including the twelve-year-old. After the dust settled, the police officer who hit

the girl was charged with assault and the charges against the family were dropped.

When the officer went to court, more than one hundred uniformed police officers appeared to protest the charges filed against him. The twelve-year-old and her grandparents were forced to pass the officers lined up on both sides of the hallway leading to the courtroom. The local NAACP president said, "It was kind of reminiscent of the civil rights struggles, with a handful of Black people walking through a sea of angry white faces in uniforms with guns." The grandmother said she stared at the officers' faces because "I wanted them to get a good look at me. Someday one of their family members might be going through what my family is going through."[1]

The police officer accepted a plea deal in which he'd be suspended four months without pay and reassigned to a different post with limited public contact, and he'd have to undergo additional training and offer an apology to the family. As he left the courtroom, he was swarmed by fellow officers who erupted in applause. He had his job, no lasting criminal record, and the full-throated support of the police force.[2] For many people, it was more evidence that police misconduct would be excused.

Minority neighborhoods were often beset by crime, and residents knew they needed the police but often felt subjugated. The paradox of needing the service, yet feeling disrespected in its provision, made objective opinions about police impossible to ascertain.

As a city councilor, I routinely heard Black residents say a police officer was racist and abusive only to have another Black resident express appreciation for the same police officer's actions. Whether an officer's actions were appropriate, I quickly understood, was in the eye of the beholder. If that eye belonged to someone in harm's way, then all actions might be deemed appropriate.

Many residents suggested that a return to an era of "beat cops" would bridge the separation between police and neighbors. If officers walked the streets, they would understand the neighborhood's rhythms, recognize bad actors, and chase them away. The reality was that policing, like everything else, had been transformed by technology. Police departments used

1. Jim O'Hara, "DA: Police Rally a Disgrace, NAACP Leader Calls Protest a 'Gauntlet of Intimidation,'" *Post-Standard*, February 5, 2000.

2. O'Hara, "DA."

sophisticated crime-tracking and prediction software to meet the public's constant demand for services. Modern tools and the public's expectations made the idea of "beat cops" a nostalgic fantasy.

## Shoot-out in Syracuse

Violence shook the city in April the year I ran for mayor. Two on-duty Syracuse police officers recognized a man on parole[3] who was suspected to be illegally carrying a silver revolver. After they spotted the man, officers called for backup and pulled the parolee over in his car at a busy intersection around seven in the evening.

As they approached his car, the driver fired his revolver, hitting one officer twice,[4] then aimed the firearm at a civilian and hit the civilian's car. The parolee ran from his car but continued to shoot. Both police officers gave chase. The second officer shot and killed the fleeing man.

That a gunfight could erupt at a crowded intersection in Syracuse sent shock waves throughout the city. It had been decades since a police officer was shot, and it was only the fifth fatal shooting involving a city police officer since 1982.[5]

Concerns over the police's outsider status became secondary to people's fear of violence.[6] Residents believed aggressive actions were necessary to subdue dangerous threats in neighborhoods. They explicitly put a premium on securing their physical safety, even if it meant sacrificing some of our most foundational constitutional rights.

That same year, 2009, Syracuse was ordered to pay almost $2 million in penalties for repeated violations of civil rights by the police department. Lawsuits were regularly filed against the police department and individual officers for using excessive force and racial epithets, sexual harassment, and other unsavory behavior, including watching pornography in police

3. Douglass Dowty, "Suspect Killed in Shootout—Syracuse Cop Saved by Vest," *Post-Standard*, April 14, 2009.

4. The police officer's life was saved by his bulletproof vest.

5. Dowty, "Suspect Killed in Shootout—Syracuse Cop Saved by Vest," *Post-Standard*, April 14, 2009.

6. Paul Riede, "City Shaken by Violence," *Post-Standard*, December 5, 2010.

headquarters.[7] Despite the egregious nature of some of the allegations, leadership's response was a collective shrug. Police had protected status, and changing the culture could be dangerous to the city and, by extension, a politician's ambition.

Yet the longer the entitlement went unchecked, the bigger the chasm between police and residents became. While neighbors and police relied on each other, the relationship was straining under the police department's lack of accountability. Meanwhile, the city had to absorb the costs of the multimillion-dollar lawsuits against it.

Trying to lead a police department acting as its own kingdom was going to be problematic for me: a woman in charge of a male-dominated culture, a reformer with a department loath to change, and a person trained to prioritize the rule of law. When I confessed my unease to a retired city hall executive, with a fatalistic smile he warned, "The police are tough, an occupying force. You have to be careful."

Once elected, my choice of police chief seemed to be the main issue the public was interested in. Despite the importance of the role, I had no idea who to appoint. As I struggled for an answer, Jack asked if there was anyone I trusted.

I immediately thought of Frank Fowler, a Black officer who had risen through the ranks to the level of deputy chief. Fowler had a gruff persona and a steely scowl. I never saw him smile or heard him say anything even approaching idle chitchat. He was all business all the time, answering questions directly and never attempting to spin. When I asked him about the officer refusing to shake Hudson's hand, Fowler said the actions were wrong. When I asked him about the large number of officers used to execute warrants, he said it was necessary to protect officers in inherently dangerous operations. He had the same manner with the public. He was respectful and honest, even when he knew his answer was difficult to hear, at times saying, "My mother named me 'Frank' for a reason."

I asked Fowler to have lunch and realized our relationship was so professional I was reluctant to use his first name. When we met, he said before we began, he wanted me to know something. This was a departure from his

7. John O'Brien, "Miner: Police Will Be Accountable," *Post-Standard*, July 1, 2010; Jonathan Perlow, "Syracuse Cops Accused of Sexist Abuse," CourthouseNews.com, July 13, 2009. https://www.courthousenews.com/syracuse-cops-accused-of-sexist-abuse/.

standard approach. He leaned across the table with a serious scowl and said, "I was raised in a household with eight older sisters and a strong mother. I have no problem taking orders from a woman." Then his face lit up in the first smile I had ever seen on him. I imagined he was remembering all the directions he was given growing up.

He told me he was raised in an inner-city neighborhood in St. Louis, Missouri. After seeing violence take the lives of friends and family, he decided he did not want his mother to mourn his death. He enlisted in the army when he was told there was a chance he could be stationed in Hawaii. He never got to Hawaii, but he traveled the world and met his wife, who was from Syracuse.

Once in Syracuse, he took the police exam to give his friends in St. Louis a laugh. When he did well on the physical test, his competitive instincts took over and he decided he wanted the job. He got it. The St. Louis kid who had once dodged the police found himself as one of a handful of Black police officers on the force.[8]

He talked about his ideas to make Syracuse a community where no one feared violence, and he shared his experiences as one of the few Black officers in the department, his founding of the Central New York Association of Minority Police Officers, and issues that came up in an overwhelmingly white department. My instincts told me he was a person who had the integrity to take on one of the hardest jobs in Syracuse. With that as a foundation, I hoped we could build a relationship.

After I named Fowler chief of police, he became omnipresent. He appeared at all serious crime scenes. He spoke to leaders and neighbors at churches, parks, and sports events. He listened to concerns and shared his plans to improve policing tools, install security cameras in high-crime neighborhoods, use a new gunshot-detection program, and pilot the use of officer body cameras. His work ethic and availability endeared him to rank-and-file officers and residents alike.

Fowler was only the second Black police chief in Syracuse's history.[9] The presence of Black police officers in the department was both minimal

8. Justin Mattingly, "Frank Fowler Made It Out of Where Michael Brown Died," My-SouthSideStand.com, November 30. 2017, https://mysouthsidestand.com/more-news/fowler/.

9. The first was Dennis DuVal, who was appointed chief in 2001.

and new.[10] Fowler's race made him a barrier breaker, but I didn't worry it would cause blowback. At the time, I thought about his position as I did mine: if he worked hard and did a good job, he would earn people's respect regardless of race. It shocks me I once thought that, but I did.

I quickly learned that gun violence increases when temperatures get warmer. And so began my annual cycle of dreading nice weather. In June 2010, my first summer as mayor, Syracuse experienced a significant rise in shootings, mostly between young Black men. It wasn't unusual for an assailant in one case to become a victim the next time. The combination of disintegrating neighborhoods and easy access to weapons meant shockingly senseless violence was becoming a regular occurrence on the streets of Syracuse in the summertime.

It was impossible to know exactly how many, but we suspected there were hundreds of illegal guns on the streets. Guns are especially dangerous in the hands of young people. Their brains haven't fully developed, so they are less likely to think rationally about the consequences of their behavior. As if the sheer abundance of illegal guns weren't enough, the weapons were also incredibly powerful. After one raid where dozens of illegal guns were seized, Fowler told me the arsenal contained some of the most powerful weapons he had ever seen, including during his military service in the Middle East.

There was hardly a weekend that I didn't receive a call from Fowler notifying me of a shooting involving teenagers. It cast a pall over everything. Fowler and I reached out to everyone asking for help, suggestions, and explanations. We instituted a public relations campaign to stop the shootings, including billboards spreading a message of nonviolence and an anonymous tip line, and we hosted and participated in meetings with young people and community leaders.

I asked the state attorney general's office for help—first from Attorney General Andrew Cuomo and later from Eric Schneiderman. At both meetings, staff members said there was nothing they could do. On occasion, I would be invited to a press conference organized by the attorney general's

10. The year Frank Fowler became chief, 481 police officers were sworn in; 93.7 percent were white, 6.3 percent were Black, and 1.7 percent were Hispanic. Syracuse's first Black police officer, Tom Seals, became a member of the department in 1966. We later served together on the city council.

office where an array of seized weapons would be displayed for the media, but substantive help from the office was not forthcoming.

In contrast, federal officials were using the Racketeer Influenced and Corrupt Organizations Act, also known as RICO, to take violent gang members off the streets, as they'd done with the mafia years earlier. Prosecutors argued that urban gangs exhibited a level of cohesion and organization that qualified them as "enterprises" under the law. RICO convictions entailed stiff sentences with no chance of parole, and those found guilty were usually sent to prisons far from Syracuse. By 2011, federal authorities had used the RICO law five times in eight years to prosecute gang members,[11] yet the prosecutions didn't slow Syracuse's violent drug trade.

Once, after a dangerous RICO joint operation, I attended an evening shift change to thank Syracuse police officers for their work. I waited for the officers to assemble, watching them put on bulletproof vests over civilian clothes and strapping automatic weapons to their legs. The officers were overwhelmingly white men with short haircuts, and quite a few had visible tattoos. They looked like warriors preparing for battle with tools of modern warfare. These were soldiers, not police officers.

Standing in that room felt like being in an alternative universe. Fowler, sensing my discomfort, reminded me they were involved in dangerous work. While I knew he was right, the sight of this militarized police force was profoundly disturbing.

## Kihary and Rashaad Jr.

One of my regular mayoral stops was at a Black men's barbershop named Blues Brothers. The man in charge was Rev. Otis Blue. Both a barber and a minister, Reverend Blue had a head of well-trimmed white hair, a stately appearance, and a glare that could stop a charging elephant. The first couple of times I stopped by when I was running for mayor, he acknowledged my presence with a glare but never spoke to me. I kept coming back.

After some time, Rev. Blue acknowledged me, but only after he was done with the client in his chair. He started calling me "the little one." I stopped in the shop anytime I was in the neighborhood. Eventually, nobody looked askance when I walked in and answered to "the little one." He would share

11. John O'Brien, "Feds Slam 13 Bricktown Street Gang Members with RICO Charges," *Post-Standard*, April 27, 2011.

with me the news and concerns of the day, from the cost of the expansion of a nearby park to the impact road construction was having on his business. In every conversation, he shared his frustration over the epidemic of youth gun violence.

Rev. Blue had a large family, which included at least one superstar. His grandson Kihary Blue was a gifted athlete with a megawatt smile. He was one of Syracuse's most celebrated high school athletes, leading both his basketball and football teams to championships as a point guard and quarterback. After graduating from Henninger High School, Kihary got a scholarship to play basketball at a community college in North Carolina.

He had recently returned to Syracuse with plans to attend Monroe Community College near Rochester.[12] On the Friday after Thanksgiving during my first year as mayor, Kihary got into a car with some friends. While Kihary was not a member of a gang, his friends in the car were. As they drove on an interstate in the middle of Syracuse, another car pulled up and fired shots into the car. Kihary was killed.[13]

Two days after Kihary died, a gang member, attempting to retaliate, drove into a neighborhood and issued a hail of gunfire into the parked minivan belonging to a nineteen-year-old gang member named Rashaad Walker. Moments earlier, Walker's girlfriend had strapped their twenty-month-old son, Rashaad Walker Jr., into his car seat in the minivan. One of the bullets hit the toddler in the head, killing him.[14]

We learned that a month earlier, a member of one gang had stabbed a member of another gang at a bar. That same night, a different gang member retaliated by firing twenty-one shots from an AK-47 assault rifle into the home of a rival gang member.[15] What had started as a barroom brawl ended in the death of a young star athlete and a twenty-month-old child.

12. Donnie Webb, "Carrying On with a Smile—Henninger Cheerleader's Spirit Honors Her Brother Kihary Blue," *Post-Standard*, March 5, 2013.

13. Douglass Dowty, "Father: Stop the Shootings—He Urges Anyone Who Wants to Avenge Son Kihary Blue's Death to Work with Police Instead," *Post-Standard*, December 2, 2010.

14. Charles McChesney, "Stray Bullet Kills 20-Month-Old in Van; Police Say Rashaad Walker Jr. Was Struck While Strapped in His Car Seat," *Post-Standard*, November 29, 2010.

15. John O'Brien, "Feds Charge 11 in Gang Sweep—Members of Group Called V-Not Accused of Using Violence, Including Killing of Kihary Blue, to Control Drug Territory in Syracuse's South Side," *Post-Standard*, May 2, 2012.

It was the worst week I ever had as mayor. The senselessness of a beloved child getting killed because he was in the wrong place at the wrong time was heartbreaking. That same weekend, I'd put my toddler nephew in his car seat just as Rashaad Walker Jr.'s mother had done. Knowing Kihary's grandfather and how he worried about violence made it even worse.

I felt bereft of tools to stop the violence. If people were brandishing high-powered assault rifles and shooting at minivans in broad daylight, what could I do? I felt like Syracuse had become a grotesque version of the Wild West.

Fowler and I went to Walker Jr.'s calling hours. We stood in line in a church packed with people and emotions so thick it was like a fog had enveloped the room. When I made it to the deceased toddler's mother, I was struck at the sight of such a young woman overtaken with profound grief. She was barely able to speak or stand as family members on either side of her offered comfort and support.

Moments later, I stood in front of Rashaad Walker. While everyone else in the receiving line was standing, he was sitting down. He, too, looked startlingly young and seemed to be trying to disappear into the pew. When the nearby adults encouraged him to greet me, he reluctantly stood up and muttered something, never making eye contact. He was obviously uncomfortable and seemed strangely out of place. When we left, I told Fowler that Walker was the only person in the church who didn't know what he had lost.

Months later, at the sentencing hearing for the man who shot Walker's toddler son, a reporter asked Walker what his message to his son's killer would be. He answered: "Missed me."[16] His comment ricocheted through the community. Syracuse was now a city where a toddler could be shot in a car seat and a father would respond to the trauma with a taunt. I could feel the police becoming more lionized. Violence and criminals were a real threat to everyone in every neighborhood, and the police were the saviors who could stop it from becoming all-consuming chaos.

---

16. Walker would create his own violent havoc, including shooting a man holding a baby in 2015. In 2017, he was sentenced to forty years to life for murdering a man bicycling home from work. Douglass Dowty, "Judge Gives 'Cold Assassin' 40 Years to Life for Murder of Man Biking Home to Work," Syracuse.com, February 3, 2017, https://www.sy racuse.com/crime/2017/02/judge_sends_cold_assassin_away_for_40_years_to_life_in _murder_of_man_leaving_wor.html.

## Adversarial Injustice

All major police-reform initiatives I was aware of involved the active participation of district attorney's offices.[17] While the state enacts most criminal laws, district attorneys decide how to enforce them. District attorneys in Brooklyn and Nassau County had instituted programs aimed at helping felons reenter the community after they were released or implemented prison diversion strategies.[18] Programs like these had improved community relationships and helped change people's perception of the criminal justice system. But I knew our county district attorney, William Fitzpatrick, was unlikely to be interested in instituting any such reform.

Fitzpatrick, who had served in the position since 1992, was powerful, smart, and deeply entrenched in the state's political leadership. He and I had diametrically different views as to how power should be used and for whom. He railed against single mothers on welfare,[19] sued judges over their insistence that the Constitution required precise language at criminal arraignments,[20] and regularly used his office to forward his political agenda by inserting himself into the center of public conflicts.[21]

17. John Worrall and M. Elaine Nugent-Borakove, eds., *The Changing Role of the American Prosecutor* (SUNY Press, 2017); Juleyka Lantigua-Williams, "Are Prosecutors the Key to Justice Reform?" *Atlantic*, May 18, 2016.

18. New York State Bar Association Special Committee on Re-entry, January 2016, https://nysba.org/app/uploads/2020/02/January-2016-Reentry-Report-2.pdf.

19. Fitzpatrick said public assistance made it easy for single women to have multiple children. When asked to explain, he said, "What I said at the Rotary is nothing different than what I've been saying for 20 years, which is that, unfortunately, the welfare system is set up to reward irresponsibility. The more kids you have, the more money you get." Rick Moriarty, "County Legislator Criticizes District Attorney's Comments on Welfare Mothers," Syracuse.com, December 7, 2012, https://www.syracuse.com/news/2012/12/county_legislator_criticizes_d.html.

20. Jim O'Hara and Greg Munno, "Courtroom Drama—D.A.'s Clash with Judges Has Statewide Implications," *Post-Standard*, April 18, 2005.

21. Fitzpatrick investigated numerous political adversaries, including the county executive, deputy police chiefs, a GOP chairman, and a political candidate running against his son. Chris Baker, "DA Defends Political Investigations: 'A DA Is Not a Potted Plant,'" Syracuse.com, September 12, 2019, https://www.syracuse.com/politics/cny/2019/10/fitzpatrick-defends-political-investigations-a-da-is-not-a-potted-plant.html; Meghan Rubado, "Fitzpatrick Refused to Prosecute His Employees' Using Cocaine at His Office Christmas Party," *Post-Standard*, December 16, 2005. He fired a staff person, Gigi Potocki, because she helped the victim of one of his investigators. John O'Brien, "DA's

I had already been a target in one of his political fishing expeditions when he investigated me after I voted against the Destiny project.[22] Under the auspices of violating the Open Meetings law, a law over which he lacked jurisdiction, he repeatedly accused me of conspiring in sinister and vague criminal activities.[23] He never closed the investigation; he just stopped talking about it.

I thought he had a regressive view of the law, and I knew that our relationship would be fraught, at best, but I hoped we could work together as professionals once I became mayor. At his request, I met with him after I was elected mayor, but before I had announced my pick for chief of police. We arranged to meet in a bar one afternoon. After he sat down, he said he hoped I didn't take the Destiny investigation "personally" and everyone told him I was honest. Before I could respond, he asked me if I wanted a beer and then proceeded to tell me who I should and shouldn't appoint as police chief, even telling me his disfavored candidate referred to women as "cunts." I listened, but Fitzpatrick's boorish behavior shut down any possibility that I'd defer to his opinion.

Soon after I took office with Fowler as chief, I got a call from Fitzpatrick's chief assistant. He greeted me warmly but informed me Fowler was exercising poor judgment toward a Syracuse University football player.[24] The athlete had been accused of a crime, and the assistant asked me to tell Fowler to let the player turn himself in. Fowler later explained to me the police had planned to arrest the football player on campus because he had failed to turn himself in on multiple occasions. Fitzpatrick's office wanted to give the athlete special treatment that would not have been given to anyone else.[25]

Staffer Says She Was Fired after Helping Victim of Well-Connected Abuser," Syracuse. com, May 5, 2016, https://www.syracuse.com/crime/2016/05/das_staffer_says_she_was _fired_after_helping_victim_of_well-connected_abuser.html.

22. See chapter 2.

23. In an interview with local television reporter Bill Carey, the district attorney said, "I'm investigating what happened at that meeting based on citizen complaints that were made to me that may—may—involve either criminality or malfeasance." Time Warner News 10 NOW, 2016.

24. Delone Carter.

25. Fitzpatrick became embroiled in accusations that Bernie Fine, Syracuse University's assistant basketball coach, had sexually abused former ball boys. This matter is not addressed because it is secondary to the issues in this chapter.

I told Fowler to do what he thought was correct. It put us on a collision course with the district attorney, but a collision was inevitable.

Months later, Fowler and his deputy chief, Shawn Broton, were told that Fitzpatrick's staff had used the crime lab to delete the recording of a racist comment the district attorney had allegedly made. Upon investigation, Fowler and Broton learned Fitzpatrick had given a speech at his office holiday party, which included a remark about a "Blacka Claus." A musician hired to perform at the event had videotaped Fitzpatrick's speech.

When they realized the speech had been filmed, several district attorney staffers asked the musician for his cell phone and video recorder. One told the musician, "If you don't give it up, we could have you thrown out the window."[26] The musician surrendered the devices. When he picked them up the following day, the footage of Fitzpatrick's speech was gone.

Broton found evidence that Fitzpatrick's staff used the crime lab to delete the recording of the comment. The conduct amounted to illegally seizing property and misusing a government crime lab. With my permission, Fowler and Broton brought the evidence of the misconduct to the New York inspector general's office, the state's internal affairs unit.

Shortly after our submission, Fitzpatrick went on a public tirade against Fowler, claiming Fowler exaggerated the number of arrests made by the department, misidentified a weapon, and wrongly claimed the victim of an officer-involved shooting was shot in the front of the head. "Reckless disregard for the facts doesn't do anybody any good," Fitzpatrick said. He continued that Fowler thought he could get away with "misrepresenting" facts "because the only guy who's yelling . . . is me."[27]

In contrast, the facts refuted each of Fitzpatrick's allegations, but his attacks against Fowler continued unabated.[28] Fitzpatrick held news conferences calling Fowler an irrelevant police chief with a "juvenile mind," as well as an "emperor" who was "undermining public safety."[29]

26. Chris Bragg, "The State Inspector General's Oversight Waned under Cuomo," *Times Union*, September 19, 2021.

27. Jim O'Hara, "Fitzpatrick Shakes a Stick at Fowler—Police Chief Denies He Misrepresents Facts to Public As DA Claims," *Post-Standard*, January 20, 2012.

28. Each of Fitzpatrick's claims was refuted with hard evidence: criminal history arrest/incident report, a video of showing Fowler at his news conference referring to a sword, and another video showing Fowler pointing to the general area at the side of his neck.

29. Jim O'Hara, "DA William Fitzpatrick Declares War on Syracuse Police Chief Frank Fowler over Bernie Fine Case," *Post-Standard*, November 23, 2011.

Soon after we sent the complaint to the inspector general's office, Fitz-patrick was appointed by Governor Cuomo to become a chair of the More-land Commission, an entity charged with investigating the state's politicians and political organizations for violations of state laws.[30] In that position, Fitzpatrick presided over a political minefield. Although Fitzpatrick was a Republican, he and Andrew Cuomo enjoyed a strong relationship.[31] Fitzpat-rick was seen as actively doing the governor's bidding on the commission, including rescinding a subpoena aimed at a firm with close ties to Cuo-mo.[32] The commission was viewed as a disaster for Cuomo when it became obvious it lacked independence. Similarly, the people associated with the commission were seen as sacrificing their integrity to do Cuomo's bidding.[33] When it became known that federal investigators were probing Cuomo's termination of the commission, Fitzpatrick published an op-ed in the *Huff-ington Post* defending the governor's actions.[34]

Meanwhile, our complaint to the inspector general remained un-answered. Around this time, Broton heard Fitzpatrick tell attendees at a meeting of local officials he was a "close, personal friend" of the inspector general, Catherine Leahy Scott. After some time, Broton was interviewed by the inspector general's office, but neither the musician nor anyone else familiar with the facts ever was.

About three weeks after Fitzpatrick was named to head the Moreland Commission, the inspector general issued reports regarding our complaint. We were shocked when both were critical of the Syracuse Police Depart-ment. The first concluded that a detective may have violated state law by using an unaccredited lab to test evidence.[35] The second report found there

---

30. See chapter 8, page 236.

31. Chris Bragg, "The State Inspector General's Oversight Waned under Cuomo," *Times Union*, September 19, 2021.

32. Susanne Craig, William K. Rashbaum, and Thomas Kaplan, "Cuomo's Office Hob-bled Ethics Inquiries by Moreland Commission," *New York Times*, July 23, 2014.

33. William K. Rashbaum and Thomas Kaplan, "U.S. Attorney Criticizes Closing of Panel," *New York Times*, April 19, 2014.

34. William Fitzpatrick, "My Moreland Mission," *Huffington Post*, April 14, 2014, https://www.huffpost.com/entry/my-moreland-mission_b_514813.

35. Sara Patterson, "Inspector General Probes Syracuse's Police's Use of Unaccredited Lab," Syracuse.com, April 19, 2013, https://www.syracuse.com/news/2013/04/inspector_general_probes_syrac.html; Office of the Inspector General, "State of New York Office

had been "no serious negligence or misconduct" committed by the crime lab[36] despite the fact there were lab technician notes showing Fitzpatrick's office sought help in erasing videos and photographs on a device matching the musician's. Neither report mentioned the deleted recording of Fitzpatrick's remarks.

I surmised the inspector general knew not to investigate Fitzpatrick because he was a friend of Cuomo's.[37] While the inspector general office was supposed to be an independent agency, the head was appointed by the governor. The first three inspector generals Cuomo appointed had worked for him when he was attorney general.[38] Moreover, when each stepped down, the governor appointed them to well-compensated positions.[39]

We were on notice the district attorney could act with reckless abandon with no adverse consequences. We understood that a necessary participant in our reforming of the criminal justice system in Syracuse—namely, the district attorney's office—would oppose and undermine whatever reform initiatives we attempted to execute.

Our conflicting views with Fitzpatrick reached another crescendo in 2014 when he appointed a man named Peter Rausch as a representative for his office on a federal drug task force. Rausch was not a police officer, but he

of Inspector General Report of Investigation of the Onondaga County Health Department Center for Forensic Sciences," April 22, 2013, https://ig.ny.gov/news/nys-inspector -generals-investigation-finds-no-negligence-or-misconduct-onondaga-county-crime.

36. Office of the Inspector General, "NYS Inspector General's Investigation Finds No Negligence of Misconduct by Onondaga County Crime Lab," April 22, 2013. https://ig .ny.gov/news/nys-inspector-generals-investigation-finds-no-negligence-or-misconduct -onondaga-county-crime.

37. Cuomo had a documented resistance to independent oversight. Michael Shnayerson, *The Contender: Andrew Cuomo* (Twelve, 2015), 147–148, 150, 160–163, 166, 172–173, 174–177, 183, 195, 197–198, 328.

38. The inspector general's office found itself the focus of heated criticism after a pattern was established where key witnesses were never interviewed in allegations involving Cuomo or his allies. According to a *Times Union* review of the inspector general's website, the office never once posted a report stating Cuomo's executive chamber had been the subject of a critical finding. Chris Bragg, "The State Inspector General's Oversight Waned under Cuomo," *Times Union*, September 19, 2021.

39. Chris Bragg, "The State Inspector General's Oversight Waned under Cuomo," *Times Union*, September 19, 2021.

was an employee of Fitzpatrick's in the DA's office.[40] Starting in 2012, while he worked as a process server, Fitzpatrick said Rauch was an investigator, which allowed Rauch to carry a gun, investigate crimes, and arrest people. Rauch was not legally qualified to be an investigator because he didn't have the required six years of experience as a police officer.

More troubling, Fowler and Broton believed Rausch did not have the judgment to carry a weapon as a government official. Rausch had exhibited problematic behavior with guns years earlier when he was arrested on a felony charge of brandishing a .380-caliber handgun in an argument at a bar in the Syracuse University area. The charges of second-degree criminal possession of a weapon and second-degree menacing were ultimately dismissed, but he continued to engage in poor decision-making, posting inappropriate pictures of weapons on social media and threatening women by brandishing weapons. Fowler and Broton felt such behavior should disqualify him from carrying a service weapon. Fowler had written to county officials saying he was concerned about a process server carrying a gun, but he never received a response.

When Fitzpatrick appointed Rausch to the federal drug task force, Fowler asked my permission to withdraw the Syracuse Police Department from participation. Anticipating Fitzpatrick's bellowing, I was tempted to tell Fowler to ignore Rauch's appointment and take part in the task force. But I hired Fowler because of his integrity; he trusted I would not compromise it, so I authorized the withdrawal.

As predicted, Fitzpatrick's spokesman said the police department had a "pathological obsession to discredit Mr. Rauch and this office." Our withdrawal was portrayed as "the latest chapter of an ongoing feud with Onondaga County's district attorney." When we cited concerns about professional qualifications, the Drug Enforcement Agency spokesperson said Rauch had gone through a "thorough background check" and it had left "no stone unturned."[41]

40. Tim Knauss, "Disgraced Investigator Accompanied DA Fitzpatrick on 50 Trips in 5 Years," Syracuse.com, November 12, 2017, https://www.syracuse.com/news/2017/11/cop _who_killed_teen_in_hit-and-run_was_da_fitzpatricks_driver_on_road_trips.html.

41. John O'Brien, "Syracuse Police Drop Out of Drug Task Force in Latest Clash with DA," Syracuse.com, March 2, 2015, https://www.syracuse.com/crime/2015/03/syracuse _police_withdraw_from_dea_task_force_citing_concerns_over_inexperienced.html.

Fitzpatrick doubled down by requesting a special prosecutor to investigate Broton for sharing Rausch's felony arrest record with a local police chief.[42] While the law allows an arrest record of a police officer candidate to be shared, Fitzpatrick's actions nevertheless forced us to hire a criminal defense attorney to defend Broton. It seemed unbelievable that we were defending a deputy police chief because of actions he took to keep an unqualified person from serving in a law enforcement capacity. Ultimately, we prevailed when the special prosecutor failed to take any action, presumably because there was no merit to the allegations, but we incurred thousands of dollars in legal expenses.

Two years later, on March 21, 2017, during a night of heavy drinking, Rauch pulled out his government-issued handgun at a neighborhood bar while "goofing off." Later that night, as Rauch drove home in a government car, he hit an eighteen-year-old pedestrian, Seth Collier, walking home from his job at Burger King. Collier was a recent high school graduate working the night shift to help support his family. Rauch fled the scene, leaving Collier injured on the street. He later died from his injuries.[43]

Fitzpatrick fired Rauch two days after the crash.[44] Rauch was sentenced to two to six years in prison for vehicular manslaughter and leaving the scene of a fatal crash.[45] Almost every story written about Collier's death failed to mention Fowler and Broton's long-standing argument that Rauch was unfit for duty.

42. John O'Brien, "DA Launches Criminal Investigation Targeting Syracuse Deputy Police Chief," Syracuse.com, May 21, 2015, https://www.syracuse.com/crime/2015/05/syracuse_deputy_chief_under_criminal_investigation_over_disclosure_of_da_employe.html.

43. Douglass Dowty, "DA's Investigator Had 16 Drinks Before Killing Man Walking Home from Work," Syracuse.com, November 17, 2017, https://www.syracuse.com/crime/2017/11/da_investigator_had_16_beers_before_killing_man_waking_3_miles_home_from_work.html.

44. Douglass Dowty, "Da Fitzpatrick on Fired Investigator Charged in Hit and Run: 'What a Betrayal,'" Syracuse.com, March 23, 2017, https://www.syracuse.com/crime/2017/03/da_fitzpatrick_on_fired_investigator_accused_in_hit-and-run_what_a_betrayal.html.

45. Samantha House, "Ex-DA Investigator Gets 2 to 6 Years in Prison for Crash That Killed Syracuse Teen," Syracuse.com, November 17, 2017, https://www.syracuse.com/crime/2017/11/ex-da_investigator_peter_rauch_sentenced_for_killing_seth_collier_in_drunken_hit.html.

## The Brick Wall to Reform

Fowler and I were determined to help to change the culture of the police department by recruiting more people of color and Syracuse residents to the police force. While I knew hiring more Black officers wouldn't solve the long-standing issues between minorities and police, I thought it would be an attainable first step in that direction. Similarly, I thought adding more city residents to the force would help build relationships and understanding between police and neighbors. It proved to be an excruciatingly difficult task.

Our first attempt aimed to require police officers to become residents of Syracuse for a certain period of time.[46] This condition needed the police union's approval, but the union refused to discuss it, arguing officers did not feel safe in any part of Syracuse. I pointed out that was a problematic message to send to the people paying their salary. While troubling, we had no way to require police to live in the city in which they served without the union's cooperation.

We used money from the police department's budget for an aggressive public relations campaign to recruit young people who lived in the city to become police officers. With the city high schools' graduation rate of only 50 percent, our pool of applicants was limited. Most of the 50 percent who did graduate went on to college or entered the military.

Another huge obstacle was the poor relationship the police had with residents in minority neighborhoods. Syracuse's best and brightest were overwhelmingly not interested in becoming police officers. To counteract this, Fowler became our greatest asset in recruiting, speaking to groups and individuals about his experience.

Despite our efforts, only 9 percent of officers were Black in a city that was approximately 30 percent Black.[47] It was one of the lowest representations of

46. State laws forbid local governments from unilaterally instituting such a requirement. We did negotiate a clause with the firefighters union requiring city residency for new firefighters.

47. We had modest success in this effort. In 2011, our first year of targeted recruiting, we had a banner year, in which nine of the twenty-three new officers who joined the department were Black, about 39 percent. The 2014 class of new officers was one of the most diverse groups to go through the police academy, with five Black officers, three Hispanic officers, and six female officers. Fourteen people from that class lived in Syracuse.

Black police officers in New York state.[48] It was yet another problem arising from long-term cultural separation. Finding a solution would require more than the earnest efforts of a mayor and chief of police.

Fowler's ascendence to chief gave minority residents a representative and a voice within the police department. While pleased with our progress, every time I asked a member of the Black clergy how we were doing healing the relationship between residents and the police, they responded that Fowler alone could not heal the wounds.

One avenue to address these ongoing issues was through Syracuse's Civilian Review Board (CRB). Created in the wake of the Rodney King beating with the noble idea of citizen oversight of the police, the CRB was supposed to hold hearings and make discipline recommendations for police accused of misconduct.[49] In practice, the CRB had been ineffective for years.

Police refused to participate[50] in the process, which was their legal right, and police officers' discipline records were sealed under state law,[51] which prevented the board and the public from learning about misconduct by officers and any discipline they may have faced. That one-two punch eviscerated the CRB's ability to meet its mission.

Officials recognized that effective civilian oversight could not happen until the state changed the laws insulating police, but supporting the oversight committee, while futile, allowed politicians to curry favor with communities demanding police accountability. Thus, politicians pledged allegiance to the CRB, knowing that the ineffective board was a threat to neither the police nor political ambition.

48. Sean Lahman, "Local Police Force Lacks Diversity," *Democrat and Chronicle*, January 21, 2015, https://www.democratandchronicle.com/story/news/2015/01/21/police-diveristy-minority-rochester-monroe-county-lovely-warren/22133689/.

49. Gloria Wright, "Citizens Give Final Review—Mayor Hears Varying Opinions at Public Hearing on the Need for a Civilian Review Board for Police," *Post Standard*, February 12, 1993.

50. The police union established there was a mandatory procedure for handling citizen complaints through arbitration. Thus, instead of being compelled to participate in CRB investigations, police officers could choose arbitration and refuse to participate with the CRB. Jim O'Hara, "Court Hands Setback to CRB a State Supreme Court Justice Blocks the Civilian Review Board's Power to Force Police Officers to Testify," *Post-Standard*, September 9, 1997.

51. William Finnegan, "The Blue Wall," *New Yorker*, August 3 and 10, 2010.

In its entire history in Syracuse, the CRB had had only one administrator, Felicia Pitts Davis, a practicing lawyer. When Davis accepted the position, she lobbied for changes to enhance the CRB's effectiveness. When her repeated efforts failed, she stopped publicly asking for change. She collected a full-time salary as the board's administrator and maintained a private law practice.[52] She was viewed as either someone not allowed to do an important job because of police obstinacy or someone taking advantage of a broken and ineffective system.

By 2010, Davis had effectively abandoned her job as administrator. She had not held a fact-finding hearing in five years, failed to forward any complaints of police misconduct, and refused to produce mandated reports. An official meeting of the board had not been held in the last seven months of 2010. The board had no website publishing its findings or explaining how people could file complaints.[53]

The need for Syracuse to have an external system to determine if police had acted inappropriately was growing exponentially. Yet my experience with the CRB made me leery of empowering volunteer civilian oversight. Subjects that inflame passion—like police misconduct—need to have a process that is deliberative, which usually means time-consuming, to ensure facts trump opinions and bias. Members of a volunteer board are frequently inspired to get involved because of a passion, and passion often makes people less likely to view issues objectively; they want answers and want them quickly.

As a city councilor, I saw board members and a city councilor use a black Sharpie to shade a picture of an alleged police victim's black eye before a public hearing. A CRB member resigned after learning members were allowed to sign in to form a quorum and leave, which allowed the CRB to work without a quorum. The CRB's leadership refused to address the issue or change its behavior even when the resigning member cited the action as a violation of the law.[54]

---

52. John O'Brien, "City Watched the Watchdog Found There Wasn't Much to See—Fired Head of Citizen Review Board Has Litany of Reasons Why So Little Happened on Her Watch," *Post-Standard*, February 6, 2011.

53. O'Brien, "City Watched the Watchdog Found There Wasn't Much to See."

54. O'Brien, "City Watched the Watchdog Found There Wasn't Much to See."

It was also problematic to have an agency whose exclusive purpose was to hold the police department accountable, which increased the city's legal liability. Thus, any adverse finding the CRB made would likely be admitted as evidence against the police department in a lawsuit. Managing a vibrant civilian review board and the police would be a blurry exercise in defending the police and supporting an agency establishing police misconduct.

Despite the risks, I decided to find a better citizen oversight model. I feared the lack of an effective forum was a bomb ready to explode. When I announced my plan to fix the CRB, Davis and CRB members accused me of undercutting the mission of the organization. They refused to admit the CRB was ineffective or take any responsibility for inaction. I called the board leadership and members, only to have them refuse to answer my calls. Like the police union, Davis and CRB leadership refused to participate in any way to fix a broken system. Finally, when Davis failed to respond to a demand to appear at a federal trial and the judge said he was considering fining the city,[55] I could no longer tolerate her multiple derelictions of duty and I terminated her.

It caused a firestorm in the progressive community. I expected support, given my battles with the police union, but I was wrong. While many progressives wanted the system to work, it didn't seem to include changing the management who had overseen years of inaction. Black clergy members told me I was wrong to have terminated Davis. The CRB and its administrator were sacred albeit ineffective cows. In the eyes of progressives, Davis had been a fighter for justice who was stopped by a recalcitrant police union. I argued she had done nothing to help foster reform and, instead, had fought it. It didn't matter. I was told she had been there from the beginning and was on Team Justice, not Team Police. Thus, she was untouchable.[56] The binary choice with this group was to support ineffective leadership or be an obstacle to social justice.

I took my lumps and continued to try to make citizen review work. We passed new legislation modeled on laws other cities had passed and hired a new administrator with the goal of effective civilian review. None of it made a difference.

55. O'Brien, "City Watched the Watchdog Found There Wasn't Much to See."

56. In 2020, Davis was elected a Syracuse city court judge.

The state continued to shield disciplinary records, effectively quashing the ability to create a constructive outlet to discuss police behavior. Some board members were more interested in vilifying the police than working to improve relationships. There remained two opposing camps separated by a border neither side was willing to cross. As for me, I felt conflicted over my duty to the police, to an agency that publicized police misconduct, and to the public.

## Reckoning

Despite the obstacles in our way, I felt good about our efforts to institute a new culture in the police department. Fowler was a respected leader. Together, he and I were regularly speaking to leaders in all the neighborhoods, both listening and reacting to their ideas and complaints. The world outside of Syracuse, though, showed the limits of our measures.

As the country started a painful public reckoning over police brutality aimed at Black men, cities became engulfed with violence and riots. When Eric Garner died at the hands of a New York City police officer, Fowler and I were together when the video of Garner uttering "I can't breathe" became public. The video was so disturbing we sat in stunned silence. When the reaction in Syracuse was limited to a peaceful protest, I attributed it to the work we had been doing to improve relationships.

Less than a month later, when Michael Brown died in Ferguson, Missouri, at the hands of a police officer, we prepared again for emotional reactions. This time we asked Black clergy to go to our high schools to talk with students about the incidents. Again, our community reacted with calm and peaceful protests. During this time, the head of a large foundation commended me for helping maintain peace through my leadership. While gratified, I feared the peace was more luck than plan.

In the predawn hours of the Monday after Father's Day in 2016, I woke to a phone call from Fowler. In June, calls at such hours were a regular occurrence, but this time when I answered, Fowler's tone was uncharacteristically hurried. He said, as he always did, "Mayor, I have a notification." This meant a death, but his tone conveyed something additionally disturbing. Forcing myself to focus, I sat up and walked to the foot of the bed to steady myself. He said, "We have a real problem," and my stomach dropped.

He said multiple shots were fired at a Father's Day gathering at a local park.[57] There was at least one person dead, a police officer seriously hurt, and hundreds of people involved. As he spoke, I heard the unmistakable sounds of chaos in the background: shouting, sirens, and marshalling of police. I felt a wave of terror, sadness, and helplessness. The only thing I could say was, "Frank, do what you need to do." I trusted he would make the right decisions, but I knew good decisions were no longer possible. Our reckoning had started.

The Father's Day picnic in one of Syracuse's poorest neighborhoods, the Near West Side, was an annual tradition. For the past couple of years, the party had become unruly and violent when the sun went down. This year, the police were tipped off that the event was likely to become violent and a permit for the event was denied.

Around noon on Father's Day, a group of seventy people gathered in the city park for the picnic. When told by the police to move, they went into the courtyard of a neighboring public housing development. People gathered for a day of cooking out, dancing, and socializing that lasted well into the night.

Around eleven at night, a twenty-two-year-old rookie Syracuse police officer named Kelsey Francemone, working alone, answered a call about an unidentified man who had collapsed on a street near the traditional picnic site. When she arrived, she didn't find anyone on the street, but saw the party of about three hundred people in the nearby courtyard. Francemone requested backup to help disperse the crowd. Minutes later, gunfire rang out.

As hundreds of people ran from the gunfire, Francemone ran toward it. She saw three men firing handguns and ordered them to drop their weapons. They refused, but she kept advancing toward them. The men separated and fled. She pursued one, later identified as Gary Porter. She saw Porter firing a gun and ordered him to drop his weapon. He refused her order, pivoted toward her, and continued to shoot. When he turned toward her, she fired seven times hitting him once.[58] Porter was killed.[59]

Immediately, a mob jumped on Francemone—ripping her uniform,

57. Catie O'Toole, "Chaotic 'Officer-Involved' Shooting Scene Near West Side," *Post-Standard*, June 21, 2016.

58. Samantha House, "Syracuse Police Officer Shot Man at Father's Day Party; Grand Jury Clears Officer," Syracuse.com, August 5, 2016, https://www.syracuse.com/crime/20 16/08/fahthers_day_shooting_district_attorney_police_officer.html.

59. Reports, "Officer Fired During Chaos; One Man Dead," *Post-Standard*, June 21, 2016.

beating and groping her, and attempting to take her firearm.[60] As other officers arrived at the scene and attempted to rescue Francemone, the crowd threw liquor bottles, rocks, trash, and even part of a bicycle at them. People yelled, "Kill the cops."[61]

A call went out over the public-safety system asking all available units in the area to respond. Police officers came from all over, including state troopers, public-safety officers from Syracuse University, and the sheriff's helicopter. Police in riot gear, armed with rifles and shields, swarmed. When Fowler arrived, he attempted to deescalate the situation, only to have people taunt him and throw things.[62]

The next morning, I went to the site. I got out of the car and walked over to an older Black woman sitting on concrete steps. She seemed separate from the buzz of activity happening behind her: police officers talking to residents, workers replacing windows, and groups of people huddling and whispering to each other. It was a sunny morning, but sadness hung in the air.

I stood silently in front of her, unable to summon any comforting words. As my eyes met hers, with great sorrow she said, "Mayor, we did nothing wrong. We were having a good time and the police just rolled up and started shooting." I knew that wasn't what happened, but I also knew she wasn't lying to me. She was processing a shocking situation informed by painful experiences—a mash-up of what had happened in the past and what just happened.

The specifics of what had happened the night before were unclear, but residents were convinced police started shooting first. Police were shaken by the violence aimed at them. Adding to the chaos, multiple one-sided accounts of the evening's events were being relayed to the media and posted on social media, one of which was that Porter was unarmed and running away when he was shot.

On Monday night, the officers posted at the site saw several men, forbidden by court order due to criminal offenses from entering the housing complex, attempt to do just that. As neighbors watched, police handcuffed

60. John O'Brien, "Officer Survived Attack by Crowd," *Post-Standard*, June 23, 2016.

61. Douglass Dowty, "37 Gunshots, Attacked Cops, a Riot on Father's Day, but Who Killed Gary Porter?" Syracuse.com, July 12, 2016, https://www.syracuse.com/crime/2016/07/37_gunshots_attacked_cops_a_riot_on_fathers_day_but_who_killed_gary_porter.html.

62. John O'Brien, "Officer Survived Attack by Crowd," *Post-Standard*, June 23, 2016.

the men and pinned one man to the ground. The police refused to explain the grounds for the arrests and a crowd gathered and started yelling.[63]

A confidential informant said he saw Porter toss a gun into the bushes just before he was shot. We knew there were at least four different guns fired, including the officer's weapon, but we needed time to determine if Porter was killed by the officer's shots or other gunfire.

We learned Porter had a history of illegal weapon possession. By Wednesday, a confidential informant said Porter's gun was in the house of a woman known to associate with a gun trafficker. The police obtained a search warrant, and as a vigil for Porter was being held nearby, forty officers in riot gear, a SWAT vehicle, and several marked and unmarked cars executed the search warrant to locate Porter's gun. The resident of the home told the media the police broke the front door jamb, three windows, a closet door, and a cabinet mirror and cracked a flat screen television. As a result, she said she had to leave her home and accused the police of harassing her.[64]

Once again, the police did not explain their rationale for executing the warrant in the manner they did. It appeared as if stormtroopers in a military vehicle ravaged a poor Black woman's home, and the police found no weapons or ammunition in the search. That lack of evidence was disastrous. While the investigation was being conducted according to well-established practices, each step resulted in further public outrage.

Trapped between recognizing the tremendous public damage police actions were causing and recognizing that the police had to investigate without political meddling, I tried to mitigate the damage by keeping lines of communication with the public open. Fowler and I were having regular media briefings, but normal investigation procedure meant the police kept everything confidential until they were ready to present evidence to the district attorney's office. The media and the community were hungry for information, and social media filled the vacuum, largely with misinformation.

While Fowler and I had reputations for being reformers, the unexplained aggressive tactics by the police, combined with social media rantings, canceled any good will we had built. To combat this, I decided to go to

63. Samantha House, "Police: Monday Arrests Are Unrelated to Shooting," *Post-Standard*, June 22, 2016.

64. Chris Baker and Ken Sturtz, "Raid Causes Tension, Anguish on Gifford Street," *Post-Standard*, June 23, 2016.

the neighborhood and hold a public forum. My steadfast supporter Bruce Connor told me I would not be welcome. More painfully, Connor told me he was skeptical about the police role at the event and was questioning my leadership. His comments were devastating. I was losing the minority community and the support of one of my most loyal friends and was not welcomed in a neighborhood I had worked hard to build a relationship with.

As I reeled from Connor's comments, Fowler called and told me he had an idea to combat the misinformation. While we had police surveillance-camera footage of the event, we could not release it under normal protocol because it would potentially taint the investigation. Fowler determined we could release it if we were asking the public to help us identify the shooters in the video. It was an elegant solution. I told him to release the video to the media. I called Connor and asked him to give me twenty-four hours. He promised me he would and tried to convince others to do the same, but I could hear the doubt in his voice.

The next day, we released the video. It begins with hundreds of people suddenly fleeing from gunshots heard off camera. Francemone appears about twenty-three seconds into the video and almost immediately begins running in the opposite direction of the crowd, toward shooters not shown in the video. Seconds later, two men pull out handguns, follow Francemone, then turn around and walk away without incident. About forty seconds into the video, a man appears, pointing a handgun in the direction Francemone had run. At the same time, at the top of the screen, a man wearing a dark shirt and dark shorts appears to fire at least two shots from a handgun toward the right of the screen as he is walking the other way. The video does not show Francemone firing her gun or Porter getting hit, which took place out of view of the camera.[65]

The video undercut all the wild speculation. The public could see with their own eyes that there was a threat that caused hundreds of people to run away. As they did, the video showed one lone officer running toward the threat. The public saw several men brandishing pistols in a threatening manner. The video proved people were in fear of their lives. The notion that police had run in and started shooting was eviscerated. Minutes after the video became public, I felt the public come over to our side.

65. John O'Brien, "Video Shows Officer As Crowd Flees Scene," *Post-Standard*, June 24, 2016.

When the investigation was complete, it established that at least thirty-seven shots were fired from several semiautomatic firearms. Multiple witnesses said Porter fired a gun, ignored commands to drop his weapon, and threw a gun during the pursuit. Though a gun was never recovered, gunshot-residue analysis on Porter's hands confirmed he discharged a weapon. Francemone fired seven times.[66] A grand jury cleared her of any misconduct, and she received a national medal of merit.[67]

The threat of a violent conflagration consuming all of Syracuse subsided, but the tension behind the riot continued to smolder. After the release of the video, a priest asked me to meet with some young mothers who lived in the neighborhood where the riot occurred. I went to the meeting alone at a church rectory. With no introductory remarks, the women shared their deep fear for their sons' physical safety. As I watched one young boy play off to the side of the room, the mothers each told me they worried every day that their sons would die at the hands of police. It was striking to think a mother would look at a son younger than ten years old and think that was a possibility.

I attempted to explain the police's actions in the riot, and they stopped me, telling me they did not want to talk about the Father's Day event. They wanted me to know the pain and anguish they lived with in a culture they believe condoned the brutalization of Black men. It was a primal scream. Their pain was obvious.

They wanted me to understand the Father's Day riot was one incident within an extensive string of events in which their loved ones were physically subjugated to the point where trust in the police was not possible. Gun violence taking the lives of young men was equally unacceptable, they said, but it was not condoned by society. They believed police violence was, and that was unjust.

Their fears pushed them to get active in the Black Lives Matter movement. As such, they told me they would be working to change the system.

66. Samantha House, "Syracuse Police Officer Shot Man at Father's Day Party; Grand Jury Clears Officer," Syracuse.com, August 5, 2016, https://www.syracuse.com/crime/20 16/08/fahthers_day_shooting_district_attorney_police_officer.html; Douglass Dowty, "37 Gunshots, Attacked Cops, a Riot on Father's Day, but Who Killed Gary Porter?" Syracuse.com, July 12, 2016, https://www.syracuse.com/crime/2016/07/37_gunshots_at tacked_cops_a_riot_on_fathers_day_but_who_killed_gary_porter.html.

67. Spectrum News staff, "Syracuse Officer Honored for Bravery During Father's Day Riot," July 26, 2017.

Fowler and I were part of that system. As I listened to their impassioned pleas, I felt their sorrow, not anger. I left the meeting sharing that sadness.

## Divided We Fail

Shortly after, I learned Black Lives Matter was organizing a march through downtown Syracuse. The organization prided itself on not having a strict hierarchy, making it impossible to garner any accurate information about their plans. There were multiple groups identifying as Black Lives Matter planning separate protests. With no dedicated, experienced organizers, it was difficult to ascertain whether the intent was to have a peaceful protest. But several seasoned social justice organizers assured me the protest would be peaceful.

Social media was filled with claims about busloads of people traveling to Syracuse intent on causing trouble. Fowler and I talked about the rumors and the lack of definitive information. Police instinct was to treat the protests as potential riots. I vetoed that approach. While it was a risk, we had no information the event was going to be violent, just fear. I reminded Fowler that Americans have a constitutional right to peaceful protest. As I did, I said a prayer that that would be the case.

On the day of the protest, several prominent downtown establishments closed early, citing a fear of violence,[68] including the federal office building. When I called the business owners and others asking where they got their information, they sheepishly admitted it was a rumor. No one in any authority had suggested the potential of violence. When I pushed an official in the federal building, he rationalized the decision to close was because of traffic issues, not safety concerns. As he haltingly stuttered his explanation, I thought about the young mothers telling me society automatically sees their sons as violent.

As the time for the initial protest came closer, the police department set up surveillance along the potential route with strict instructions not to look obtrusive. Fowler came to city hall, and we set up a command center

68. Patrick Lohmann, "'Everyone Wants to Be Proactive': Concerned About Storefront Access and Traffic Flow, Some Downtown Businesses Closed Before Black Lives Matter March," *Post-Standard*, July 21, 2016.

in my office. The police were uncomfortable with the limitations I ordered, and I was worried my decision to show restraint might backfire. We both anxiously waited.

As we watched on social media and television, the demonstration kicked off with hundreds of people peacefully gathered. The crowd was made up of the young and old and a mix of people of color and white people. They said they were there to protest "ongoing murders of Black people" around the country and "police brutality against Black residents" in Syracuse.[69] One of the mothers that met with me shared her message with the media: she feared for her nine-year-old son's future because he was Black. She was marching to stop police from making decisions based on race or lack of understanding of the communities they serve.

One of the organizers of the protest, Shaunna Spivey-Spinner, demanded action to stop all violence, including from members of her community. "Hell, yeah, I'm angry," she said. "I'm pissed off and discouraged. I'm afraid that at any given moment one night of me trying to enjoy myself will turn into the last night of my life."[70]

As the crowd marched, Fowler was notified that a police officer thought a protester was carrying a gun. In a tense series of deliberations, I told Fowler we needed to be sure before we authorized the police to extract a protester from a peaceful march. The repercussions of such an action would be devastating, but gunfire would be equally devastating. The officer said he could not be sure, and the decision was made to watch the protester closely but not intervene. The protestor continued to march without incident.

The crowd arrived at city hall shouting for me and Fowler to come out and speak to them. I told Fowler I was going, and he said not without him by my side. I told him he needed to take his gun off if he wanted to join me. He was stunned, and I told him it was the only way he could accompany me. It seemed the right thing to do. I wanted to demonstrate we were one community. A gun was a symbol of fear. It was inconceivable to me my

69. Catie O'Toole, "Live Coverage of Black Lives Matter March, Rally," Syracuse.com, July 18, 2016, https://www.syracuse.com/news/2016/07/live_coverage_of_black_lives_matter_march_rally.html.

70. Patrick Lohmann, "Syracuse Mayor Speaks to Black Lives Matter Rally after Group Arrives at City Hall," Syracuse.com, July 18, 2016, https://www.syracuse.com/news/2016/07/syracuse_black_lives_matter_rally.html.

community would hurt me or Fowler. I like to think that was true, but it may have just been foolish.

Fowler removed his gun, and we walked out unarmed. When we stepped out the large front doors of city hall, we were greeted with loud cheers. I asked the assembled crowd for their help. "Each of us has a responsibility to . . . make it better for all of us."[71]

When one protester loudly criticized the police department for the small number of Black police officers, Fowler responded by asking the young man to come forward. He spoke privately to him about joining the police department.[72] After the conversation, Fowler told the crowd we wanted people from the community to join our police force. After we spoke, the crowd walked peacefully to its next location.

I felt good about the events and was hopeful it would serve as a first step toward a community solution to the issues we had as a city. I reached out to one of the main BLM organizers asking for a meeting with her and anyone else she wanted to bring. Echoing my comments at the march, I told them we welcomed their help in any way they felt comfortable. Fowler and I both offered to have regular meetings with them and coordinate any efforts at change.

We had one or two meetings, but they never took me up on recurring meetings. They never met with Fowler after the initial encounter. My attempt to funnel anger and energy failed. Maybe the people with the energy were young and had other things they needed to attend to, maybe they thought working with us would be seen as acquiescing to the system, or maybe the daily slog of finding solutions was more than they could muster. Much later, I received an email from a main organizer apologizing for not following up, but she said she was busy with school and contemplating becoming a police officer.

What remained was deep-seated anger. We were two camps: for the police or against the police. The idea of one community seeking to enable justice for all was, for the present, ethereal.

71. Lohmann, "Syracuse Mayor Speaks to Black Lives Matter Rally after Group Arrives at City Hall."

72. Lohmann, "Syracuse Mayor Speaks to Black Lives Matter Rally after Group Arrives at City Hall."

## Postscript

Syracuse, like other cities, continues to be ravaged by gun violence. In the wake of George Floyd's 2020 murder at the hands of police, the state repealed Section 50-a,[73] which sealed police disciplinary records, but there is still a lack of effective accountability for police behavior.

Many years ago, I suggested to Governor Mario Cuomo he shouldn't say the criminal justice system is a mess. "But it is," he answered. I agree.

73. Finnegan, "The Blue Wall."

# Economic Development

## Show Them the Money

"Mayor, are you okay? Do you need me to do something?" my security officer asked in a concerned tone. It was the evening of December 20, 2013, and she had driven me to an annual toy and homemade blanket giveaway at a recreation center. I sat in silence, not moving. The Onondaga County Executive Joanie Mahoney had called me moments earlier and breezily said the governor was going to announce a new state-financed stadium for Syracuse University. I was gobsmacked and could only muster, "I have no idea what you're talking about." Smoothly, she responded, "Oh, I thought you did."

As I tried to wrap my mind around the notion of a multimillion-dollar stadium being dropped on Syracuse, I heard my security officer and realized I needed to snap into the moment for the event. My phone buzzed with a text message from Mahoney, saying she was "under the impression I was being kept in the loop." After the event, I responded, "I'm totally out of the loop," knowing that had likely been the plan all along.

## 19 Days to a Stadium, Really?

My head was swimming: "A stadium. Really, of all things . . . a stadium?" Syracuse was experiencing record-breaking poverty, our infrastructure was crumbling underneath us, and our schools were performing poorly—and the governor wanted to spend money on a stadium? While stadiums are perfect political sugar highs, they are notorious money pits, sucking public resources and failing to provide a return, particularly for the people who live adjacent to stadium sites, who are usually poor and Black.

My questions piled up like a highway car accident: Where would the stadium be located? Which neighborhoods would be affected? What services would be impacted? How long would this process take? But my real question was: "What the fuck is going on?" In a mere nineteen days, including Christmas and New Year's, the governor was scheduled to unveil a plan for a new stadium for Syracuse in his State of the State address. It was incomprehensible.

When I told Richard Brodsky[1] about the situation, he said it was bad economic development coupled with bad process. With characteristic bluntness, he said the maneuver was done deliberately to reward Mahoney's joyful cheerleading for Cuomo and punish my criticism by showing that I, as mayor, was superfluous. "She smiles at him, and you don't," he said. When I responded, "What the fuck does that have to do with anything?" He told me to "grow up," and after a long pause, he said, "Show them it doesn't."

I alerted my staff about Mahoney's call. After some digging, we learned COR Development had created schematic drawings of a stadium just east of a site known as Kennedy Square. My staff ascertained the county executive and leaders from Syracuse University had been meeting for months with the governor's staff to put together a plan for a $500 million stadium on the east side of Syracuse. It was another shocking piece of information. Syracuse University was in the midst of a leadership change. The former chancellor had left, and the newly appointed chancellor had not assumed the job. It seemed crazy that an institution would go forward with discussions over such a major decision without a sitting chief executive.

When my office contacted university officials, they attempted to artfully deny participation in any discussions about a stadium, but eventually said they did so at the behest of the county executive and governor's office. We learned the university had undertaken a feasibility study. When we asked for a copy of the study, the request was denied. A private institution was refusing to share a taxpayer-funded study with the top elected official of the jurisdiction where the stadium would be located, another mind-boggling break in public policy. My staff and I were stunned by the disrespect and deceitfulness of officials with whom we worked regularly. It was unprecedented. All of it.

As each piece of information came to light, one person's absence became

1. See chapter 2, page 55, for Brodsky introduction.

notable: Todd Howe, COR's lobbyist and Cuomo whisperer. Three years earlier, in the fall of 2010, at an informal meeting in my office, Howe casually said Syracuse University might need a new stadium. While it was common knowledge the university's Carrier (now JMA Wireless) Dome was getting older and lacked the amenities such as luxury boxes that were so lucrative in modern stadiums, I told him I had heard nothing other than the speculation common in a sports-obsessed community and dismissed it.

He then turned to the third person at the meeting, Bill Eimicke, a Columbia University professor. Howe introduced Eimicke as a noted academic who routinely authored important economic-development studies and was looked upon by the Cuomo team with great admiration. Howe asked Eimicke for his thoughts. In a tone that clearly conveyed he, an Ivy League professor, was going to educate me, a small-town politician, about the finer points of economic development, Eimicke spewed out numbers, cost factors, and important-sounding theories and concluded a stadium would be "transformative" for Syracuse.

I had spent a lot of time looking for successful economic-development programs and knew stadiums were losers.[2] I saw Eimicke's presence at the meeting as an attempt to intimidate me, but I wasn't having it. I told him and Howe I knew of no stadium in the United States that had transformed one neighborhood, much less an entire city. I finished by sharply stating, "I've looked, not one." To up the ante, I offered to review any examples Eimicke could share, knowing full well he would not be able to meet the challenge.

Howe, sensing my mood, said, "No, Mayor, you're pretty clear—no stadium," laughing to defuse the tension. Howe later shared that when he worked for Andrew Cuomo at the Department of Housing and Urban Development, one of his primary jobs was to ensure no one got a meeting with Cuomo who wanted money for a stadium or convention center. And yet, in a few days, Cuomo was scheduled to announce a stadium as a major economic development project for my city.

As I struggled to make sense of it, I decided to gauge the feelings of other elected officials. I called Assemblyman Bill Magnarelli, the senior Democrat representing Syracuse, coyly asking if he had heard anything about a proposed stadium. He responded he had not, but it sounded like something he would support.

2. Andrew Zimbalist and Roger G. Noll, "Sports, Jobs, & Taxes: Are New Stadiums Worth the Cost?" Brookings, June 1, 1997.

Next, I called Senator John DeFrancisco, the senior Republican representing Syracuse, and asked him the same question. He said, no he had not
heard of anything and, as the head of the Senate Finance Committee, he
expected he would have been briefed on such an important matter. When I
explained to him what I knew, he responded with characteristic bluntness,
"That's stupid." He was clearly irritated he was just hearing about it. I told
him I would keep him in the loop, and he said he'd do the same.

My final key call was to the soon-to-be-installed chancellor of Syracuse
University, Kent Syverud, who was leaving a job in Missouri to come to
Syracuse. I reached him while he was driving, and I apologized that our first
discussion would have to be controversial. I told him I thought a stadium
project needed more evaluation and was unsure it would be economically
beneficial to the region.

Having read he was a Cardinals fan, I casually pointed out that while
baseball stadiums have dozens of games, basketball and football have far
fewer. He laughed and said such a project should be assessed. He volunteered that he had enough on his plate without immediately having to worry
about a new stadium being built. I wished him a happy holiday and got off
the phone, thinking I had two key parties on my side: the Senate Finance
chair and the new head of Syracuse University.

After Mahoney's phone call and texts about the stadium, I started receiving dozens of phone calls and texts from Steve Aiello, one of the founders of
COR Development. Aiello was a longtime family friend and his role in this
was a stinging betrayal of our friendship. After a few days, I regained my
composure and arranged to talk to him at my office.

Aiello arrived, looking deeply apologetic. He sat down and said, "I didn't
know if you were ever going to talk to me again." I told him I wasn't sure
I would. He said the stadium plans had been just talk until Mahoney got
involved. Casting blame on her, he said she wanted the stadium, and she
pushed it before anyone could talk to me. I knew it was an excuse, but I
wanted to forgive him and move forward.

I did let him know, though, that I was deeply wounded. "This isn't just
my job Steve; it's my life." He said he understood, and he would keep me in
the loop in the future. As the meeting ended, he sheepishly said his wife gave
him Christmas cookies to give to me and Jack, but he was afraid I would
reject them. I laughed and accepted them. Those cookies foreshadowed a
bitter end for us. In a little over a year, a relationship that went back two

generations on my side, and included my husband and our immediate family, would be permanently severed.

Shortly after my meeting with Aiello, Howe contacted me to tell me that earlier in 2013, the governor had asked Mahoney for suggestions for a significant state-funded project to boost his reelection and Mahoney had suggested a new stadium. Mahoney, he said, was good friends with SU's athletic director Daryl Gross, who had apparently been talking up the idea for some time. Shortly after getting the green light from the governor, Mahoney arranged for the nonprofit Syracuse Convention and Visitors Bureau, funded by the county, to give $50,000 to Syracuse University to help pay for a feasibility study.

Like Aiello, Howe blamed the whole thing on Mahoney, conveniently omitting that COR's stadium renderings were done in 2011. The governor asked her for an idea and Mahoney told him a stadium would be great for his reelection. She wanted to curry favor with the governor by ordering everyone to keep me in the dark. It was common knowledge that anything done to slight me was looked upon favorably by the governor.

Mahoney came to my office shortly before the State of the State to tell me all the elected officials, including DeFrancisco, were in support of the stadium. "It's all up to you," she said. She clearly did not realize I was in contact with DeFrancisco and knew that was not his position. I did not respond to her entreaties, which was a response in and of itself, but was cordial and noncommittal. Mahoney had become Cuomo's acolyte—the merit of the proposals or other relationships did not matter.

Days later, Howe asked me if there was an avenue for compromise. I responded I was open to a discussion and reminded him that Syracuse needed money for infrastructure. The Sunday before the State of the State, Howe told me to expect a call from the governor's powerful secretary, Howard Glazer, to negotiate a compromise.

On the day of the call, I gathered my senior staff, along with Jack, in an empty city hall. We talked about what to expect, and the consensus was our sports-obsessed community would be enthralled with a new stadium. As consolation, Jack told me I was like the famous Chinese man who stood in front of the tank in Tiananmen Square to protest injustice. I reminded him that guy died.

Moments before the expected call from Glaser, Kent Syverud called. He apologized, saying he would have to backtrack on his initial commitment. He explained he was new to New York state politics and had been convinced he could not cross the governor. Thus, he would support the stadium. I tried to be gracious and thanked him for letting me know. I relayed the news to my staff, realizing we could not stand against the governor and the new university chancellor without enormous political costs.

The meeting took on the air of a funeral when my phone rang. Howe got straight to the point. The governor had called DeFrancisco about the stadium and the senator said it was a terrible idea. DeFrancisco's Senate leadership position would make him a formidable opponent. As a result, the governor ordered the stadium pulled from the State of the State. Just like that, it was all over, except for the assignment of blame when the matter became public.

Within days, Mahoney had her supporter, Ryan McMahon, the County Legislature chairman, tell the media the governor wanted to provide state funding for "a significant economic development project," and she had asked the governor for a new stadium for Syracuse University. "A lack of enthusiasm from city hall"[3] prevented the project from happening. It was, I thought, a harbinger of things to come.

The next day, as I braced for the fallout, a staffer walked into my office and dropped a newspaper story on my desk. "You're going to like this," he said. It was a column by Brent Axe, a local sportswriter, titled "5 Questions About a Potential New Syracuse Sports Arena," which read in part:

> One of the selling points of this project, if and when it is officially proposed, will surely be the economic impact it will have on the Syracuse-area. My advice to you and our local leaders is to do your research on that before making such a claim. A quick Google search will find you lots of examples of stadium projects that did not provide the economic boost they promised.
>
> Governor Cuomo, Onondaga County Executive Joanie Mahoney, and anyone else that would stand at a podium and explain how this project will be paid for needs to be upfront with the taxpayers and residents of Syracuse

3. Tim Knauss, "Mayor Miner Is Blocking New SU Sports Arena, County Legislature Chairman Says," Syracuse.com, January 14, 2014, https://www.syracuse.com/news/2014/01/mayor_miner_is_blocking_new_su_stadium_proposal_county_legislature_chairman_says.html.

and Onondaga County about how this project will be funded and why it seemingly is taking priority over a city's basic needs.[4]

Sports writers are among the most-read and well-regarded journalists in Syracuse, so Axe's column was an unexpected victory for us.

The day it appeared, I walked to a downtown jewelry store to get a watch battery. A man I did not know stopped me and said I was "the only grown-up" in political leadership. Proceeding to eviscerate the officials who were proposing a stadium, he said, "They suddenly announce they want to build a stadium! Our roads and pipes are what they should be paying attention to, like you've been saying." It was surprising but telling, revealing that Mahoney and the governor had wildly misjudged the popularity of a stadium.

The governor apparently understood the negative consequences. Howe and Aiello told me independently they were called to a meeting where the governor screamed at them about the stadium debacle. Howe told me the governor kept referring to me as Howe's "girlfriend." At the time, I assumed he said it sarcastically. When I asked Aiello about it, he became deeply uncomfortable. Clearly wanting to stop the discussion, he said he had never seen anyone as angry as the governor. Aiello said it was so awful, at one point he wondered what his father would have thought about him being subjected to the governor's epic tantrum. It was enough for me to stop asking questions. The explosive conversation would become the subject of legal scrutiny much later.

## Corruption State of Mind

The year I became mayor, the state was in the process of seating its third governor in four years. Eliot Spitzer had been elected in 2006 and resigned in 2008 after news broke that he was a frequent customer of a high-end escort service. His successor, David Paterson, almost immediately became embroiled in rumors of official misconduct.

It was a time of momentous political upheaval in the state. The comptroller, Alan Hevesi, had just resigned as part of investigations related to

4. Brent Axe, "Five Questions About a Potential New Syracuse Sports Arena," Syracuse.com, January 13, 2014, https://www.syracuse.com/axeman/2014/01/five_questions _about_a_potenti.html.

his use of state resources to aid his ailing wife. Subsequently, he was sent to prison for his role in a "pay-to-play" scandal with the state's pension fund.

Joseph L. Bruno, the former state Senate Majority Leader, was the subject of an ongoing federal investigation, and Bruno's successor, Pedro Espada Jr., was also the subject of several criminal investigations. Anthony Seminario, a longtime assemblyman, had resigned from office after pleading guilty to taking bribes. These were just the highlights of a political culture so rife with misconduct, New York was considered one of the most corrupt states in the nation.[5]

I was part of a political system constantly on edge over corruption rumors and criminal convictions. It was akin to swimming in a cesspool having become impervious to the smell.

One person who smelled opportunity in the scandals rollicking the state in 2010 was Andrew Cuomo. His gubernatorial campaign announcement was held in front of the Manhattan courthouse named for Boss Tweed, the infamous corrupt political boss of Tammany Hall. "Unfortunately, Albany's antics today could make Boss Tweed blush," he said. It was great theater, but time would show that was all it was.

Cuomo's election for governor was a forgone conclusion in 2010, but speculation had already begun that he would inevitably make a play for the White House. Political wisdom held that he would have to reverse upstate's economic fortunes to craft a successful presidential campaign narrative, especially to compete in states like Ohio and Pennsylvania. To do so, he would have to execute a perfect political maneuver by appealing to upstate sensibilities while leveraging New York City money and influence.

Shortly after the gubernatorial election, I learned COR had partnered with Upstate Medical University to redevelop a long-vacant and blighted site called Kennedy Square[6] into a mix of office, housing, educational, and retail space. When I expressed my surprise at COR's new business direction, Aiello told me his retail partners wanted access to the nearby college students. He piqued my interest when he said he would ensure the project paid

5. Alan Greenblatt, "How New York Became One of the Most Corrupt States," NPR. org, May 10, 2013, https://www.npr.org/sections/itsallpolitics/2013/05/10/182852131/how -new-york-became-one-of-the-most-corrupt-states.

6. Kennedy Square was the name of a site of a four-hundred-unit public housing project built in the 1970s. When it closed in 2008, it was tax-delinquent and badly blighted. The state transferred ownership to Upstate University in 2008.

property taxes. Typically, upstate economic-development arrangements demanded the government waive property taxes for a significant period to incentivize the developers. Moreover, because one of the partners in this project was a hospital-educational institution, there was a strong argument the development would be exempt from property taxes because it was part of a nonprofit institution. If Aiello could deliver on his promises, it would be a game changer in how these projects were carried out.

Just months later, I was at a press conference announcing the redevelopment plan, and Lieutenant Governor Robert Duffy was praising newly appointed Governor Cuomo for cutting through bureaucratic red tape to move the project forward. When the head of Upstate Medical University publicly committed to paying taxes for the project,[7] I looked at Aiello and he smiled and nodded.

While architectural renderings were shown at the press conference, the developer and Upstate Medical University leadership didn't provide specifics for the site or cost estimates for the project. Bill Eimicke, the Columbia University professor, even put together a study that estimated the project would create seven thousand temporary jobs during the construction phase and three thousand permanent jobs. I wondered how a study could determine that when the underlying details hadn't been hammered out.

Duffy said a new day was dawning in Albany thanks to Cuomo and called the project a victory for the local economy. At the end of the event, Howe ebulliently approached me and asked how big the headline in the paper would be the next day. "Front page, right? It's got to be, such a big jobs announcement." Throwing cold water on his enthusiasm, I disagreed. He responded, "Come on, Mayor, 3,000 jobs? When has an announcement like that happened?" I told him plans promising huge economic benefits happened all the time in Syracuse and never actually came to fruition. Sure enough, the story did not make the front page. Howe acknowledged I was right but said this time was going to be different with a new governor and new developers.

Days after the Kennedy Square announcement, I received an unusual request to meet from Tom Young, who was the mayor of Syracuse from 1986 to 1993. Young came to my office, which once had been his, to tell me

7. James T. Mulder, "Upstate Medical Teams Up with Private Developer to Give Kennedy Square a Makeover," Syracuse.com, December 1, 2011, https://www.syracuse.com/news/2011/12/upstate_medical_teams_up_with.html.

Syracuse's Inner Harbor could finally be redeveloped. The Inner Harbor, originally known as the Barge Canal Terminal, was an industrial waterfront created in the early 1900s to help move goods like coal, lumber, and oil through the Erie Canal system.

Starting in the early 1980s, Syracuse leaders, including Young, and state officials viewed the Inner Harbor as ripe for redevelopment but failed to make it happen. Young told me Aiello could redevelop the property with Howe's contacts in the Cuomo administration. In fact, Young told me he put Aiello and Howe together and disclosed he was going to be a paid consultant on the project. In short order, Howe, Aiello, and Young put together plans. They determined it would be easier to work through the regulatory burdens with Syracuse and its officials rather than the state bureaucracy. I agreed. They told me the state would transfer the Inner Harbor land to Syracuse for redevelopment if I requested it.

One hot, muggy day, I traveled to Manhattan to do just that. I was dropped off at the offices of the Metropolitan Transportation Authority, where the Thruway Authority board was meeting. I was running late, looking sweaty and disheveled, and showed my mayoral identification and mayoral police badge to the security guard. He looked at it and asked me, "When is the mayor coming?" I pointed at my picture and answered, "That's me. I am the mayor." He blushed, looked at the identification again, apologized, and ushered me to a private elevator.

I got off the elevator, relieved to find the meeting had not started. I was escorted to a chair on the side of the room and watched as a fleet of technical engineers scurried around inserting people from across the state into the meeting via video monitor. There were about thirty people seated around a large conference room table and lots of hovering staff members doting on the attendees.

Howard Milstein, the appointed head of the Thruway Authority, came in and sat down. He looked at me briefly and looked away. Howe had warned me that Milstein was a big personality who could be difficult but was one of the governor's biggest financial supporters, so I was to defer to his demands. When it came to the agenda item to transfer the land to Syracuse, Milstein looked around and asked if the mayor of Syracuse was present. I raised my hand and he apologized for not recognizing me.

I succinctly said the Thruway Authority had not been able to develop the land and I thought we could. Milstein looked at me and asked, "How much time do you want?" Without much thought, I said, "Two weeks more than you want to give me." Everyone in the meeting laughed. Saying he liked my style, he proposed two and half years, and I agreed. The motion passed unanimously.

Howe called later and told me I had charmed everyone, even the notoriously difficult Milstein. I told Howe the next step would be an open process to bid on the development so there could be no question of favoritism. "Absolutely," he said. "Aiello wouldn't want it any other way."

We put out a request for bids for the development of thirty-four acres of land, with the city keeping five acres of land for public use. I appointed a committee from a cross-section of the community to review the proposals.[8] When the deadline came for submissions, there were only three proposals, and COR's was "big, bold," and the most detailed, with sketches of a 150,000-square-foot satellite campus for the local community college; a three-story hotel, 432 apartments, and retail stores on the ground floor; and a marina and a community boathouse.[9] Not surprisingly, COR was the unanimous selection of the committee.

In the span of one month, COR had announced two large real estate redevelopment projects in the area, with the state being a major funder of both. Howe had orchestrated every move from behind the scenes. He had direct access to decision-makers in Albany, stayed out of public view, and got things done. He was the governor's guy.

## The Brotherhood

It was an accepted aphorism that the only way to become a "made guy"[10] with Andrew was service in Mario's administration. Later, I was to learn the

8. The committee included City Councilor Patrick Hogan, CenterState CEO President Robert Simpson, City Council President Van Robinson, Deputy Onondaga County Executive William Fisher, and the former president of the Greater Syracuse Chamber of Commerce, Darlene Kerr. Tim Knauss, "Panel Picks COR Development to Transform Syracuse's Inner Harbor," Syracuse.com, January 13, 2012, https://www.syracuse.com/news/2012/01/panel_recommends_cor_developme.html.

9. Knauss, "Panel picks COR Development to Transform Syracuse's Inner Harbor."

10. The Cuomo team, including Howe, used this term with me to describe themselves and others.

"made guys" referred to themselves as "the brotherhood."[11] Howe was first of the brotherhood who came to see me when I was mayor.

Howe was a "made guy" of the highest order: He had worked on Mario Cuomo's campaigns and for Andrew Cuomo at the Department of Housing and Urban Development. He had a game-show host look to him, was exceedingly polite, and gave me the impression he listened. Unlike other Cuomo confidants, he did not shout or scream. Instead, he would punctuate disagreements with an agreeable "I understand" and follow up with, "But you know how these guys are," communicating he just wanted to help you.

Howe knew who was important, who was on the list for an important job, and who was on the list of enemies. His information was always accurate. He told me Rochester mayor Robert Duffy would be selected as lieutenant governor and later alerted me Duffy would leave at the end of the governor's first term. He could get things done; he once represented, secured, and delivered the transfer of $2.5 million in state funding between two competing developers.[12] He was the preeminent Cuomo administration whisperer, fixer, and influence peddler.

Much to my surprise, his key client in Syracuse was my family friend Steve Aiello and his company, COR Development. Aiello was from the same neighborhood as my mother's family, and the Aiellos and my great-aunts and great-uncle were all longtime members of St. John the Baptist Church, a tie that binds in Syracuse. His father had installed the flooring in my great-aunt's house and, according to her, teased he would have married her if he had not married Aiello's mother.

Aiello was something of a gentle giant. He was physically imposing but understated with an "aw shucks" demeanor and a sly smile. Separately, Aiello was close with Jack and his sons. Those personal friendships crossed into professional relationships. Terry Mannion, Jack's second son, served as the outside attorney for many of COR Development's legal transactions, and Kerry Mannion, Jack's youngest son, was a real estate broker who operated under the name of COR Real Estate.

11. Shane Goldmacher, "How Albany Really Works: Cuomo Loyalist Exposes Pay-to-Play Culture," *New York Times*, February 16, 2018.

12. Tim Knauss, "Embattled Lobbyist Involved As $2.5 Million State Grant Takes Odd Path to Syracuse Building," Syracuse.com, May 13, 2016, https://www.syracuse.com/ne ws/2016/05/embattled_lobbyist_involved_as_25m_state_grant_takes_odd_path_to_sy racuse_buildi.html.

COR had developed about five million square feet of commercial real estate projects across upstate New York. While Aiello contributed to my campaigns, I thought of him as a generous family friend. He never discussed any interest in public work. During my mayoral campaign, one of my opponents sent out a negative mailer accusing Aiello of contributing to me to garner work. Aiello was hurt by the accusations and made it clear to me he wanted nothing to do with politics and government. A year later, COR hired Howe and it became apparent something had changed.

## The Enforcer

Howe's clout emanated directly from a guy he had hired and someone I had become acquainted with at the beginning of my political career: Joseph Percoco. Howe hired Percoco for his first job on Mario Cuomo's campaign.[13] Howe would call him "Joseph" when he needed Percoco to understand something was a serious matter. They were like brothers and spoke to each other every day.

After Mario lost, Percoco joined Howe working for Andrew at the Department of Housing and Urban Development. He was with Andrew Cuomo during the lowest period of his career—his humiliating withdrawal from the 2002 governor's race and subsequent divorce from Kerry Kennedy. Percoco set up the announcement when Cuomo dropped out and went fishing with Cuomo to start the healing process a few days later. He became part of the Cuomo family firmament.[14]

In his 2014 memoir, Cuomo praised Percoco as "the total package: trained as a lawyer, he had the guts, brains, and stick-to-itiveness necessary to attack any project—hard." During the "worst of times," Cuomo wrote that Percoco "could make us laugh."[15] During his eulogy at Mario's funeral, Andrew referred to Percoco as "my father's third son, who I sometimes think he loved the most."[16]

13. See chapter 1.

14. Tom Precious, "As Innermost Advisor to Cuomo Since '90s, Joe Percoco Was Family's 'Third Son,'" *Buffalo News*, September 28, 2016.

15. Andrew M. Cuomo, *All Things Possible: Setbacks and Success in Politics and Life* (New York: HarperCollins, 2014), 147.

16. NYS Executive Chamber, "Governor Andrew Cuomo Gives Eulogy at Mario Cuomo's Funeral," YouTube, January 6, 2013, https://www.youtube.com/watch?v=85j2ii7tSoQ.

Percoco and his wife and daughters lived in the well-appointed Westchester enclave of South Salem, about fifteen miles from the house Cuomo shared with his girlfriend, the TV cooking-show host and author Sandra Lee. Cuomo was known to ride his motorcycle over to the Percoco house,[17] and Percoco was said to be the first and last person Cuomo spoke to every day. He was Cuomo's all-purpose troubleshooter, alter ego, and enforcer. His relationship with Cuomo, his bark, and his forceful manner made him the second-most-feared man in state government.

Yet Percoco and I had snapped at each other for a lot of years, and I wasn't afraid of him. We had both gotten older since we first met and, hopefully, wiser. He did yell at me, but he always seemed to respect that I was elected in my own right. He always addressed me as "madam mayor," even when he was furious with me. He always called personally to address disagreements and was often self-deprecating about our most recent blowup.

## The Darling

Percoco had orchestrated Joanie Mahoney's surprising endorsement of Cuomo in 2010. Mahoney, a Republican, told me Percoco was charmingly relentless in his pursuit of her support for Cuomo, and it was easy to understand why he had been so dogged. Mahoney had an ever-present smile and sunny disposition. Along with these God-given attributes, she inherited significant name recognition as the daughter of a well-known local politician.

She shocked both the Republican and Democratic Party establishments by endorsing Cuomo in 2010. It was an unusual and highly risky endorsement that was beneficial to the Cuomo candidacy. The governor seemed forever grateful for her actions. In every appearance he made in the region, he extolled her leadership.[18] Mahoney became a trusted and influential member of Cuomo's orbit.

---

17. Julie McMahon, "NY Corruption Trial Spotlights Bond Between Cuomo and Defendant Percoco," Syracuse.com, February 2, 2018, https://www.syracuse.com/state/20 18/02/ny_corruption_trial_highlights_bond_between_cuomo_and_defendant_perco co.html.

18. Mahoney took a state job created for her at a salary of $275,00.00. Tim Knauss, "Onondaga County Executive Joanie Mahoney Steps Down Midterm," Syracuse.com, September 24, 2018, https://www.syracuse.com/news/2018/09/onondaga_county_exec _joanie_mahoney_announces_early_retirement.html.

Having served with her on the city council, I knew Mahoney's strengths, and after an initially bumpy start, our relationship was collegial. I attributed Mahoney's convivial attitude with state leaders to the fact she did not have the same existential challenges I had as mayor. She did not have the pension bill crisis, the aging infrastructure, or the climbing poverty rates. Given the needs of my constituents, I had no choice but to be a relentless, vocal advocate. I simply did not have room for error, because many of my constituents lived on the precipice. Good government programs were often the only way to withstand the brutal effects of poverty. Many of my constituents were always at risk of sliding further into oblivion, and this reality didn't engender an air of sunny optimism.

I was also naturally brooding and analytical, and some found that challenging. Many civic leaders told me my demeanor was problematic—they expected me to be the region's prime cheerleader because I was the mayor. I did not see the role that way. I thought my job was to advocate for an idea if it had merit, not just because I was asked to. I was deliberately exacting, because my constituents trusted me to make sure they were well-served in a political environment that had chronically failed to do that.

Mahoney's advocacy was the opposite: it was unreflective and easily given. I was told countless times by people lobbying me that all they had to do was ask Mahoney for support and she would provide it. I would acknowledge their point but continue to ask the tough questions. While Mahoney and I had distinct dispositions and styles, we had been able to successfully work together because we respected each other—or so I thought.

Mahoney's unswerving loyalty to the governor paid off when he appointed her to serve on the Moreland Commission, which was formed to "crack down" on public corruption in the state.[19] Appointing her meant the governor had complete confidence in her fealty. The commission's objective to expose political corruption ensured it was a major focus of the state's political world.

Months into the work, Mahoney appeared on a statewide political talk show and was asked if the commission intended to investigate those who had appointed the members—namely, the governor or the attorney general—for political corruption. She responded, "I think we're making a mockery of this whole process if we try to pretend that a group of us that's

19. Jimmy Vielkind, "Bold Move to Unearth Political Corruption," *Times Union*, July 3, 2013.

been appointed by the attorney general and the governor is investigating the attorney general or the governor. . . . So, I never subscribed to that notion to start with, and there has been no conversations."[20] Mahoney's comment was immediately interpreted as an extraordinary admission. Cuomo's critics attacked her, the attorney general immediately distanced himself from her, and the commentariat lashed out at her political stupidity.

I called Mahoney in the aftermath of her Moreland comments. After my *New York Times* op-ed, I knew what it felt like to be politically ostracized. She told me it had been awful, and the governor told her she had done real damage. As we wrapped up, we discussed my recent reelection, and she thanked me for my call.

Two weeks later, she breezily told me about the pending stadium announcement.

## The Doctor

Another key player in the economic development process was Dr. Alain Kaloyeros, the head of SUNY Polytechnic. I knew him by reputation only. He was said to be brilliant, and if you doubted it, he would tell you. He had spearheaded the development of SUNY Polytechnic, which was also known as the nanotechnology school. He had attracted millions of dollars of outside investment and oversaw more than $14 billion in campuses, labs, and scientific clean rooms across the state. Known as both "Dr. K" and "Dr. Nano," he was the state's highest-paid employee, with an annual salary of $800,000. He sported a trendy three-day beard growth, dressed in couture T-shirts and expensive jeans, drove a Ferrari Spider with a "Dr. Nano" license plate, and posted pictures of scantily clad women reclining on sports cars.

He had gotten his start in government under Mario Cuomo and, as such, was seen as a "made guy." Kaloyeros had quietly hired Howe[21] to represent

20. Associated Press, "Onondaga County Exec Joanie Mahoney Says Moreland Commission Won't Investigate Cuomo," Syracuse.com, December 3, 2013, https://www.syracuse.com/news/2013/12/onondaga_county_exec_joanie_mahoney_says_moreland _commission_wont_investigate_cu.html.

21. Julie McMahon, "Dr. K Hired Lobbyist Todd Howe's Firm to Work for SUNY Poly for $25K a Month," Syracuse.com, June 20, 2018, https://www.syracuse.com/state/2018 /06/dr_k_hired_lobbyist_todd_howes_firm_to_work_for_suny_poly_for_25k_a_mon th.html.

his interests with Andrew Cuomo, who had described Kaloyeros as "a visionary in the field of nanotechnology" and "probably the single greatest economic development mind New York state has." Cuomo promised that vision would be "transformative."

COR's highly publicized projects were a complete departure from Aiello's normal operating process. He had always expressed an aversion to politics and was not an active campaign donor. That changed when, unbeknownst to me, Howe counseled Aiello to be "strategic about who you support and who you reward." COR's strategy, Howe said, should be to maximize the benefits received from campaign contributions.[22]

Howe put the strategy into place and identified Cuomo as a "growth area." Inviting COR officials to a Cuomo fundraiser in New York City in April 2011, Howe told them he thought the governor would be receptive to developing a relationship because Syracuse had been identified as a target of economic-development projects. When Howe learned a COR official was a Corvette afficionado, he accurately predicted Cuomo would be thrilled to talk to him about the muscle car. Aiello later proposed a small invitation-only fundraiser in the executive's Corvette garage. The invitation list included COR executives, Howe, Mahoney, Tom Young, and Eimicke. The fundraiser amassed $125,000 for Cuomo, and Howe advised Aiello to split the money over five of his thirty-five corporate entities, specifically ones that did not include the name "COR," to avoid media scrutiny.[23]

Despite the effort to obscure its contributions, COR was recognized as one of the governor's biggest upstate campaign donors. Aiello's change was startling to me. In the beginning, he confided in me that he was not used to politics: how people spoke to each other, the threats, and the complicated web of alliances and enemies. Our conversations had stopped, and Howe became the one to tell me what Aiello wanted or was thinking. Howe repeatedly said they were thrilled with the work they were getting done in Albany and spun it as being "great for the community."

It was concerning, but Aiello was my friend, and I knew him to be a good person. If he and Howe were succeeding, I told myself it would be

22. Julie McMahon, "Facetime, Donation, and Corvettes: Todd Howe Reveals How Syracuse Developer Wooed Cuomo," Syracuse.com, February 6, 2018, https://www.syracuse.com/state/2018/02/facetime_donations_and_corvettes_todd_howe_reveals_how_syracuse_developer_wooed.html.

23. McMahon, "Facetime, Donation, and Corvettes."

good for Syracuse, because the Kennedy Square and Inner Harbor developments would create two new vibrant neighborhoods.

## Kiss of a Bully

In spring 2013, when Cuomo was scheduled to travel across the state announcing economic development programs, Howe called and asked me to attend an event in Syracuse where the governor would unveil a program for forgiving all state taxes if a business located to New York. The event would be the first time the governor and I had been together since my *New York Times* op-ed appeared.[24] Howe told me the governor wanted to put our disagreement behind us. I thought my presence would demonstrate the disagreement was based on policy, and I agreed to attend.

On the day of the announcement, I arrived at the SUNY Upstate Medical University campus and was ushered into a room with other dignitaries. As we waited for the event to begin, Robert Simpson, the head of a preeminent business advocacy organization called CenterState CEO, entered the room saying he had just learned the details of the announcement. Cuomo was going to announce a program called Start-Up New York that would allow businesses moving near a state college campus to pay no taxes for ten years. I corrected him and said, "No state taxes." No, he said, the program is absolutely no taxes—no property taxes, no corporate taxes, no sales taxes, and no income taxes. While no one in the room knew the program would be so sweeping, I was the only one who depended on property and sales tax to pay for key services like police, fire, snow, and trash removal.

I had been sandbagged. The Cuomo administration wanted to use my presence as evidence of support for the flawed program. The Start-Up program was a rehash of the state's disastrous Empire Zone program, which had doled out a panoply of tax incentives for commitments to create or retain jobs in the state.[25] The program, initially celebrated as transformative and a once-in-a-lifetime opportunity, was eventually revealed to be an epic disaster that gave away billions in tax benefits and failed to create economic

24. See chapter 4.

25. John O'Brien, "Inside Planning Destiny USA: It Was All About the 'Golden Cow' of Tax Breaks," Syracuse.com, July 1, 2012, https://www.syracuse.com/news/2012/07/inside_planning_destiny_usa_it.html.

growth.[26] It was the shallowest of pandering. Cuomo's message was that upstate's economy had suffered because taxes were too high. Just erase taxes and we'd magically have a better economy. Except it did not work, ever. It was a fiasco if one cared about public policy, but it was intoxicating if one just cared about optics. Andrew Cuomo was clearly in the latter category.

As we proceeded into the room, I was escorted to a front-row seat to ensure that everyone saw I was present. Like a superhero, the governor took the stage and said he was promising business would be tax-free. "I mean tax-free," he said. "That's why I said tax-free." Cuomo described the program as "big" and "bold," saying it was "directed primarily to upstate New York . . . because that's where we have an economic problem."[27]

I seethed. At the end of the event, the governor's staff grabbed me and ushered me to the receiving line, ensuring the media could see the governor greet me, thus confirming my support of the program. I was being manipulated but had no real choice. If I refused, it would cement me as someone who could not work with the most powerful elected official in the state. I felt like a trapped animal, and I knew my face gave away exactly how I was feeling. I looked up the line and saw Joanie Mahoney beam and the governor greet her with a kiss. As if things could not get worse, I thought, what if he tries to kiss me?

When Cuomo got to me, he grabbed my hand and, with a big smile on his face, leaned in to kiss me. I instinctively leaned out, feeling myself flush red, and murmured a hello while the cameras snapped. Given that he was about six feet tall, and I was five three, he was able to easily envelop me. I told Jack that I must have looked terrible when the photographer captured the scene. Later Jack took one look at the photo and said, "You were right. You look awful."

To be clear, I was furious about the manipulation and the illusory economic-development promises, not the kiss. It wasn't the last time Cuomo would kiss me. When he came to Syracuse to deliver his State of the

26. Citizens Budget Commission, "It's Time to End New York State's Empire Zone Program," December 12, 2008; Tim Knauss, "Empire Zones, NY's Failed Aid to Companies, Still Costing Taxpayers: $3 Billion Plus," Syracuse.com, August 9, 2017, https://www.syracuse.com/state/2017/08/empire_zones_nys_failed_aid_to_companies_keep_costing_taxpayers_3_billion_plus.html.

27. Teri Weaver and Michelle Bridenbach, "Gov. Andrew Cuomo to Businesses: Yes, I Said Tax Free," Syracuse.com, May 23, 2013, https://www.syracuse.com/news/2013/05/gov_andrew_cuomo_to_businesses.html.

State address in 2017, I was given a prominent seat. I wondered why until after the speech, as I watched him make his way down the row where I was seated. As his cameraman furiously clicked away, Cuomo greeted everyone with a hug or a kiss. I was in the middle of the row with multiple people on either side of me. There was no escape. When he got to me, he surrounded me and kissed me.

Several people commented that the governor now clearly "liked" me because he had kissed me, which was surely his intention. I assumed he did it because he knew I was popular, and he wanted to show people we had a relationship as he prepared for reelection. Did I want that? No. Was it clear from my body language, my facial expression, and everything he knew about me I did not want that? Yes, which is why he did it: to show his political dominance.

As a female politician, I was routinely referred to using various terms of endearment and greeted with a kiss by men (and women). Some of the men were creeps, and some of them were dears. Somehow, I'm usually able to distinguish between the two. Most women I've talked to about it have the same sense. Maybe it's an anachronism to call it female intuition, but there were men who routinely kissed me, and I was charmed by it. With others, I turned my head. I did not want to give up the former because of the latter. I had the agency to manage it. Many women do not.

With Andrew Cuomo, his kissing me was about power. I never viewed it as sexual. We were gladiators in a public ring and that's how he showed he was boss. I did not find it any more objectionable than the other ways he bullied me. It was part of the rules of engagement as a politician. I chose to be in the arena, and his kisses were the least of his control tactics.

## A Peek at the Truth

On October 19, 2013, I took a break from my reelection campaign to attend my mother's induction into the American Academy of Nursing in Washington, DC. I had been there for less than twenty-four hours and was rushing around a hotel room getting ready for an event when Howe called and said he needed to speak to me. Pressed for time, I put him on speakerphone while I multitasked.

After some pleasantries, he asked if I had seen an email he sent to my private account a couple of days earlier. I had and the email was a series of forwarded emails from other people about a "nano RFP." It was so random, I wondered if he had sent it to me accidently.

Giving him a quick, "Yeah," Howe proceeded to tell me the "nano project" would be great for Syracuse if Aiello got it. The "nano project" referred to a request for proposals from the state to build a nanotechnology facility, which would manufacture items at an extremely small scale. Cuomo had made the creation of nanotechnology hubs across upstate a cornerstone of his economic-development policy. The selected proposal would be extremely lucrative to the winning developer.

I felt like Howe was dropping me into the middle of a conversation in which I'd never been included. He talked a bit more about how the project would transform the area and then casually remarked how terrible it would be if the "Pyramid guys" got the work. After asking me if I thought any other major developers would bid on the nano work, I took the phone off speaker and put it to my ear.

I told Howe Pyramid had their hands full, but others might be interested. When I mentioned a couple of names, Howe dismissed them by saying they were not liked by the governor. In any event, he continued, the advertisement had been so buried it would likely be missed by everyone, and he chuckled about the convoluted process to get a legal notice published in the Syracuse newspaper. As he spoke, I had a sick feeling and wondered if every building project had similar origins.

Hours later in the airport, I juggled my coffee and iPhone and carefully reread Howe's email. On October 3, 2013, at 4:51 a.m. Howe sent an email to Steve Aiello, Joseph Gerardi, and Jeff Aiello, all principals of COR Development. The email said, "According to dr k the rfp should be printed in the hard copy of the syr paper today. Let me know. It took a few days because u understand the paper isn't printed each day . . . make sense?" The "dr. k" was obviously Kaloyeros and SUNY Polytechnic Institute was the arm of the state bureaucracy responsible for the nanotechnology request for proposal.

Just over three hours after Howe sent the email, Gerardi, COR's legal counsel, confirmed the advertisement was in the paper, attached a copy of it to the email, and said he would respond. The email attachment showed an advertisement buried in the classifieds. It started with the heading "LEGAL NOTICE" and continued in a long column of text with font smaller than the advertisements for lost pets appearing next to it. It was so inconspicuous that someone, I assumed Gerardi, had it circled with a wide tip pen to ensure the reader saw it. The email chain ended with Howe sending it to me saying, "this is the NANO rfp, which is expected to be turned around quickly."

As I waited for my flight back to Syracuse, I understood Howe was getting valuable inside information about a lucrative contract and, with COR's participation, was attempting to rig a multimillion-dollar state contract.

When I shared the information with Jack, he was crestfallen. Aiello, he said, had become "intoxicated" with being welcomed into the Cuomo world. "He's not used to guys like that or that world," he said. We both knew that world offered the illusion of being an insider, with all the power and access that came with that. The price of admission was ongoing campaign contributions, and the rewards were seemingly endless.

Aiello's deceit with the stadium and what I surmised after reading the nano RFP email was hard to process. We were friends, our families were friends, and we had been for a long time. I always assumed I would have the same friends when I entered the mayor's office as when I left office. I was painfully wrong.

While I was uncomfortable, there was simply nothing I could do to change the dynamic. I was used to developers manipulating the levers of power. Even if I thought there had been something illegal going on, which I did not, there was no one to report it to.[28] More to the point, I had no evidence anything illegal was underway, just an educated suspicion and a dodgy email.

Later, I realized Aiello was in too deep when I learned he had attended Mario Cuomo's wake, despite not having known the former governor. Aiello was told he was part of the Cuomo family by Howe and Percoco. They ensured he had exclusive access to the event, mingling with the family and friends, while other mourners waited in line outside by the hundreds.

The guy I knew, raised in St. John the Baptist, would never have violated such a solemn occasion for someone he did not know. Howe and Percoco had convinced Aiello he was family so his money would keep flowing, even when it involved a sacred event. It seemed to me Aiello abandoned his Syracuse values and accepted a cloak of political power in exchange.

28. The Onondaga County district attorney and the state attorney general had both been leaders in the Moreland Commission, which became mired in controversy. Susanne Craig, William K. Rashbaum, and Thomas Kaplan, "Cuomo's Office Hobbled Ethic Inquiries by Moreland Commission," *New York Times*, July 23, 2014.

While I did harbor a small hope Aiello would reach out and say he had made a big mistake getting involved with the Albany world and was sorry, it was not to be. I'll never be sure exactly what happened. Was it the allure of millions of dollars for the taking? Was it a slow and steady number of compromises until it was too late, or was it, as Jack said, intoxication? I would come to peace with my lack of answers. I don't know if Aiello ever did.

## Hollywood Comes to Onondaga?

The demise of the stadium project momentarily quelled the governor's appetite for transformational economic-development announcements, but by March 2014, the rumor mill was churning with stories about other potential projects. On the day of the county executive's annual State of the County address, news broke that the governor was going to attend the event to unveil something big.

Hours before the event, Howe called and told me a film company with which Kaloyeros had connections was going to locate to the Syracuse suburbs as part of the state's nanotech development program. The project would be built by COR in its suburban industrial park, because the area was "shovel ready." It went without saying that while Kennedy Square was shovel ready, too, the governor would not allow an important development project in my jurisdiction.

It was clear Howe was assigned to ensure I didn't rain on the governor's parade. By this time, I no longer had enough fire in my belly to do so. I had questioned public policy on pensions, infrastructure, and the stadium, and, in return, I'd been brutalized.

When I arrived at the venue, which was within view of city hall, I learned the governor's staff, always trying to ensure only Cuomo's friends felt the warmth of his power, had violated the rules of protocol by burying me in the middle of a section and off to the side so it would be hard to see me. The front-row seats were for the governor, the county executive, Aiello, Kaloyeros, and a film executive. When Howe talked to me about the nano RFP five months earlier, which now felt like a lifetime ago, he exhorted me how good a nanotechnology facility would be for the region. Here was the evidence their scheming had paid off.

When everyone took their seats, the lights dimmed, and an announcer asked the audience to welcome the governor of the State of New York,

Andrew Cuomo, and the Onondaga County executive, Joanie Mahoney. They emerged from behind a blue curtain, looking like a reality show couple, beaming and waving as they took their seats. They were surrounded by Aiello, Kaloyeros, and another guy I assumed to be the film executive.

Aiello looked uncomfortable with the attention but obviously not enough that he avoided it. Kaloyeros looked small next to Aiello, but his demeanor was one of bored disapproval. The other guy was slick-looking enough that I guessed he was the film guy—rumor had it he portrayed the "green Power Ranger" in a series of forgettable films. Howe was nowhere to be seen, but I knew he was there watching his work come together.

Mahoney took the podium, clearly bursting with excitement. She rushed through her State of the County remarks as though they were secondary, before getting to the true purpose of the event. "In our business in politics, we're here for just a minute and sometimes we make decisions that are short-term for instant gratification, because we need to see the results before the next election day," she said. No truer words will be spoken tonight, I thought. She continued, "But occasionally there are decisions that are made that are in the best long-term interest of the people that are being served." Kaloyeros did this, she said, by creating economic rewards with the Buffalo Billion, part of the governor's much ballyhooed announcement to invest $1 billion in Buffalo, and now it was Onondaga County's "turn." As she spoke, I thought, my God, she believes this is good policy.

Following Mahoney's paean, Kaloyeros came to the podium, opening with the obligatory praise of the governor's leadership. "As you know, Governor Andrew Cuomo has created a successful and effective formula . . . establishing New York as a world leader in the 21st century innovation economy." *Nope*, I thought, *people do not know that*. He continued that he was "honored and privileged to announce a public-private partnership to establish the Central New York Emerging Nano Industries Hub with the first tenant being 'the Film House.'" The Film House would spend $150 million in private money over seven years, create 350 high-tech jobs, and include a film school utilizing nanotechnology.

He finished with an attempted rhetorical flourish, subtle as a sledgehammer, but delivered in a flat monotone. "In language that I'm sure all of you Orange fans will appreciate, this announcement is the equivalent of putting Derrick Coleman, John Wallace, Carmelo Anthony, and Gerry McNamara all on the same team . . . but instead of Boeheim, we have Coach Cuomo."

The head of the Film House, Ryan Johnson then took the podium and said he was a "producer of a bunch of movies over the last couple decades." He and his partner were "expanding" and looking to "drop anchor in a place where we could grow and build a labor force and an infrastructure that would support going somewhere." He, too, paid homage to the governor. "Governor Cuomo has transformed New York into a business-friendly destination, especially for the film and TV industry," he said. Johnson finished by looking down and reading his talking points, which was strange for someone in the entertainment field. Then it was time for the main event.

Everyone in the audience, including me (much to my chagrin), stood and applauded. The governor took the stage and said, "It is great to be in Onondaga." With his Queens accent, he butchered the pronunciation of Onondaga, but his point was clear: he would not say Syracuse. He showered praise on the county executive and riffed on the genius of Kaloyeros. He misstated data regarding Syracuse city government and said he was done having the state subsidize insolvent governments. The message was obvious: he had brought this amazing gift to the people of the community, and if I had played by Cuomo's rules, I could bask in the glory of the moment, but I had not, so I would be punished publicly.

I listened half-heartedly and snapped back to attention just as the governor said, "Hollywood comes to Onondaga. Who would've ever guessed?" No one, I thought. No one thinks Hollywood or the film industry is going to come to central New York and rescue our economy. No one. The governor continued that this gift was made possible by putting the "Start-Up Zone together with the film tax credit, a powerful one-two and it can really start an entire cluster economy, and that is exactly what you're seeing here." It was a cluster all right.

When I left the film hub announcement, I happened to walk out behind Robert Simpson, the head of CenterState CEO, and James Fayle, the regional director of the state's regional economic development office. Simpson, who was clearly frustrated, sarcastically said how glad he was that the business community had put so much thought, time, and effort into the idea of locating a nanotechnology near the Lockheed Martin[29] radar facility,

29. Lockheed Martin, a large employer in the region, had a business operation focused on technology. Mark Weiner, "After layoffs, Lockheed Martin Sees Robust Future in CNY," Syracuse.com, August 8, 2013, https://www.syracuse.com/news/2013/08/leaner _lockheed_martin_corp_still_sees_robust_future_in_central_new_york.html.

only to have the nanotechnology facility become a film hub. Fayle, who had seemingly been part of the Lockheed Martin discussions, shrugged and bemusedly agreed.

Shortly after that event, the governor announced that Soraa, a LED lightbulb manufacturer, was relocating its global operations to a building next to the film hub. The move would create 420 new high-tech jobs, which was possible thanks to $90 million in state investment for the facility's construction. Soraa would lease the factory for $1 a month for ten years and, of course, the project would be developed by COR.

The insiders and the media were beside themselves with glee and anticipation. Simpson became a fervent public backer of the film hub, Soraa, and the governor's economic-development process. Simpson's organization received significant funds from the state, and if he disagreed with the governor, he risked having those funds—almost half a million dollars—taken away as punishment.[30] It was widely understood that any entity in line for state funding would not question any of the governor's policies for fear of retribution. No one doubted the governor's ability to punish dissent.

The area's elected officials remained supportive of the initiatives. With some officials, like Mahoney, it was not clear whether they thought the policy was good or if they just wanted to go along to get along. Other civic leaders told me to stay quiet because my dissent threatened resources for Syracuse. It seemed implausible that we would become by fiat a "Hub for Emerging Nano Industries." That these multimillion-dollar state contracts were going to the governor's highest campaign contributor in the region was so obviously ethically, if not legally, corrupt, it was almost painful.

The local media's coverage of all this was particularly superficial. If the local media had investigated, they likely would have found that Johnson, the film producer, had a history of legal and financial issues, including two judgments against him for fraud and breach of contract, for which he owed at least $1.6 million. Another suit, involving nonpayment of film crew workers, found him liable for $100,000. The company's Los Angeles address

30. Office of the State Comptroller, Open Book New York, 2013, 2014, 2015, 2016, 2017.
2013 = $291,527.40
2014 = $411,214.16
2015 = $473,389.26
2016 = $635,410.88
2017 = $736,386.00

was actually the address of a Sephora in a strip mall in Marina del Rey, California.

Instead of investigating or questioning the economic-development announcements, the community's institutions and leaders stood in line to receive their state monies and told the public the Cuomo administration was delivering on its promise of transforming the region's economy.

## "All That Most Maddens and Torments"

As we worked on our own economic-development projects,[31] COR and my administration were in near-daily contact pushing through the bureaucratic red tape necessary to get the Inner Harbor project off the ground. By design, Aiello and I spoke even less frequently after the film hub announcement, but the Inner Harbor project moved forward.

COR announced the Aloft Hotel would be built as part of the first phase of the development, and Aiello proclaimed he would not seek any special tax breaks to build the hotel. It was evidence he was following through on the commitments he made to have his developments pay taxes. It also was a confirmation of something Aiello had said to me on December 26, 2013, at our meeting about the stadium.

After apologizing about the stadium proposal, Aiello told me he was going to finance the Inner Harbor project without a special tax agreement known as Payment in Lieu of Taxes (PILOT).[32] I was intrigued, because

31. We modernized the Syracuse Airport, allowing it to become competitive; spurred the transformation of downtown into a popular mixed use of residential and retail development; and oversaw the renovation of the Hotel Syracuse, Syracuse's oldest and grandest hotel. Syracuse Regional Airport Authority (n.d.), 2016 Annual Report to the Community, Message from the Executive Director, 3, https://syrsraa.com/wp-content/uploads/2013/01/SRAA-Annual-Report-2016.pdf; CenterState CEO (n.d.), ReInvention Annual Report 2012–2013, 11, https://www.centerstateceo.com/sites/default/files/CenterState%20CEO%20Annual%20Report%202012-13.pdf; Editorial Board, "Rebirth of Former Hotel Syracuse Is a Touchstone Moment," Syracuse.com, August 26, 2016, https://www.syracuse.com/opinion/2016/08/rebirth_of_former_hotel_syracuse_is_a_touchstone_moment_editorial.html.

32. Local governments can reduce property taxes by entering into an agreement, known as a Payment in Lieu of Taxes (PILOT), with commercial property owners. The property owner agrees to make property improvements and, in return, gets a schedule of reduced payments to the government for a period of usually between ten and twenty years. The PILOT payments are lower than the taxes on the property would be. In practice, shrewd

I was looking for a financing model that avoided the unequal bargaining power between shrewd developers and financially challenged cities like Syracuse. Traditional PILOTs, in my experience, abused the public's interests.

When I asked Aiello to explain what he meant, he said he could do the development without any additional incentives, only what he was entitled to under the law. It was in keeping with what he had committed to do for Kennedy Square, which had been part of the public announcement. I told him it would be a groundbreaking change in how these development projects typically played out. He laughed and told me he thought I'd like it.

By fall 2015, Syracuse was set to sell the final parcels of Inner Harbor land to COR for the development, as well as finalize commitments to give COR $1.5 million to build roads and other infrastructure on the site. These final steps prompted a public debate over what requirements COR should have to fulfill to be able to develop public land. Several community activists forcefully argued COR should commit to training and hiring marginalized city residents.

There was room for compromise on commitments, but we had to manage the situation carefully because COR could bypass Syracuse by going to Onondaga County for a tax agreement without any commitments. Developers typically came to the Syracuse industrial development agency for assistance with projects within the city's borders and had gone to the county's agency, the Onondaga County industrial development agency, for projects outside the city. Yet, the county's industrial development agency was authorized to assist development projects anywhere in the county, including Syracuse's Inner Harbor.

Thirteen days after we transferred the last of the land to COR, my economic development director walked into my office with a sickly gray pallor. "Mayor," he said, "I just got a call from COR saying they are going to go to the county for the Inner Harbor." COR had effectively cut out the city from a role in the development and rid itself of any substantive obligation to hire city residents. The director was told I had received a call from Terry Mannion explaining everything. I had gotten no such call.

Once my staff left the office, I called Terry and asked him what was going on. He told me he had been instructed not to say anything to me. I knew as COR's attorney he had an ethical obligation to follow such directives. I

developers set the terms of the PILOT by telling the municipality they will not develop the property unless given lucrative tax breaks.

told him COR was telling people that he had called and spoken with me. It was such a profound betrayal I knew it was the end of my relationship with Aiello and I worried it might be the end of my relationship with Terry, too.

While I understood his ethical obligation, I loved Terry. Apart from my relationship with Jack, Terry was my friend. It was a painful betrayal. Terry was too smart not to know that. The last thing I said to him was, "Aiello's going to get in trouble. He's being too greedy." Terry answered, "I don't think so. He's done nothing wrong."

In a matter of days, COR secured a fifteen-year tax break worth approximately $45 million. Most of the taxes waived were owed to the Syracuse City School District and city government. It was all accomplished in record time and with an astonishing repudiation of the public—refusing to let city residents speak at meetings where the tax agreement was discussed; refusing, contrary to law, to release the details of the tax agreement; and illustrating an overall contempt for engaging with the public.

The day before the county voted to confer the tax breaks, I got a phone call from a reporter telling me Aiello was holding a small, private fundraiser for the governor at Albany's private Fort Orange Club.[33] The reporter told me Mahoney, the governor, Percoco, and the secretary to the governor, Bill Mulrow, attended. The reporter asked me if I knew what was being discussed. While I demurred, I imagined Aiello and the attendees were luxuriating over their blunt political move of gaining control of the Inner Harbor land without having to pay taxes or hire underrepresented people while, as a bonus, punishing me.

The governor, while professing to fight for equity and justice, instituted an economic-development process giving lucrative projects to generous campaign donors who, in turn, refused to negotiate a commitment to ensure community benefits. As a show of fealty, COR knifed an enemy and threw an exclusive fundraiser for the governor that raised $25,000 from five COR associated entities.

It was maddening. The whole seamy transaction was the worst personal loss of my political career. I was devastated by Aiello's betrayal, and Jack was blindsided by its aftermath. He had always been able to help me put things in perspective and move forward, but with this he could not. I was too hurt and angry.

33. Jimmy Vielkind, "Cuomo Attended December Fundraiser with Embattled Lobbyist, Aide, and Developer," *Politico*, May 12, 2016.

While I was polite at family gatherings, I seethed with anger. I had worked so hard, only to be done in by the people closest to me. Jack was in the middle, with no one willing to talk to him about it, much less resolve it.

Over and over, Jack would say to me, "This is awful. You won't talk to Terry and Terry won't talk to me." I would feign professional distance and tell him Terry ethically could not talk about it, but it felt like a huge compromise on my part. I knew it was wrenching for Jack to watch his beloved family implode. He would repeat, "This is awful." And it was.

I felt completely victimized. In retrospect, I'm not sure what I could have done differently. Perhaps I could have required that COR sign a legal agreement formalizing the commitment. But when you enter a long partnership to develop a complicated project, it's not practical to ask the other partner to reduce every commitment to an enforceable legal document.

Most of all, though, I could never have imagined Aiello was capable of this kind of treachery and duplicity. I couldn't function if I cynically assumed that every friend I had could commit the most egregious betrayal, but only that level of distrust would have protected me in this situation.

The only recourse was to file a lawsuit against COR for reneging on its promise to not seek tax breaks for the project. I believed at the time, and still do, that there were emails and text messages setting forth a plan to defraud Syracuse by getting the land and then moving to the county for the tax benefits. In COR's response to our suit, Aiello acknowledged he told the city council COR was not seeking a PILOT agreement "at that time." However, he said he told the council at the same meeting that COR might request a tax deal for "certain portions of the project in the future." As for my statements about COR's commitment not to seek special tax breaks, Aiello said I was lying.

My staff drafted a letter to the editor about COR's refusal to commit to hiring minorities. Bruce Connor, a member of my kitchen cabinet, went to several ministers and asked them to sign the letter. When they did, it was sent to the newspaper.

The letter appeared during the lawsuit and the Onondaga County district attorney, William Fitzpatrick, opened an investigation into it.[34] We had drafted the letter to the editor, but it was standard practice to do so.

34. Tim Knauss, "Misleading Letter to Editor Was 'Smear Campaign' not Free Speech," Syracuse.com, June 2, 2016, https://www.syracuse.com/news/2016/06/prosecutors_say _letter_to_editor_was_smear_campaign_not_free_speech.html.

Fitzpatrick investigated saying the letter was part of a "nefarious" effort by my administration to manipulate public opinion to win our lawsuit against COR.[35] It seemed to be the worst type of prosecutorial abuse, but the district attorney had a history of defending developers.[36] He'd also recently received $2,500 in contributions from COR.[37]

Within weeks after announcing the investigation, we were told by a trustworthy third party that if we withdrew the lawsuit against COR, the investigation against the letter to the editor and Connor would go away. We refused, and Connor was charged with a misdemeanor accusing him of sending a bogus letter to the editor. Connor spent thousands of dollars on a private attorney to represent him and the case was thrown out of court with a scathing opinion by the judge.[38]

When the court dismissed our lawsuit against COR, Fitzpatrick launched a separate investigation into my dealings with the company. It was the second time the district attorney had investigated me because of my opposition to a prominent developer. Admitting he was acting at the behest of COR, he said he was looking into an "orchestrated effort" by me and my allies to spread lies in support of a city lawsuit against COR.[39] Amid this investigation, COR donated $1,360 to the district attorney.

As a result of the investigation, multiple city hall officials were forced to hire lawyers and spend months feeling pressured and intimidated by the district attorney's office. A judge who blocked one of Fitzpatrick's subpoena requests called the foray a "fishing expedition." While grand jury proceedings are supposed to be secret, the media frequently asked me to comment on information taken straight from the proceedings. I refused, but I assumed they got the information from the district attorney's office.

35. Tim Knauss, "Judge Throws Out Criminal Charge in Letter to the Editor Case as 'Serious Injustice,'" Syracuse.com, July 6, 2016, https://www.syracuse.com/news/2016/07/judge_throws_out_criminal_charge_in_politically_tinged_letter-to-editor_case.html.

36. Rick Moriarty and Tim Knauss, "Tax Free from the Start: Destiny Dictated the Deal," Syracuse.com, January 10, 2012, https://www.syracuse.com/news/2012/06/destiny_dictated_deal.html.

37. Williams Fitzpatrick's Board of Elections Fundraising Filing, July 2015.

38. Knauss, "Judge Throws Out Criminal Charge in Letter to the Editor Case as 'Serious Injustice.'"

39. Tim Knauss, "Two COR Executives Charged in Federal Probe of Cuomo Development Projects," Syracuse.com, September 22, 2016.

While we continued to fight the DA's efforts, I knew I had already lost. My staff was collapsing under the pressure, and I was doing my best to keep a stiff upper lip, but I was beaten. The foundation of my personal life was buckling, with my husband and family torn apart by the events. Professionally, the truth of how economic-development policy worked in the state—rewarding campaign donors with state money to garner headlines for illusory transformative projects—tormented me.

One night, I was standing in our bedroom unconsciously squeezing my hand around the end of the bed frame. When Jack saw it, he told me I needed to let things go. In his words, "let some air out of the balloon." I wanted to. I told him that I'd been repeating words from a prayer I had memorized in childhood but seldom thought about as an adult: "Forgive those who trespass against you." I just could not do it. While I had once been a happy warrior, now I was consumed with rage that "cracks the sinews and cakes the brain."[40] Try as I might to take Jack's advice of letting things go, I failed.

At the end of April 2016, I was in Rhode Island to attend funeral services for Jack's niece, Maura, who had died suddenly. Maura's death was a blow to the heart of the family, particularly for her husband, daughters, and mother. I was at the wake when a news alert came over my phone saying federal investigators were looking into Percoco's role in the nanotech projects, and it looked like COR might be involved, too. Moments later, Cuomo publicly cut ties with Percoco. It was huge news, foretelling a major scandal.

My immediate thought was, "Happy birthday to me." I was desperate to leave the funeral home and start making calls to see what the Albany gossips were saying about this momentous political development. As I looked toward the exit, preparing my excuse to leave, I caught sight of Maura's daughters and became overwhelmed with disgust . . . at myself.

*Who have I become?* I thought as I watched them deal with this profound loss. How had I become so callous to suffering that I was willing to slide over it to engage in idle political speculation? What had become of me that the thought of the likely ruin of someone I had known my entire adult life, who had a wife and children, was a "birthday present"?

I put away my phone and sat in silence. I realized my anger toward the Cuomo administration, its goals, and its tactics had caused me to become

40. Herman Melville, *Moby Dick* (New York: Harper and Brothers, 1851), 247.

like them—win at any cost, stoop to conquer, luxuriate in the humiliation of the other side. That was never who I wanted to be.

I was not ready to forgive Percoco or the others, but I started to see the whole thing as more than a political loss; it was a human one, too. It certainly was not the end of my feeling of animosity, but it was the start of "letting some air out of the balloon."

## "All Truth with Malice in It"

During the third week of September 2016, I had spent the night at my cousin Kate's house in Long Island. I had several events scheduled in New York City, including a discussion with a *New York Times* reporter about infrastructure. Kate and I packed onto the Long Island Railroad train into Manhattan and parted at a mobbed and smelly Penn Station. As I walked up the subterranean stairs onto the sidewalk, my phone started vibrating ceaselessly.

When I answered, my press secretary breathlessly told me Aiello, Gerardi, and several Buffalo Billion developers had been woken up that morning by federal government investigators and taken into federal custody.[41] Preet Bharara, the former US attorney for the Southern District of New York, was scheduled to announce a blockbuster federal indictment later that afternoon.

At his press conference, Bharara said the complaint against Percoco, Aiello, Kaloyeros, and others "shines a light on yet another sordid side of the 'show me the money' culture that has so plagued government in Albany." In each case, "the bids were rigged, and the results were preordained. Companies got rich and the public got bamboozled." Over a rushed cup of coffee, the *Times* reporter acknowledged the news was such a bombshell, he didn't have the time to discuss infrastructure. It was another way corruption robs public policy.

The accusations formed a compelling narrative of three trusted counselors to the governor conspiring to help favored contractors by rigging bids worth millions of dollars and doling out favorable treatment. Within twenty-four hours of the arrests, William Fitzpatrick had a hastily composed

41. Tim Knauss, "Two COR Executives Charged in Federal Probe of Cuomo Development Projects," Syracuse.com, September 22, 2016, https://www.syracuse.com/news/2016/09/two_cor_executives_charged_in_federal_probe_of_cuomo_development_projects.html.

letter, as evidenced by the typos and grammatical errors, delivered to me at city hall, informing me he was terminating his investigation of my office. Shortly after Bharara's press conference, I was notified that I was a potential witness for the prosecution in the federal case.

Howe became a problematic star witness for the federal prosecution.[42] His testimony was unvarnished and damning. He described setting up fundraisers for Cuomo with developers seeking state business, arranging fishing trips between developers and Percoco, and other steps he took to get developers into Cuomo's good graces.

As part of his testimony, Howe spoke about the fateful conversation he and Aiello had with me about the stadium demise, how angry the governor was, and Cuomo's reputation as a bully.[43] Admitting Percoco was like a brother to him, he discussed facilitating more than $300,000 in payments to Percoco, including $35,000 from Aiello and Gerardi through a shell corporation he set up to help secure state contracts. The payments were called "ziti," a reference to money that they'd picked up from *The Sopranos*. Howe described how he and Percoco sought to actively sell influence in Albany to companies seeking state contracts.[44]

Percoco's trial shined a harsh light on Aiello. Testimony, emails, and text messages demonstrated that Aiello was eager to get the attention of state officials, was exuberant when he thought he had maneuvered around regulations, and was left smarting when he felt overlooked by officials. When Aiello's son, who worked in state government, did not receive as large a raise as he had expected, Aiello texted:

> "The administration has embarrassed me in my community." . . . "I have been loyal as the day is long. They insult us like this. I'm finished!!!"
>
> "Everybody else gets what they need and want. I keep giving," he continued. "It's a sad statement!"

42. During his testimony, he admitted he attempted to defraud his credit card company while he was cooperating with the government. Benjamin Weiser and Vivian Wang, "Todd Howe, Key Witness in Albany Corruption Trial Is Jailed," *New York Times*, February 9, 2018.

43. Vivian Wang, "Key Witness in Corruption Trial Tells a Tale of Cuomo," *New York Times*, February 15, 2018.

44. Jesse McKinley and Benjamin Weiser, "In Albany, Percoco Secretly Strained to Keep the 'Ziti' Flowing," *New York Times*, February 6, 2018.

Howe alerted Percoco, who saw to it that Aiello's son got a 10 percent raise. A state official testified Percoco had conveyed that Aiello was upset because he had not been invited to drinks the night before a gubernatorial event.[45]

In 2014, Aiello and Gerardi asked Howe for help in avoiding a state requirement to hire union employees for the Inner Harbor project. Howe asked Percoco to intervene, and soon after, the state lawyers reversed the requirement. Aiello's emails showed he was thrilled. "Totally amazing," he wrote to Howe. "The power of TH, JP!"—a reference to Howe and Percoco.[46]

Hearkening back to my phone call with Howe years earlier, the prosecutors said COR executives got a copy of the Syracuse RFP before it was released to the public or competing firms. The government said a COR executive emailed Howe with the company's qualifications and experience, which ended up in the bid documents word for word. Prosecutors established the requests for proposals were tailored to ensure SUNY Polytechnic awarded contracts to COR in Syracuse worth more than $100 million.[47]

## "The Lees of Things"

Howe pleaded guilty to eight felonies and received a sentence of five years' probation, with no prison time.

Percoco was convicted on three charges of soliciting and accepting bribes from executives working for companies with state business, including COR. He was sentenced to six years in prison.[48]

Kaloyeros was convicted of wire fraud conspiracy and wire fraud and sentenced to three and a half years in prison.[49]

Aiello was convicted of conspiracy and fraud by juries in two Buffalo Billion trials and sentenced to a three-year prison term.[50]

45. Vivian Wang, "Witnesses Tell How Percoco Gave Developers Access to the 'Albany Game,'" *New York Times*, January 3, 2018.

46. Wang, "Witnesses Tell How Percoco Gave Developers Access to the 'Albany Game.'"

47. Benjamin Weiser and Vivian Wang, "Looking for 'New York's Secret Weapon'? For the Next 42 Months, Try Prison," *New York Times*, December 11, 2018.

48. Laura Nahmias, Terry Golway, and Daniel Lippman, "Percoco Sentenced to 6 Years in Prison for Corruption," *Politico*, September 20, 2018.

49. Larry Rulison, "Kaloyeros, Ex-Albany Nanotech Chief, Starts Prison Term Next Month," *Times Union*, February 24, 2022.

50. Mark Weiner, "Syracuse Developer Steve Aiello Sentenced to 3 Years in NY

Gerardi was convicted of conspiracy, wire fraud, and making a false statement and sentenced to two and a half years.[51]

Projects celebrated by the establishment were so corrupt a federal judge said they fed the view that state government was "all about who knows who and who's greasing whose palm."[52]

Hollywood never did come to Onondaga. The CNY Film Hub remained empty and was eventually sold to Onondaga County for $1.[53] Soraa, the California-based LED lightbulb manufacturer, never came to the region.[54] The Buffalo Billion program, in addition to being mired in a federal corruption trial, was a substantive failure.[55]

I once swam in the cesspool of the state's political culture, never thinking the stink would rub off on me or impact my ability to do my job. At the end of my term as mayor, I was a potential witness in a federal corruption trial involving one-time close friends and people with whom I had started my political career.

Never again would I be blind to the waste and destruction corruption wreaked.

Corruption Trial," Syracuse.com, December 7, 2018, https://www.syracuse.com/news/2018/12/syracuse_developer_steven_aiello_sentenced_in_ny_corruption_trial.html.

51. Tim Knauss, "Syracuse Developer Joe Gerardi Sentenced to Two and a Half Years in NY Corruption Trial," Syracuse.com, December 6, 2018, https://www.syracuse.com/news/2018/12/syracuse_developer_joe_gerardi_sentenced_in_ny_corruption_trial.html.

52. Vivian Wang, "A Cuomo Insider Was a Big-Money Lobbyist Who Drove a Porsche. Then Came a Stunning Fall," New York Time, April 5, 2019.

53. Jesse McKinley, "New York Spent $15 Million to Build a Film Hub. It Just Sold It for $1," New York Times, June 1, 2018.

54. Tim Knauss, "Soraa Walks Away from $90 Million Factory That NY Built; $15 Million More Brings New Tenant," Syracuse.com, December 20, 2017, https://www.syracuse.com/news/2017/12/soraa_walks_away_from_90m_factory_that_ny_built_but_15m_more_brings_new_tenant.html.

55. The state spent $2.2 billion in projects with claims it would create eight thousand jobs and spur an equal number of indirect jobs. Employment in the technology sector fell in western New York between 2011 and 2017, employment in advanced manufacturing fell by 2.1 percent and by 2.6 percent in life sciences. A state comptroller audit of several of the high-tech projects funded through the Buffalo Billion initiative found the Cuomo administration allowed the required number of jobs to be both reduced in number and quality and failed to do any serious analysis before doling out taxpayer funds to the projects. Office of State Comptroller, "Empire State Development: Oversight of Select High-Technology Projects," August 2020, https://www.osc.state.ny.us/files/state-agencies/audits/pdf/2017-S-60_0.pdf.

## Postscript

On May 11, 2023, the Supreme Court unanimously vacated federal fraud and corruption convictions arising from the Buffalo Billion program. *Ciminelli v. United States*[56] invalidated the Second Circuit's right-to-control fraud theory, and *Percoco v. United States*[57] invalidated the test used by the district court for determining whether a private person may be convicted of honest-services fraud. These decisions, along with others, have been viewed as evidence of the Supreme Court's effort to limit federal fraud prosecutions in the context of public corruption at the state and local levels.[58]

---

56. 598 U.S. ＿＿＿ (2023)

57. 598 U.S. ＿＿＿ (2023)

58. Adam Liptak and Luis Ferré-Sadurní, "Supreme Court Throws Out Fraud Convictions in Albany Scandals," *New York Times*, May 11, 2023; Aidan Mulry et al., "*Ciminelli* and *Percoco*—Federal Public Corruption Prosecutors Suffer Two More Unanimous Losses at the Supreme Court," *Arnold & Porter*, May 24, 2023, https://www.arnoldporter.com/en/perspectives/blogs/enforcement-edge/2023/05/ciminelli-and-percoco-federal-public-corruption.

# Politics

## Running on Empty

As my tenure as mayor was drawing to a close, people began to cajole me to run for another office. The 2016 presidential election galvanized people, and I was frequently asked to speak at meetings focused on the public policy implications of President Trump's agenda. One meeting I agreed to address had a standing-room-only crowd in the city council chamber in city hall. I was preparing my remarks when I saw out of the corner of my eye an unfamiliar man appear next to me. As I smiled at him quizzically, he stood in front of my microphone and opened his jacket to the audience, exposing a homemade T-shirt that read, "Run, Stephanie." As he did, people began to stand and chant "Run, Stephanie, run"—an exhortation for me to run for Congress. What should have felt like the pinnacle of flattery was a trapdoor into anxiety. Not only was I not going to run for Congress but, most troublingly, I felt I had no options for my post-mayoral life.

At home after the event, Jack tried to lift my spirits. "It has to be pretty heady to have all those people begging you to run," he said. He shook his head as I told him once again I felt only existential dread. The conversation ended as they all did, with Jack telling me that only I could determine what would make me happy.

## The End of the World as I Knew It

My term was approaching its end on January 1, 2018. At midnight on December 31, 2017, I would be mayor, and at 12:01 a.m., I would not. I was not prepared for the dramatic, instant change. Being mayor was a great job.

Even with its burdens, I felt relevant and believed I could positively impact people's lives. It was a position where the art of politics could be used constructively. I wanted—needed—another role that gave me those feelings. As I considered what to do next, I was haunted by a comment Chicago mayor Richard M. Daley made to me almost eight years earlier.

I had followed Daley into a room in the White House before the 2010 U.S. Conference of Mayors meeting with President Barack Obama and Vice President Joe Biden. When I introduced myself, Daley asked how long I had been mayor and I sheepishly admitted only a few days. With unbridled excitement, he told me it would be the best job I would ever have because I would be able to really help people. He lowered his voice and told me people in Washington think they help, but mayors are the ones who do the work. "That's why," he concluded, "we don't ever do anything else."

Many of my mayoral peers shared with me they were done with elected office once their terms ended. The rewards of other political jobs were not worth the personal sacrifices. I understood, but politics had consumed me for the better part of twenty years, and I enjoyed it. I also feared I had no other skills.

In 2017, a prominent statewide political blog citing unnamed sources said I was going to run against John DeFrancisco, a Republican state senator who represented an upstate district that included parts of Syracuse. I called Brodsky to chuckle over it, telling him it was news to me. He had read the piece, too, but instead of laughing, he asked me if it was true, seemingly hurt I had not told him first.

When I pointed out I lived in a different senate district, he shocked me by saying I should move so I could run against DeFrancisco. I was stunned he would so cavalierly tell me to sell my house and move solely to mount a political campaign. I told him that thinking was exactly what I detested about the Albany mindset: ambition trumps everything.

"Think about it," he said. I sarcastically told him I would as soon as he told Jack we should uproot our whole life to move a couple of miles away so I could run against a person we both liked. With that, Brodsky suggested that I rent an apartment in the district; I wouldn't have to live there. Yes, I countered, what could possibly be wrong with that?

"You upstate people don't get it," Brodsky said. "The important thing is you're in office." No, I said, he didn't get it. We didn't see disingenuousness in the pursuit of power as a virtue. Maybe you should, he retorted.

Maybe he was right—if that were the case, I might not be experiencing such turmoil.

Perhaps this was a by-product of not recognizing the toll governing had exacted on me. While I thought I was successfully dealing with an inordinate amount of stress, the fact was I couldn't focus on anything for longer than a few minutes. My mind was constantly unsettled.

I would joke it was mayoral-induced attention-deficit disorder—cue the laughter—but I couldn't remember the last time I had read a book or watched an entire movie. I would clean up meals before Jack had finished eating. I would sit at the dinner table anxiously looking at my phone, waiting for him to finish so I could get up and leave. He was exasperated by my behavior, and I would respond that it was just part of my job, though I knew that wasn't quite true.

I ignored the fact I hadn't slept for more than a couple of hours at a time in years. The longer I was mayor, the less I slept. I could tell the time by the radio program: midnight was *Fresh Air*, *BBC News* from 1 a.m. to 5 a.m., and then NPR's *Morning Edition*. In my view, I was a hypervigilant mayor. Sure, I internalized tragedies, but I was intent on not wasting a minute of my term, telling myself that sending emails to staff at three in the morning was proof I was dedicated to the job.

But the job I loved was ending. I was burying my insecurity about my future under a frenetic exterior. All the while, I heard people saying, "Run, Stephanie, run" . . . for Congress, state senate, or even governor.

Running for Congress seemed like an obvious choice. In the short span of my electoral career, the Syracuse seat had become nationally important.[1] Syracuse was the district's population center, and I was the city's mayor and the most prominent elected Democrat in the congressional district.

When I was on the city council, New York's 25th congressional district was a solid Republican seat that had been held by Rep. Jim Walsh for twenty years.[2] But by 2008, because of the Republican Party's continued purge of social moderates and voters shifting between parties, the seat had become a rare swing district, meaning a candidate from either party had a fair shot

1. Mark Weiner, "John Katko Victory Makes Syracuse the No. 1 Swing District in Congress," Syracuse.com, November 5, 2014, https://www.syracuse.com/news/2014/11/john_katko_victory_makes_syracuse_the_no_1_swing_district_in_congress.html.

2. Mark Weiner, "Rep. Jim Walsh Announces Retirement," Syracuse.com, January 24, 2008, https://www.syracuse.com/news/2008/01/congressman_jim_walsh_retiring.html.

at winning it. The seat became a battleground for both the Democratic and Republican national parties.[3]

Democrats had been recruiting me to run for Congress since I had won election to the city council in 2001, so I'd had many honest conversations with its members. After I told them I wouldn't run, many volunteered they were trying to find ways to get out of Congress. It was grueling to run every two years, raise so much money, never see their families, feel ineffective, and watch the atmosphere get more toxic. Even on the worst of days, the mayors I knew never felt so disenchanted.

There were other factors, mostly unspoken. By this time, Jack was eighty-one and slowing down. He was conscious our time together was limited. I knew that but could never think about it. I did not want to be in DC with him in Syracuse. He had no interest in being in DC. "Our life is here," he said, and he was right.

## Nancy Says Relax

As my term drew to a close, I was in DC to participate in an event celebrating the public service of Paul Volcker, an economist who'd been chairman of the Federal Reserve.[4] I was listening to erudite discussions on federal policy when my phone rang. I slipped out of the grand auditorium to take the call. It was Joe Crowley, a gregarious congressman from Queens who was a friend of mine and Jack's. Crowley had heard I was in DC and wondered if I was up for having some fun. I told him I was always up for fun, but "no recruitment." He told me not to worry and gave me instructions for where to meet him.

When I arrived on the Capitol grounds, I was met by a Crowley staffer who escorted me through a labyrinth of hallways to a committee room with a hearing in process. When I walked in the room, Crowley got off the dais to greet me. He bent his giant frame down to give me a kiss on the cheek, whispering to follow him.

We walked to the middle of the room, and he said, "Watch." As I followed his eyes, I saw a congressman jump up from the dais, get on his

3. Mark Weiner, "5 Reasons to Pay Attention to New York's Congressional Primaries," Syracuse.com, June 28, 2016, https://www.syracuse.com/politics/2016/06/5_reasons_to _pay_attention_to_new_yorks_congressional_primaries.html.

4. Volcker Alliance Symposium, Washington, DC, November 9, 2017.

phone, and scurry out of the room. Crowley laughed, telling me it was the congressman in charge of Republican reelections. My presence was a signal I might be considering challenging one of his colleagues. "What would he do if I really kissed you?" I said jokingly. Crowley roared and said he wanted me to meet someone.

This time he escorted me through a series of ornate hallways. As we made twists and turns, he happily greeted everyone by name or with a wise-crack. Finally, we stopped at a desk in front of an ornate door. I glanced at the closed door—it was Nancy Pelosi's office. I realized I'd been had by my charming friend Joe. I was going to get the hard sell from Pelosi herself.

Pelosi's office was elegant, with yellow walls, tastefully matched, uphol-stered furniture, and several American flags. Somewhat surprisingly for a high-ranking politician, I didn't see any framed, autographed pictures of Pelosi with dignitaries in the room. Within seconds, Pelosi walked into the room from a different entrance. She flashed her million-dollar smile and shook my hand. Within moments, we were joined by a photographer who took pictures of the three of us, then just me and her, and then repeated the whole thing with Crowley's phone. The latter, I assumed, would soon be used for a tweet to send the GOP into further fits.

Crowley left Pelosi and I alone. She invited me to sit in a chair and she sat on an adjacent couch. With effortless and easy charm, she talked about the important role Congress currently had in fighting for democratic values. She said the GOP wanted to undermine everything the Democratic Party had accomplished since the New Deal, giving examples of gender equality and reproductive rights. As she talked, I felt myself falling under her spell. She looked directly into my eyes and made me believe she was fighting for important values at a time when it mattered. Communicating ideas were important, and advocates were crucial to ensuring our country's progress did not backslide. When she leaned in and said, "Stephanie, everyone says you're the person for this seat. We need you." I was hypnotized.

I stuttered and thanked her for being so gracious. I summoned my cour-age and told her the truth, "I'm exhausted." She smiled and said, "I know, Stephanie. I know what it's like." And, of course, she did—outside of her own political career, her father and brother had both been mayors of Balti-more.[5] "As a mayor, you have to be on all the time. Every time you go out of

5. Thomas D'Alesandro Jr. (mayor from 1947 to 1959) and Thomas D'Alesandro III (mayor from 1967 to 1971).

the house, go to the grocery story, or the phone rings," she said empathetically. I was entranced and leaned toward her.

She was breaking down my defenses—I didn't want to disappoint her. After a pregnant pause, she said, "You can come to Congress and relax." With that, her spell was broken. I could never go to Congress and relax. The district was too volatile. I'd have to campaign tirelessly, raise millions of dollars, constantly spin on social media, all without seeing Jack for days, if not weeks, at a time. I respected her skills, but I was not buying. I thanked her and left, charmed but not seduced.

## The End of the World as We Knew It

I thought Hillary Clinton was the best candidate for president in 2016. That could be seen as hypocrisy. After all, my part of the country had been left behind for decades, and Clinton was deeply entrenched in a dysfunctional system where the elites in both parties made impossible promises of transformational changes to come. She stood beside generous campaign donors at countless scripted press events, pledging another surefire way to revitalize the country.[6] But I believed she was someone who made concessions to survive in a corrupt political system and, most importantly, I liked her. She was whip smart, she understood the political system, and she was interested in people's well-being.

Even if I ignored her deep roots within a debased political system, I should have recognized how flawed her campaign was after I attended a meeting in Brooklyn in 2016. In early autumn, I joined about one hundred mayors from across the country at the Clinton campaign headquarters to receive high-level briefings from Bill Clinton, her campaign chair, John Podesta, and her campaign manager, Robby Mook.

After a series of presentations, Mayor Mike Duggan of Detroit stood up to ask a question of Podesta and Mook. He said Clinton had been in Detroit over Labor Day and there were a lot of voters who wanted to know why they should vote for her. These were people who aspired to make a better life for themselves and their families, he said. What should I tell them? Mook did not have an answer other than important suburban swing voters liked Clinton more than Trump, and Podesta remained silent.

6. Charlie Savage, "A Donor's Gift Soon Followed Clinton's Help," *New York Times*, January 3, 2009.

A few mayors said they agreed with Duggan and asked again. At that point, several other mayors got up to defend Clinton, their general argument being that Hillary Clinton was not Donald Trump. Other mayors pointed out that a vote against a person is not the same as a vote for a person. I quietly observed hoping someone would share an answer that I could use too. The debate began to get more heated, and Mayor Ras Baraka of Newark stood up and forcefully said that if Duggan didn't know why his constituents should vote for Clinton at this point, he should leave. Accusations of disloyalty were thrown back and forth. Mitch Landrieu, the mayor of New Orleans, stood up and out of deference to his leadership the room quieted. Landrieu said he agreed with Duggan, and we needed an answer. If not today, then soon. We never got an answer.

It was astonishing: weeks away from the general election, her top-level campaign staff and many top mayors from across the country—some of the best minds of the Democratic establishment—could not enunciate one simple reason to vote for Hillary Clinton. Perhaps it should not have been so surprising Trump won, but, of course, it was.

I had spent election night in a room at the Hotel Syracuse with plans to address the victory party in a ballroom below when it came to fruition. Instead, I left the hotel room, got into the elevator, skipped the ballroom, and drove home in the wee hours of the morning. As I drove, I ignored dozens of calls from Democrats across the state who were in a similar state of shock. There was simply nothing I could say.

One of the first reactions to Trump's victory was an energized progressive base in the state. Progressives were spoiling to exact consequences for Governor Andrew Cuomo's broken commitments from 2014, when he pledged to fight for robust public campaign-finance reform, help seat a Democratic state senate, and support an increase in the state minimum wage.[7] He cynically made those pledges to win over more liberal-leaning Democrats and effectively put an end to a gubernatorial challenge from the progressive hero Zephyr Teachout.[8]

As Cuomo readied for reelection in 2018, none of the commitments he

7. Blake Zeff, "A Year After the Cuomo-WFP Bargain, Everyone's a Sucker," *Politico*, June 1, 2015, https://www.politico.com/states/new-york/city-hall/story/2015/06/a-year -after-the-cuomo-wfp-bargain-everyones-a-sucker-089811.

8. Sam Raskin, "Cuomo's Progressive Promises Reminiscent of Four Years Ago, Received Differently," *Gotham Gazette*, April 14, 2018.

made had been realized. The Working Families Party (WFP), a third-party founded by an alliance of union and progressive groups, were especially smarting from Cuomo's behavior four years earlier.[9] WFP was planning to stand behind a Democratic primary challenger against Cuomo.[10]

I had a positive relationship with the WFP. It had helped me get elected mayor[11] and I had enacted policy actions the party supported, one of which was unilaterally raising the minimum wage of full-time workers in Syracuse government to fifteen dollars an hour in 2015.[12] As such, WFP leaders encouraged me to challenge the governor. I seemed to be an ideal candidate: a woman, a principled challenger to Cuomo's policies, and a WFP supporter.

While the Working Families Party was focused on finding a challenger to Cuomo, it was facing an existential crisis of its own. Several unions that were beholden to state contracts, and by extension Cuomo, said they would stop financing the WFP if it proceeded with challenging Cuomo. The loss of revenue would devastate the party and its ability to mount any campaigns at all.[13]

At the same time, many WFP members felt that not challenging Cuomo undercut the purpose of the party, which was to fight the forces standing in the way of progress for working people. Some members threatened to leave the party over the issue, and such an exodus would gut the ability to execute any campaigns and put its ballot status at risk.[14]

During this time, some of the party's leaders asked to meet with me. The meeting was in a nondescript Brooklyn conference room with about twenty people, most of whom I didn't know. It was a diverse group: it included

9. Molly Ball, "The Pugnacious, Relentless Progressive Party That Wants to Remake America," *Atlantic*, January 17, 2016, https://www.theatlantic.com/politics/archive/2016/01/working-families-party/422949/.

10. David Freedlander, "Working Families Party Mulls All-Out War With Cuomo," nymag.com, June 7, 2018, https://nymag.com/intelligencer/2018/06/working-families-party-mulls-all-out-war-with-cuomo.html.

11. See chapter 2.

12. Patrick McGeehan, "Syracuse Leader Raises Public Workers' Minimum Wage to $15," *New York Times*, October 21, 2015.

13. Shane Goldmacher and Jesse McKinley, "Flexing Their Support for Cuomo, Key Unions Leave Working Families Party," *New York Times*, April 13, 2018.

14. David Freedlander, "Working Families Party Mulls All-out War With Cuomo," *Intelligencer*, June 7, 2018, https://nymag.com/intelligencer/2018/06/working-families-party-mulls-all-out-war-with-cuomo.html.

men and women, young and old, and several people of color. One by one, they introduced themselves and said the group was united by social and economic causes. They were also deeply frustrated by the political culture in Albany, and most of all, by Andrew Cuomo.

We agreed that enacting policy should be a corruption-free process, but as the discussion progressed, it became increasingly clear that my views were much more centrist than theirs. Those around the table seemed to feel more money was the answer to every problem. In my experience, it was not. I saw money routinely wasted on failed economic-development projects and ineffective programs funded each year because they became a vested interest within the state's government-industrial complex.

As the meeting wrapped up, WFP head Bill Lipton confirmed in front of everyone that I was a lawyer. He ended the meeting saying, "so we have choices." If I lost the Democratic primary, Lipton was insinuating, the WFP party would remove me as its gubernatorial candidate in the general election and give the WFP line to Cuomo.

The state's election laws give parties the ability to remove an unsuccessful primary candidate from the general-election ballot by having them run for a different office in the general election. This maneuver is easy if the losing candidate is a lawyer who can run for a judgeship. Lipton had signaled that a challenge to Cuomo was more about a power struggle than the integrity of the system. There was little chance Cuomo would lose in a primary. Lipton's statement was an acknowledgment the WFP would capitulate to Cuomo. I was not interested in being a pawn in the WFP's feud.

I would not be the WFP standard-bearer and charge into the Cuomo Valley of Death. I believed elections should not just be about transactional power battles. Moreover, my policy views, which sprang from the responsibility of running a city, not ideological purity, were different enough from the WFP that my candidacy would have required major compromises that I wasn't ready to accept.

The WFP quickly united around the actress Cynthia Nixon's gubernatorial bid,[15] and admittedly, Nixon was a better WFP candidate than I would be. While politically inexperienced, she was enthusiastic, and she had instant name recognition—something that I would later learn cost millions to earn. She took positions to the left of what I would have been comfortable

15. Vivian Wang, "Nixon Tops Working Families Ticket, but Party Remains at 'Crossroads,'" *New York Times*, May 19, 2018.

with, accepted an endorsement from the democratic socialists, and carried out stunts like wielding a coat hanger when addressing abortion rights.[16] While she and the WFP ran a vigorous campaign, I never doubted she would lose.

After she lost the Democratic primary, WFP leaders engaged in intense wrangling with its members to get them to give the WFP line to Cuomo. As telegraphed by Lipton, the party nominated Nixon to run for an Assembly seat. I thought the behavior undercut the integrity of the process. Cuomo publicly dithered about whether he would run on the WFP line.[17] Many speculated Cuomo would kill the party once he was reelected.

## Fusion

During the WFP's recruitment efforts, I received a phone call from a man who introduced himself as Mike Berland. Berland owned a research and analytics firm and had deep political connections, having served as a pollster for both Michael Bloomberg and Hillary Clinton.[18] He said he and his friend, Joe Rose, had an idea they wanted to discuss in person. Rose was a politically active scion of a wealthy New York City real estate family with connections to Manhattan's elite.[19]

A few days later, Jack and I met with Berland and Rose at Syracuse's Century Club. After a few niceties, we shared our view that Trump's election was evidence of the public's frustration with the status quo. Armed with data from a recent statewide poll that Rose had commissioned and Berland conducted, they said the state's voters were primed to shock the political system in the upcoming gubernatorial election.

They believed a strong candidate representing a new third party could

16.  Clarrie Feinstein, "Democratic Socialists Back Former 'Sex and the City' Star Cynthia Nixon in Bid for New York Governor," *Salon*, July 31, 2018; Lisa Ryan, "Cynthia Nixon Holds Hanger, Talks Mom's Illegal Abortion," *Cut*, July 18, 2018, https://www.the cut.com/2018/07/cynthia-nixon-mother-abortion-wire-hanger.html.

17.  Jesse McKinley, "Cuomo Accepts the Working Families Ballot Line, Ending Feud. For Now," *New York Times*, October 5, 2018.

18.  Azi Paybarah, "A Clinton Pollster Sues a Bloomberg Pollster," *Observer*, June 26, 2007. https://observer.com/2007/06/a-clinton-pollster-sues-a-bloomberg-pollster/.

19.  Andrew Rice, "Mighty Joe Rose: Third-Generation Builder Battles Skyscraper Elite," *Observer*, April 3, 2000. https://observer.com/2000/04/mighty-joe-rose-third -generation-builder-battles-skyscraper-elite/.

win the governor's race by creating a viable alternative to the Republican and Democratic Parties, and they thought I would be the perfect candidate. Moreover, even if I lost the governor's race, I would hold a position of power and influence in a new party.

New York state election law allows a process called fusion voting, in which a new political party could be created if candidates running under that party's name garnered at least fifty-thousand votes in a general election. Once the fifty-thousand-vote threshold was met, the party was entitled to ballot status in the state for four years. The new party's placement on future ballots is based on how many votes the party's candidate receives in the general election. So if I were to run for governor and receive fewer votes than the Democratic and Republican candidates but more than every other party's candidate, the new party would be third on the ballot for four years.[20]

Rose and Berland were presenting the rare case in politics where a candidate can win if they lose. If I received fifty-thousand votes in the general election, the new party would be entitled to a ballot line across the state for the next four years, a powerful tool to push an agenda, and there was no shortage of issues in the state that needed a new approach.

Rose said he was committed to personally raising a million dollars for the effort. As he said it, I watched him put a poll sheet in his pocket with his name listed alongside other potential candidates. Based on the size of the poll sample I saw, he was not exaggerating when he said he had already expended a significant amount of money on the effort.

At the end of my mayoral term, I accepted a position at the NYU Robert F. Wagner Graduate School of Public Service as a visiting professor in January 2018. Jack had agreed to relocate for a couple of months, and I had visions of attending plays, baseball games, and restaurants as I tried to figure out my longer-term plan.

One winter morning in early 2018, I was in my NYU cubicle when I was startled by the desk phone ringing. Since I didn't know the number yet, I had never given it to anyone. I answered tentatively and a booming voice said: "Stephanie, it's Tim Onoff. Long time no talk, but my Syracuse family keeps me in the loop. Great job."

20. Annie McDonough, "Odd Ballot Lines Flourish with New York's System of Fusion Voting," *City and State NY*, October 12, 2018, https://www.cityandstateny.com/politics /2018/10/odd-ballot-lines-flourish-with-new-yorks-system-of-fusion-voting/178036/.

Onoff and I had both worked for Mario Cuomo decades earlier.[21] In the intervening time, I had spoken with him perhaps twice. But acting as if we'd been in regular contact, he said he had a wealthy client interested in infrastructure looking to hire a consultant familiar with urban issues and government. Naturally, he thought I would be perfect for the role and wanted to put us together. I thanked him and wondered what he had been promised if he could eliminate me as a potential Cuomo challenger.

It was just one of several lucrative, unsolicited job offers coming from people associated with Cuomo. Each offer came with a confession that the governor was a bully, and I was to be celebrated for my principled opposition to him. Then, like clockwork, I was offered a position or asked what I wanted. The Cuomo insiders' aim was obvious: promise anything to ensure I did not run for governor. I did not seriously consider any of the offers.

Once I was living in New York City, Rose engaged in a diplomatic but persistent recruitment campaign. He invited me and Jack to sit with him at his VIP seats at Yankees games, be his guest at black-tie events, and attend lots of lunch meetings with notable people to discuss politics and governing, during which insiders and activists would admit a lot of people were unhappy with the current system and looking for a new path. While these people recognized there were challenges, they also saw opportunity. Rose was energized by every conversation and punctuated each with "what we can do," conveying that we could provoke much-needed change and reform in the state.

As I contemplated my decision to run, Rose and Berland were doing the groundwork necessary to start a new third party. They regularly met with consultants and election professionals. It was legally and strategically necessary for me to be excluded from these meetings. While Rose and Berland were recruiting me, there were no commitments being made. If either one of us decided I was not the right candidate, it would be problematic if I walked away with important information.

Campaign-finance laws are murky about the separation between legally funding a party and legally funding a candidate.[22] Any blurring of Rose's efforts to start a new party and my candidacy could have also been portrayed

---

21. It was the birth of Onoff's eldest son that had prompted Mario to say "mazel tov" in my red-faced meeting so many years ago. See chapter 1.

22. *Upstate Jobs Party et al. v. Kosinski et al.*, No. 6:2018cv00459.

as an illegal use of resources. If we made a mistake and resources were found to be unlawfully combined, it would undercut a message of change and reform. With Cuomo controlling the election bureaucracy, it was imperative to hold bright-line distinctions, which we did.

During this process, Rose paid Berland to conduct a statewide poll with my name and attributes designed to help me decide if I should run. It was understood I would not be allowed to see the full results of the poll, just as I had not been allowed to see the full results of the first poll they did.

Sometime in first quarter of 2018, they gave Jack and me an overview presentation of the results of the second poll. They showed that a message of reform and change and my background made me a formidable challenger to the governor but even more so as someone who could help create a strong new third party. I conveniently overlooked that polls are conducted with a context of perfect information. Pollsters provide people with information and ask questions in the context of that information. In a real campaign, there's no guarantee voters will get accurate information, or any information at all.

I thought the idea of being elected governor was a long shot, but I was captivated by the idea of helping to create a new party. New York was becoming a one-party Democratic state focused on only one region: New York City. The Democratic Party was being pulled to the far left, just as the Republicans were being pulled to the extreme right. In the process, a huge number of people were being ignored. As the leader of a new third party, I could choose the issues, organize for meaningful change, and focus on ethical behavior.

Rose had brought the idea to me, recruited me, and promised to raise money. His message was "there is everything to gain and nothing to lose." I could speak about the issues I thought were important, he would do the fundraising, and together we would build a party that could influence policy and the political process. Personally, it provided me a way to stay politically active and avoid the question of who I was without politics. I eventually bought into Rose's vision that there was huge potential with little risk involved, and I agreed to run.

I should have known that there is no such thing as "risk-free" when it comes to politics.

After hearing about the poll results, I took a train to Albany to meet my old friend Sherman Jewett for coffee. Jewett owned a communications consulting firm. We had known each other for a long time, and he had briefly worked for me when I was mayor. A press operative by training, he was an Albany fixture.

We went to a small diner away from the train station. Jewett looked around to ensure we could talk freely, and I confided in him about the third-party idea, showed him the slimmed-down poll results, and told him about Rose's fundraising promises. He was smitten with the idea. I asked him if he'd be interested in running my campaign and assured him it would at the very least be an adventure, but he said he needed to talk with his wife. I knew by his reaction, though, he would join. Beth Rougeux, my former director of administration, agreed to be my campaign treasurer, taking on the onerous responsibility of doing the financial filings.

Rose brought two more high-powered people to the team: Stephanie Junger-Moat and Richard Bryers. Junger-Moat had worked with Henry Kissinger, was fluent in multiple languages, and owned her own consulting firm. Bryers had worked for the legendary political consultant David Garth. Rose paid for Bryers to spend a week with me, with the idea that if we liked each other, he would work on the campaign.

We had the foundation of a successful operation coming together: a campaign manager (Jewett), an operations director (Junger-Moat), a communications expert (Bryers), and a treasurer (Rougeux). Berland had conducted two statewide polls, and Rose had committed to raising the money. We had a good team in place and the promise that other big names were ready to lend support. It was exciting. Too exciting, in retrospect.

## Another SAM Enters

One of the many lunches Rose arranged was with John Avlon, who was a political commentator at CNN at the time. Over lunch at a swanky downtown eatery, Avlon said there were important people thinking seriously about a third-party alternative to the current system. He suggested we contact a group of people in the New York area calling themselves the Serve America Movement.

The Serve America Movement, or SAM as it became known, was created in the aftermath of the Trump election. Eric Grossman, a lawyer working for Morgan Stanley, and a handful of others from both parties felt there should be another way to fix the broken political system. One of the movement's foundational principles was the importance of civil dialogue, and Grossman and others recruited people from all political ideologies to form a party focused on consensus and problem-solving. Many thought it was naive, but they were at least committed to trying to build something rather than just complaining.[23]

Rose and I met for lunch with a SAM representative named Michael Wilner, a retired cable executive who had left the Republican Party after Trump's ascendance. Shortly thereafter, Rose and I met with a handful of other SAM representatives in a midtown Manhattan conference room. Scott Muller, a former federal prosecutor and partner in the Davis Polk & Wardwell law firm, was a key leader of the SAM movement. After a discussion about SAM's mission, I talked about my experiences as a mayor trying to solve problems while being forced to confront corruption and why I had decided to run as a third-party candidate.

When I finished, Muller, exuding enthusiasm, said, "You're exactly what we're looking for. I want to introduce you to people right now. What can we do to help?" At that point, I pointed out my initials were SAM and joked that our partnership was predetermined. I was ecstatic—we had found the right group of people to help our effort, and Rose immediately got to work, estimating how much money SAM could contribute.

One of our first priorities was finding the right person to join me on the ticket as a lieutenant governor candidate. This was urgent because the whole effort could collapse if we didn't have enough time to get petitions printed and circulated. I wanted someone who I got along with and was also a true believer in good government, someone I could trust to share the burdens of campaigning and who had the passion to fuel the effort. Rose indicated he was in talks with a young, wealthy high-tech executive, but nothing had come of it. Then the SAM folks suggested someone they thought might be interested.

A couple of days later, I walked into another Manhattan law office and met Michael Volpe, a lawyer and the then-mayor of Pelham, a small town in Westchester County.[24] Volpe had been a Democrat and then a Republican.

23. Sonali Basak and Max Abelson, "A Morgan Stanley Star Wants You to Back His Political Movement," *Bloomberg*, July 2, 2018, https://www.bloomberg.com/news/featu res/2018-07-02/a-morgan-stanley-star-wants-you-to-back-his-political-movement.

24. Jon Campbell, "Stephanie Miner Picks Pelham Mayor, a Republican, as Running Mate in NY Governor's Race," *Lohud*, June 25, 2018, https://www.lohud.com/story/news

Apologizing, he said he didn't have much time because he had a meeting about a zoning issue. I asked him about the issue, and for the remainder of the meeting, we swapped stories about planning and zoning. I liked him right away. He was smart, straightforward, and concerned about the effect government dysfunction had on his constituents. As the meeting broke up, Volpe told me he got involved with SAM because he was concerned about his children's future.

As Rose and I walked away from the meeting, I asked what our backup plan was if Volpe decided not to join the ticket. He mentioned the high-tech executive he was sure to run into at an event on Long Island that weekend. We ended up at a Manhattan restaurant that he said was one of his favorite places. Settling onto barstools in an empty barroom, he asked what my biggest worry was and I said raising enough money to be formidable. He agreed and said it would be difficult, but he was confident we could accomplish great things.

But an uncomfortable pattern was beginning to emerge. Rose had failed to fulfill several important commitments. Not only had he not secured a candidate for lieutenant governor, but it also didn't seem he'd had any substantive discussions with qualified people. He had promised to make the maximum personal campaign contribution of $44,000, but he had not. He promised to raise at least a million dollars, but he had not secured any contributions.

When I asked him about this, Rose acted as if it was just an oversight. He would say he had just had a conversation with someone who was going to help the effort or was scheduled to talk to someone important at an upcoming event in Manhattan, the Hamptons, or at one of his clubs. He asked the maximum amount members of his family could contribute and for a reminder of the name and address of the campaign account.

By this time, I was committed to running. I had arranged my life to take up the challenge and was excited by the possibilities, in large part because of Rose. I liked him and trusted him, and I believed he was committed to the effort. When I asked Berland what was going on with the unmet obligations, he agreed Rose was committed but said I shouldn't run unless Rose put money in my campaign account. It was the last conversation I was to

/politics/politics-on-the-hudson/2018/06/25/stephanie-miner-running-mate-pelham
-mayor/729345002/.

have with Berland. Likely, I assumed later, because Rose stopped paying for his professional advice.

Rose kept saying his check—and others—were imminent. People who knew him said he just needed managing. The whole effort was his baby, after all; there was no way he'd come this far and fail to hold up his end of the deal. Rose was, in effect, holding my campaign hostage, but I was refusing to acknowledge what was happening because my identity had become so wrapped up in my candidacy. I felt if I was not in politics, then I did not exist.

In late spring, SAM's leadership said its commitment of support would require me to run as a candidate of the Serve America Movement party. SAM had spent a great deal of time and money to arrive at that name long before they met me. If the SAM folks wanted to name the party, I was fine with it, because we needed them to be a foundational part of the campaign. Rose told me he did not care about the name, but he took issue with it nonetheless. The failure to determine the party's name threatened the entire effort, but Rose didn't have an alternative suggestion to resolve the issue.

Volpe, who had not decided whether to join the campaign, and I continued to talk. I confided in him that despite what Rose was saying, I didn't think we could win, but I thought it could be a spark igniting a real change. He agreed and said he needed to talk with his wife, but he would let me know soon.

We had to finalize the details immediately, so Rose, Volpe, Jack, and I set up a meeting with SAM leaders and several lawyers. The crux of the meeting was Volpe would not run without SAM's blessing, and the SAM folks would only support the campaign if Serve America Movement or "SAM" was the name of the party.

SAM's demand, we discovered, raised a potential legal issue. Under New York state election law, a party can't have the word "America" in its name.[25] In response, SAM's leadership committed to paying for any legal defense required to fight an effort to knock it off the ballot. Rose refused to commit to SAM, arguing he would not give money to a campaign that could be pulled off the ballot. When the SAM folks asked Rose if he would commit to supporting the campaign if it survived any potential legal challenges, he did not answer.

25. NYS Election Law Section 16–104.

Jack then stepped in and asked everyone to say what they were willing to commit to. The SAM folks said they would support the effort if the party's name were either Serve America Movement or SAM. They would fund any legal effort necessary to ensure the name was on the ballot and help raise money for the campaign. Rose grudgingly said he would donate the legal maximum of $44,000, far less than the $1 million he once promised.

I asked to talk with Volpe, and we left the room. I confessed to Volpe I thought something else was behind Rose's reticence. The fact that he hadn't given any money to the campaign and his failure to meet other commitments seemed to indicate he'd had a change of heart or had another motivation. Volpe and I decided we would run under SAM's banner. We went back to the room and announced our decision. The SAM folks were thrilled. Rose got up and left without any comment.

After the meeting, I talked to Rose. I told him I considered him a friend. The campaign was originally his idea and I wanted him to be a part of it. He reiterated that he was committed to the effort and to me. Shortly after, he told the *New York Times* he had pledged to raise money for the campaign.[26]

Yet, by July 4, Rose had disappeared. He failed to return multiple calls from me and Jack. His contributions never materialized—not the $44,000, much less anything close to the $1 million he had so firmly committed to raising months earlier in Syracuse. In total, he donated $10,000, which paid for Bryers initial consulting visit.

It was a stunning rejection. Some speculated Rose was not prepared to do the tedious work required to raise money for an underdog campaign. Another rumor floating around was that Cuomo had called Rose and offered to make him the head of the New York City Housing Authority.

Later, I came to believe that Rose thought he knew what the message should be and thought he was the best messenger. I recalled seeing his name as a potential candidate on the first poll results. Perhaps he wanted to be the candidate or even the lieutenant governor candidate. I suppose he could have argued he wanted more control of the effort and so dropped out, but he never gave me an explanation. He just evaporated.

It was a shocking turn of events. He recruited me, made commitments, spoke with me almost daily, and then just disappeared. It was breathtaking to the people who knew him, many of whom told me he would resurface.

26. Shane Goldmacher, "Stephanie Miner to Make Independent Bid to Challenge Cuomo," *New York Times*, June 18, 2018.

He never did. I didn't have time to speculate on his motives because the campaign's ambitions needed to be scaled down and my role scaled up.

## The Making of the SAM

The immediate aftermath of Rose's withdrawal was the reality that a campaign planned around a budget in the millions would need to be radically scaled back. As we were doing this, several political consultants said Rose had failed to pay them for services. Some of the service providers were people Rose and I had met with to talk about the idea. I realized then that part of their openness to a third-party may have been driven by the potential they would be able to cash in on the effort.

The idea of staging an electoral upset was replaced by the goal of starting a new party. It was a Sisyphean effort. Volpe and I started splitting obligations as they arose. He volunteered to plan and appear at events, meet with local leaders, activists, and funders, and communicate with lawyers. Jewett retooled the budget. Junger-Moat[27] absorbed multiple campaign roles. A young man named Owen Stone joined and helped draft policy positions and anything else he was asked to do. Steadily, others joined the effort, helping with management and fundraising. It was inefficient and messy, but it was the reality after the lost time and retooled expectations.

We couldn't gather the resources to mount a robust yet affordable digital strategy, which had been the cornerstone of our campaign plan. The lack of a cohesive digital strategy, including a strong social media presence or even a better-than-average website, bedeviled the entire campaign, from organizing volunteers to conveying a message to voters. It was the Achilles' heel of our entire effort.

After Rose disappeared, the onus to fund the campaign fell to me. Resources were needed immediately, or the effort would collapse. While raising money through small donors was a possibility, we needed a dynamic website to make the process work. To do that, we needed to pay the costs up front, which meant we needed more money.

I spent most of my time in New York City because that's where the biggest donors are. With the lease in my apartment in the city running out, Wilner and his wife, Gretchen, offered me a bed and bath in their apartment.

---

27. Bryers left when the campaign's goals changed.

Michael and Gretchen quickly became like a second family, ensuring I had everything I needed, like lots of coffee, and things I didn't think I needed, like coconut-water lemonade for energy.

My days became consumed with doing what I once had consciously avoided: raising money by calling strangers. I spent hours at a desk in the donated bedroom using my cellphone to call potential donors. I called dozens of people a day, most of whom didn't answer or never returned my call. The next day, I would start again. I'd do the same thing the next day and the day after that.

There were people who told me they would donate but refused to when I said I would not take checks from limited liability corporations, or LLCs. New York State is notorious for having the one of the weakest campaign-finance laws in the country. One of the biggest and most frequently used finance loopholes was something known as an "LLC contribution." This provision allows corporations to create a limited liability corporation for the sole purpose of giving money to candidates and political parties. One firm can, and often does, create multiple LLCs, which effectively erases contribution limits.[28]

LLCs hide who is donating because the contribution is usually attributed to an anonymous entity. In 2018, the state's Senate Democrats received $25,000 from at least three donors—2332 7 Ave LLC; 207 Silver Lane LLC; and 228 W 132 LLC. All the donors shared the same address: 223 West 138th Street in Manhattan, the home of a real estate management company.[29]

This is why it's so difficult to trace donations and thus who is influencing policy decisions. Not surprisingly, many of the state's numerous corruption scandals[30] involved the use of LLCs. I had stopped taking LLC contributions several years earlier.

When I started raising money to start the new party, I encountered effects of my position. When I told potential donors I didn't take LLC donations, they rescinded their support for fear of retaliation from the Cuomo administration. Donors from different parts of the state in different lines

28. Vivian Wang, "NY Democrats Vowed to Get Big Money Out of Politics. Will Big Money Interfere?" *New York Times*, November 22, 2018.

29. Wang, "NY Democrats Vowed."

30. William K. Rashbaum, "Albany Trials Exposed the Power of a Real Estate Firm," *New York Times*, December 18, 2015.

of work all worried the governor's people would hurt their interests if their names appeared on my filing. These donors were not giving, relatively speaking, large donations or harboring the illusion I was going to win. Instead of simply saying no to me, as many did, many went out their way to tell me they feared retribution from the Cuomo administration.

It was perverse. People from across the state wanted to contribute to help fix the system, but they would not, for fear of retaliation from the system I hoped to fix. I was being sacrificed on the altar of my own ethics, making the arduous task of raising money almost impossible.

The unvarnished reality was that without millions of dollars in donations, our campaign could not get a message out. A campaign to break the death grip monied interests have on the political agenda was destined to fail in New York because of a lack of contributions from these same monied interests.

## Petitions

Given the election-law language banning the use of "America" in a party name, the decision was made to run under the party name of SAM. Petitions could start to be circulated on July 10 and submitted to the board of elections by August 21. Our entire summer was focused on getting enough signatures on petitions to qualify to be on the general election ballot.

What seems like a straightforward task, getting voters to sign a petition, is in practice an exercise in the tedious oversight of details. A well-run campaign will have a daily running tally of how many signatures have been collected and, of those, how many are "good." Campaigns hire people with experience reviewing signatures and petitions to excise faulty petitions before they are submitted.

We had a hodgepodge list of volunteers for the petition effort. Yet, such an effort by itself was not going to be enough. With volunteers, the assumption is they will gather half of what they commit to, and half of those signatures will be deficient. They are volunteers, not professionals. We did not have the manpower or technology to oversee their work on a daily, or even weekly, basis.

To ensure we had enough signatures that could hold up to scrutiny, we supplemented our volunteer efforts with paid canvassers with three different operations across the state—one in Buffalo, one in Rochester, and one in the New York City area. It would consume the lion's share of the money raised from June to September.[31]

We had regular updates from volunteers and professional canvassers. July rain and heat slowed the effort, but the numbers of signatures we gathered ticked up steadily. Weeks into the effort, our consultant out of Rochester stopped communicating. When we were able to get in contact, we were told a subcontractor named Robert Scott Gaddy had collected only half of the signatures he was hired to provide. There were accusations and half apologies, but there was little we could do.

When Gaddy submitted his petitions, we saw the signatures were in the same ink with similar handwriting and had serial addresses and dates, which was indicative of fraud. The reality of going door-to-door to gather signatures is that they will be in different ink because people use their own pens. People living on the same street will never all be home at the same time, allowing a canvasser to bounce from house to house to gather signatures in sequence. And, of course, people have vastly different handwriting. The money we paid up front was wasted. It was agonizing.

As if the potential fraud was not enough, Gaddy demanded to be paid the remaining money owed to him and said he would accuse the campaign of failing to compensate needy Black people unless we paid him. We refused and Gaddy did exactly that. The post gained some attention online but failed to get any real traction. Less than a year later, Gaddy was indicted by a federal grand jury in a separate matter for participating in a bribery plot.[32]

Our volunteers gathered hundreds of signatures, but we became dependent on our New York City consultant to deliver the bulk of the signatures needed to qualify. The consultant started demanding full payment, but we were still stinging from our Rochester fiasco. When we asked to see the signatures, they refused, but we'd been told the reputation of the firm was built on delivering good signatures. We were in a complete cash crunch and spending the money on sight-unseen signatures seemed like a foolhardy

31. $396,247.43

32. WROC staff, "Local lobbyist Robert Scott Gaddy Pleads Guilty to Theft of Government Money in Bribery Scheme," *Rochester First*, September 16, 2020, https://www.rochesterfirst.com/crime/local-lobbyist-robert-scott-gaddy-pleads-guilty-to-theft-of-government-money-in-bribery-scheme/.

risk that could end the campaign. But the campaign would end without the contracted signatures.

This reached a crescendo—risk bankrupting the campaign for signatures that would not withstand scrutiny or not pay for signatures and fail to qualify for the ballot—on a day Volpe and I were interviewed on a Fordham radio program. As we walked out of the stately academic building onto a gorgeous tree-lined campus in the middle of the Bronx, I admitted to Volpe I was afraid we faced an embarrassing disaster if we failed to even qualify for the ballot.

Just then, my phone rang. Jewett, Wilner, and Muller were on the line. Muller and Wilner's wives agreed to loan the campaign $25,000 to ease the cash crunch and resolve the issue. Volpe stepped into the breach to negotiate a successful resolution. The New York City consultants ultimately produced what they had committed to, and the loaned money got us to the point where we were able to submit forty thousand signatures gathered by volunteers and consultants by the deadline.

We waited to see if the petitions would be challenged. Challenging petitions is the standard method to get a candidate knocked off the ballot. It's also used to create protracted legal battles, forcing challengers to spend money in legal costs. Every phone call and every visit to the mailbox became filled with anxiety. Everyone held their breath as the time to challenge slowly ticked by. Suddenly, just as the window to challenge was about to close, Volpe learned there would be no challenge—not to the signatures and not to the name SAM.

## Underdog's Reality

It was dark when I walked out of a subway stop on the Upper West Side of Manhattan. My day had started early with making money calls, then doing some media interviews, making more money calls, and it finished with an appearance at a small event in lower Manhattan, all to raise interest and votes for our quixotic campaign. I inhaled the ever-present smell of New York City—a combination of food, exhaust, and other things best left unobserved—feeling weary and surprisingly hungry.

I found an all-night pizza joint and pointed at the closest slice. As one clerk put the slice on a paper plate and into a brown paper bag, another stood behind the cash register and said, "That'll be five dollars." It took a second to register—five dollars for one slice, really? I silently handed over the money and grabbed the paper bag. I walked out into the quiet neighborhood, wondering how I found myself so alone and so exhausted, holding an overpriced slice of pizza. With bitter resignation, I acknowledged I had done it to myself, and I ate the pizza with no satisfaction.

I was not prepared for the reality of running an upstart campaign. I never contemplated it because I believed someone else would provide the infrastructure. I decided it was important enough to move forward, despite the fact the promised help had evaporated. I thought the devotion to the cause would blunt the edges of running an underdog campaign. It didn't.

While successful underdogs are heralded in folklore, the reality is, they mostly fail. The political system is designed by the winners and vested interests who use their power to narrow, almost to the point of exclusion, challenges. To contest the status quo is to toil in ignominy, and it's by design.

As we entered the general election, our strategy was to raise our profile enough to garner the requisite number of votes: 50,001. We could not afford to do any polling, but the public polls released indicated we were invisible. There was no recognition of our candidacy. We were trying to get traction on issues of competency, reform, ethics, and innovation but struggled to gain traction. Our website lacked functionality. We put together a small digital strategy that attempted to gain the attention of voters interested in reform, but without more money, we struggled to measure the effectiveness of the efforts.

We were excluded from events with the oft-used explanation that people are not interested in minor-party candidates. It may seem reasonable that the attention should favor the candidates likely to end up in the office at stake, but it constricts dialogue and depletes the marketplace of ideas. People crave alternative ideas and solutions, but the system is designed to ensure they don't receive them.

Given this, it is no surprise people are tempted by demagoguing populists and attention-seeking celebrities. Minor-party candidates who are famous, such as Cynthia Nixon, engage people's curiosity.[33] Celebrity name recognition is worth millions of dollars in attention, a key facet of a

33. In one example, Al Lewis, who played Grandpa on "The Munsters," ran for governor of New York in 1998 on the Green Party ticket.

political candidate. It's one reason celebrities have become serious political contenders.

Similarly, social media's ability to grant name recognition inexpensively makes it powerful, even if recognition is triggered by doing something notorious. During the campaign, I was scheduled to make an appearance at a public broadcasting radio show in Rochester, and I spilled coffee all over my lap in my car. As I tried to mitigate the damage, I thought maybe if I took a picture of my coffee-stained lap and tweeted something provocative, it might go viral, and the attention would translate into awareness. I didn't tweet it out, but other candidates would have. The system incentivizes bizarre or ridiculous behavior by people who want to hold jobs that are important and serious.

In the face of these forces, Volpe and I continued to meet with small audiences, pushing a message of reforming a broken system. I struggled to keep my spirits up in the face of the daily slog of campaigning to challenge the system. We had no idea if we would get fifty votes or fifty thousand, but we kept plugging away.

## Good to Be King

The state was effectively run by one man: Andrew Cuomo. The party had closed ranks to prevent further negative fallout from the Buffalo Billion scandal. Even though it had been an unprecedented year for political corruption, public ethics inquiries were pursued by the US attorney's office alone.

The state's political press corps, once celebrated as hard-driving and aggressive, had become a shadow of its former self. Where once there had been a Capitol press room filled with reporters from news media across the state, now there were only a hardy few from a handful of outlets. The press room was largely quiet, with empty desks once occupied by famed reporters. The entire second floor of the office was filled with detritus like crumbled note paper, old pens, half-used notebooks, empty coffee cups, but not reporters.

As the changing profit model for journalism forced consolidation of the media, a state agency spokesperson role was seen as the one of the few jobs available to an out-of-work reporter. As the once powerful New York Daily News shrank, many speculated that its chief statehouse reporter, Ken Lovett, would soon be looking for work. Lovett was known as an aggressive reporter, but by 2018, his stories seemed to have lost their edge. Insiders speculated he was worried about his job and wanted to keep a positive relationship with the Cuomo administration. A year after the election, he became a senior advisor to Cuomo's Metropolitan Transportation Authority.[34]

Those who remained in the press trenches could easily be overwhelmed by a governor with a big bullhorn, a huge bureaucracy behind him throwing up barriers to providing information, and an administration united by a fanatical belief in bullying. Whether they were simply overwhelmed or considering their own murky futures, the press corps let Cuomo escape accountability for governmental corruption, policy failures, and seamy campaign tactics throughout the campaign. On the eve of Rosh Hashanah, Cuomo's campaign sent out a mailer misrepresenting Nixon's views on Israel and accusing her of ignoring anti-Semitism. Cuomo denied knowing anything about the mailer. A top Cuomo staffer said he authorized the mailer but did not look at the side with the accusations.[35] It strained credulity that the staffer forgot to turn over a piece of mail the campaign paid for. Shortly after the story broke, it came to light a Cuomo aide was shopping a story about Nixon's alleged support for the pro-Palestinian movement the day before the mailer went out.[36] Yet the media accepted the Cuomo campaign's explanations and the story died.

Cuomo ran as if he was unopposed. His campaign appearances were highly scripted and controlled. He continued his well-known practice of avoiding joint appearances with opponents.[37] During the 2018 race, he waited until the last possible moment and agreed to only one televised debate in both the primary and the general election.[38] The Cuomo team ensured strict

34. Ken Lovett (@klnynews), "Some Personal News: Lovett to Become MTA Senior Advisor," Twitter, November 21, 2019, 4:59 a.m., https://twitter.com/klnynews/status/11 97469600981684224.

35. Nolan Hicks, Carl Campanile, and Anna Sanders, "Mail Linking Nixon to Anti-Semitism Was Approved by Top Cuomo Aides," *New York Post*, September 12, 2018, https://nypost.com/2018/09/12/mailer-linking-nixon-to-anti-semitism-drafted-by-top -cuomo-aides/; Jesse McKinley, "Former Cuomo Aide Drafted Language for Inflammatory Anti-Semitism Flier," *New York Times*, September 12, 2018.

36. Anna Sanders and Bruce Golding, "Emails from Cuomo Aide Cast Doubt on Claims over Anti-Semitic Mailer," *New York Post*, September 11, 2018.

37. Editorial Board, *New York Post*, September 30, 2018.

38. Vivian Wang, "Cuomo Agrees, Finally, to Debate Nixon on Aug. 29," *New York Times*, August 13, 2018.

ground rules about everything, including the room temperature.[39] While Nixon and the Republican challenger, Marc Molinaro, attempted to raise issues surrounding Cuomo's gubernatorial record, neither was successful and both forums degenerated into name-calling.[40]

One day during the campaign, I ran into Molinaro at a Starbucks near the Brooklyn Bridge. As we waited for our coffee, we shared our astonishment at the lack of scrutiny Cuomo had received. Molinaro said Cuomo's campaign "just keeps saying I'm Trump; I'm not." I thought "our political system now only allows two choices: Trump Republican or Cuomo Democrat." I was neither and, consequently, there was no room for me.

## A Minor, but not Miner, Party

When the polls closed on Election Night, my campaign sent out a tweet from my account, conceding defeat. I went to bed confident that whatever happened, I had done the best I could. After hours of uninterrupted sleep, I awoke the next morning to dozens of text messages. The last one was from Wilner, sent in the wee hours of the morning. He had stayed up late to confirm we received 55,441 votes—just enough to pass the required threshold. The SAM Party had won ballot status in New York state.

There was little time to rest. This was a new political party that needed to build an infrastructure, hammer out policy positions, and build awareness and respectability. With my full blessing, Volpe became chair. He and others put together a party apparatus and started vetting candidates. I had decided to stay in Syracuse, not for days or months, but permanently. My belly was empty of fire.

The system I believed was sacred no longer functioned in a way I thought was inherent to its existence. The process, the campaign, and the outcome had broken a part of me that was once unshakable. I had to face the painful reality that I'd chosen to believe in a fantasy of a successful campaign because I was too scared to face the unknowns of a life outside of politics. Now,

39. Gregory Krieg, "Nixon and Cuomo Are Talking Climate (of the Room Where They'll Debate)," *CNN*, August 29, 2018, https://www.cnn.com/2018/08/28/politics/cynthia-nixon-andrew-cuomo-debate-heat/index.html.

40. Jesse McKinley and Shane Goldmacher, "Cuomo-Nixon Debate: Six Takeaways," *New York Times*, October 23, 2018; Vivian Wang, "Cuomo and Molinaro Spar in Bare-Knuckled Debate, Trading Shouts and Jousts," *New York Times*, October 23, 2018.

I had to confront that possibility and wondered if all the work I'd done and battles I'd fought amounted to anything other than hubris.

I was to discover the answer in an unsurprising, but still shattering, way.

## Postscript

In the 2019 state budget bill, a little-noticed item was inserted that allowed the formation of a commission to create a new public campaign-finance system. The commission's rules required minor parties to draw either 2 percent of all the votes cast or 130,000 votes in a general election vote for governor or president every two years. (As opposed to garnering 50,000 votes every four years in a gubernatorial election.)[41]

The rules were widely seen as Cuomo trying to kill the Working Families Party and other troublesome minor parties. Putting the commission's recommendations into the annual budget bill meant there was no debate or discussion over the impact or fairness of the rule changes. As a result, SAM lost ballot status in 2020. Two years later, the SAM Party merged with the Forward Party.[42]

41. Samar Khurshid, "NY's Smaller Political Parties Must Quickly Meet New Ballot Thresholds," *Gotham Gazette*, April 13, 2020.

42. Rebecca C. Lewis, "Only Two Minor Parties in New York Will Keep Their Ballot Access," *City State NY*, November 4, 2020, https://www.cityandstateny.com/politics /2020/11/only-two-minor-parties-in-new-york-will-keep-their-ballot-access/175486/; Shawna Chen, "Yang Announces New Forward Party with Other Centrist Groups," *Axios*, July 27, 2022, https://www.axios.com/2022/07/28/andrew-yang-forward-party-mer ger.

# The Light of Belonging

I was in bed, awake but so disoriented I had to remind myself I was actually conscious. In my liminal state, I found myself watching a fuzzy black-and-white YouTube video of Robert Goulet as Lancelot singing "If Ever I Would Leave You." Even in my disassociated state, I found my actions strange. I am not a fan of Robert Goulet, the musical "Camelot," or that song. Yet there I was in the wee hours at the start of the Memorial Day weekend 2019, endlessly viewing the video. The first lines of the song are: "If ever I would leave you, it wouldn't be in summer." Hours earlier, Jack had died after taking a fall. I was on the precipice of a nervous breakdown, as evidenced by the inexplicable fact I was watching this video endlessly.

The next day, I went through Jack's overstuffed wallet. Among the credit cards, receipts, and coffee shop punch cards was a folded blue piece of paper. I immediately recognized it as his handwritten playlist. Jack could play piano by ear. Name a tune and he could play it. Yet when called upon to "play anything," his mind would go blank, so he kept a playlist in his wallet. The list would change with the arrival of holidays, the football season, or on a whim when he found a new song to add to his repertoire. I knew the lists well and his rotating favorites, which would form the last bars of every song he played until replaced by a new beloved. Sometimes it was Nat King Cole's "Unforgettable," the Notre Dame fight song, or Duke Ellington's "Satin Doll."

When I unfolded the creased blue paper, I was stunned to see "If Ever I Would Leave You" as the first song on the list. I don't remember ever hearing him play it or even talking about it. Yet, there it was, in my hands and in my head from the previous night. Maybe it was God, maybe it was the universe, maybe Jack, or all the above. I only knew I was in the midst of something so overwhelming, I wasn't sure I could survive, or if I even wanted to. All I could do was bear the pain as long as I was conscious, and often in my subconscious, too.

## Breaking's Aftermath

With the disappointment of my race for governor and the chaos of Trump's tenure, I was experiencing a reckoning over my democratic ideals. I watched in disbelief as the values I held as sacred were pulverized daily. There seemed to be no consequence for lies, bad acts, or hypocrisy. I wondered if everything I believed in and worked for was meaningless, or worse, a romantic fantasy. While Jack shared my disbelief, he bridged my cynicism with an inherent faith in the system. He was, as always, my sounding board, therapist, and champion. Still, I struggled, feeling like I was experiencing loss every time I read the news.

Then the inconceivable happened—Jack died—and I learned what loss really is.

The sight of that song in Jack's handwriting marked the beginning of an existential struggle for me. Everything had changed, and I was unalterably broken. Shockingly, the rest of the world continued to function, and I could not understand how that was possible.

My beloved city felt so foreign, I felt myself a stranger in an unfamiliar place. A person without purpose, meaning, or desire, who once had an embarrassing abundance of everything. I would see people and think, "Why are they laughing when everyone they love is going to die?" I felt like I was dying, though I knew I wasn't. But I hoped I was.

Everything I relied on disintegrated. As I had done for twenty-five years, I reflexively thought, "What does Jack think?"—only to be crushed by the painful reminder of his death and the totality of my loss. Every second of every day, this painful cycle repeated until I was physically exhausted.

I confided in my sisters that I wasn't sure I could survive and not sure I wanted to. My sisters did not disagree or tell me "things will get better." Instead, they listened during daily phone calls, texted with me at all hours, and issued mandatory dinner invitations. The Mannions, too, made no attempts to downplay the grief. During one phone call, Patrick said, "No one wants to be on this road, but we are. Together." A handful of friends made offers I could refuse without consequence. I felt as if I had nothing but time and tears.

## The Unexpected Light

In the depths of this, the dog food ran out. While I cared little about my own well-being, I knew Jack would be upset if I did not take care of our—now my—dog, Figgy. Forced to venture out to buy dog food, I found myself standing in the entryway of BJ's Warehouse completely overwhelmed.

As I reminded myself to "just function," a voice beside me said, "Hey, aren't you the mayor?" I turned to see a man in his sixties who I didn't know. I attempted a smile and said, "I used to be," thinking, I used to be a lot of things. He said enthusiastically, "Oh my, God, you look great! I can't believe how young you look, and I'm a Republican!"

Then I really smiled, because I knew I looked terrible. "Well, I don't feel so young," I responded. With a gentleness I will never forget, he said, "I'm really sorry about your husband." I nodded and he filled the emotional moment by asking what I was doing there. I told him Jack bought the dog food and I was trying to figure out where it was.

"Come with me," he said. "I'll show you." I followed him as he prattled on about how he had unsuccessfully proposed to a city employee multiple times, but she wouldn't marry him even when he begged. We found the correct aisle, and he put the dog food in my cart. When he was finished, he asked if I needed anything else. Unable to speak, I shook my head no. He smiled and said he would make sure to tell the object of his unrequited love how great I looked. I watched him walk away, feeling I was watching a manifestation of grace.

Days later, I happened upon the garbageman taking my empty garbage can from the curb to the side of my house. I summoned enough energy to thank him for his extra effort as he was only required to leave the empty can at the curb. As he walked back to the truck, he turned and said, "It's not a problem. After all, you always think of us." I swallowed and looked away, afraid I might break down. His generous throwaway comment offered a small beam of light in my dark world.

A couple of months later, I was in the grocery store when an employee stepped out from behind the deli counter, complete with her hair net and plastic gloves, and followed me into an aisle. She pulled me aside and said quietly, "I haven't seen you to tell you how sorry I am about your husband." By that time, it was easier to say thank you without falling apart. I thanked her, wondering if it would violate public health rules if I hugged her. It was the first time I was able to think about something other than my grief. I did not hug her, but I held her generosity of spirit close.

Piles of handwritten notes filled my mailbox, with heartfelt words meant to alleviate my suffering. Many were from people I did not know writing to tell me they were thinking of me. Some were from people I knew with different political beliefs. Former Republican adversaries sent notes and called, and even the local Conservative Party donated to a homeless organization in Jack's name.

As I slowly emerged from my isolation, people would approach me on the street or in a store, often sharing their own grief over the death of a spouse, a parent, a child, or a loved one. All of them were offering a connection they knew I needed but I would not consciously recognize I needed for some time. I worked through my grief thanks to the grace of many strangers and some former opponents, each offering compassion unrelated to party, philosophy, or any of the common ways we willingly separate ourselves.

These acts of kindness made the days somehow bearable. It did not fix the brokenness, but it helped me come to terms with it. Slowly, I began to see that while I felt like a stranger, people wanted me to know I was not, and I was not alone in my suffering. This new, strange land was the same place I once reveled in. I was seeing it in a different light. A light of belonging.

## Community

I had certainly witnessed grief while I was in public office. I saw mothers lose sons to violence, children lose parents, people learn of loved ones diagnosed with cancer—all types of loss and tragedy. As mayor, I regularly attended funerals, wakes, and memorial services. People at these events would routinely tell me that they did not know the departed, "but I want to pay my respects." Sometimes they shared a distant connection: "My friend knows a cousin and I'm here for her," or even something as simple as "I just had to do something." I heard these things and never really recognized how remarkable it was that this kind of empathy was routinely given by and to strangers.

At the end of my term, there was a particularly terrible house fire where six members of an extended family, including four children, ranging in age from seven to thirteen, died.[43] As I waited to pay my respects, I watched hundreds of people gather in line holding poster-board collages of smiling children, arrangements of candy, and handwritten notes to share with the grieving family.

I wound my way into the room of six caskets, four of them child-sized. Each casket was surrounded with homemade signs and pictures illustrating the community's love. When I got to the grieving family, they expressed such gratitude over the compassion of the community and made a point to say many of the people who had been so generous were strangers.

The tragedy burned into my psyche. Still, at the time I didn't fully understand what the community's compassion indicated about the human condition, in general, and about Syracuse, in particular. Nor did I understand it even in the immediate aftermath of Jack's death, when I was in the throes of existential grief.

It was only in the slow, painful passing of time and in processing my loss with the help of others that I was able to recognize how profound the gift of freely given empathy is. Sometime in that period, I learned to acknowledge and accept grace. I realized I had witnessed countless examples of community members selflessly fostering healing.

Neighbors offering a bond that would not be severed, even in the face of great loss: I had been present for it many times throughout my tenure as mayor. I saw it given to those perceived to be in need. It was offered regardless of notoriety, neighborhood, race, class, religion, or any of the ways we divide ourselves. I saw it enough to know that, now, it was being given to me, not because I was the former mayor but because I was a part of this community. They wanted me to know I belonged. They offered me a light to help me move through my darkness.

They cared enough about a neighbor to stand in the presence of suffering—perfect strangers going out of their way to extend compassion to another in a time of need, not for money or attention but out of humanity alone. At our best, we help heal trauma in the ways we can, because we belong to each other. When I was most vulnerable, I benefitted from the

43. Ken Sturtz, "Six Victims of Deadly Syracuse Fire: Who They Were," Syracuse.com, May 7, 2016, https://www.syracuse.com/news/2016/05/syracuse_house_fire_victims .html.

greatest virtue a community has—compassion for its members. They had no guarantee their kindness would make a difference to me, but they acted upon that desire anyway by giving of themselves. Thus, they created "public" and "good" by taking care of each other.

I had once preached the virtues in Syracuse of doing good through public service. I believed it, and the voters believed in me. As mayor, I tried to ensure that local government served the public good by attempting to solve problems—ploughing snow, picking up trash, educating children, and providing working infrastructure. It was only after I was mayor, when I was most vulnerable, that I understood the ultimate importance of the political system was the honest effort to try to build community.

What I was experiencing in upstate's drumlins was saving me. I started noticing every day, commonplace acts of generosity by people: the simple act of holding a door open for someone, waving from across the street, or helping to wrangle an escaped pet.

The winter after Jack died, there was a large snowstorm followed by a cold but unusually sunny day. As I drove through Syracuse, I saw the familiar sight of people with shovels. As I looked closer, I realized people were shoveling out fire hydrants, a task that typically fell to the fire department. Nobody told them to do it; nevertheless, across Syracuse that day, everyone had taken it upon themselves to excavate the hydrants.

## COVID

Winter was on the precipice of becoming spring when the COVID-19 pandemic shut down the world. It felt oddly normal for me because I had viscerally experienced a shutdown of sorts after Jack's death. As the world suffered through unimaginable loss, I continued to process my own grief. Gradually, the accumulation of these everyday object lessons helped me understand that belonging to this community was easing my loss.

The anger and disappointment I had once harbored toward Andrew Cuomo and the political system was replaced with gratitude. I was grateful part of my inheritance was belonging in Syracuse, thankful I had decided to stay in Syracuse, grateful for feeling as if my work as mayor had helped strengthen my community and grateful that community helped save my life.

I was even grateful I lost the governor's race to Cuomo. If the outcome had been different, I might have been tempted to travel and hit the hustings, which would have kept me apart from Jack for the last six months of his life. Instead, I spent every day of those months with him.

As I was coming to peace, Cuomo's political world was unraveling. He became embroiled in a crisis over how many of the state's nursing home residents died because of the virus. Evidence was uncovered that Cuomo's aides had tried to hide the true number of COVID fatalities and that state employees had helped write Cuomo's book about his leadership during COVID.[44] His final undoing, though, were accusations that emerged that he had sexually harassed several women.[45]

I was not surprised by the allegations. "Power tends to corrupt and absolute power corrupts absolutely."[46] Cuomo had near absolute power. He resigned when it became likely he would be impeached.[47] When Cuomo's demise became obvious, I started hearing from Albany insiders that had once been aligned with him. They unctuously compared me to "David" finally seeing "Goliath" fall and asked if I was planning on running for office or going to work in state government. I was not. The drive I once had to be part of the hurly-burly political world was gone.

## Keeping the Faith

In its place was a desire to continue to build community and share the light of belonging with other people who needed it. I decided to write a book about my experiences. I began teaching political science to students at Colgate University. I mentored new mayors, many of them women, with the Bloomberg Harvard City Leadership Initiative program. I supported public-sector innovation as a member of the board of the Volcker

44. Michael Gold and Ed Shanahan, "What We Know About Cuomo's Nursing Home Scandal," *New York Times*, August 4, 2021.

45. Yoav Goen, "Cuomo Made Staffers Work on His $5M Pandemic Book for His 'Personal Gain' Investigators Charge," *City*, November 22, 2021, https://www.thecity.nyc /2021/11/22/22797615/cuomo-staffers-work-pandemic-book-investigators-charge; Luis Ferré-Sadurni and Mihir Zaveri, "Sexual Harassment Claims Against Cuomo: What We Know So Far," *New York Times*, November 11, 2021.

46. Acton Institute, Acton Research: Lord Acton Quote Archive, https://www.acton .org/research/lord-acton-quote-archive.

47. Michael Scherer, Josh Dawsey, and Ted Gup, "Cuomo Announces Resignation in Effort to Head Off Likely Impeachment After Devastating Report on His Conduct," *Washington Post*, August 20, 2021.

Alliance and represented children in need of legal counsel in family court. My post-politics work has been varied, interesting, and constructive. It's allowed me to forge new relationships and strengthen my existing relationships, and it's given me precious time to think about public policy.

I have come to understand contrary forces are ever present in our political system. Integrity and honesty coexist with corruption and malfeasance and have throughout our history, and in all places. To me, the important fight is to see the presence of goodness and not abandon a desire for better outcomes—to not cower in the face of injustice. Demand substance and solutions even if it seems futile. While sometimes all this work is futile, other times it takes a surprising and unexpected direction resulting in progress.

My grandmothers had a habit of saying goodbye with "Keep the faith." As an adult, I have come to think of it as an overt reminder to refuse to let darkness dim hope. After all I experienced, I had ended up where they told me I should be.

Like them, I, too, decided to keep the faith.

# Acknowledgments

Sometime in the winter of 2018, Jack and I were walking up the hill to Christ the King Retreat House and he said, "You should write a book. You can just tell people you are writing one and it will buy you time to figure out what you want to do." Moments later when we got to Christ the King, Father Mike Carmola greeted me by saying, "You should write a book." I was stunned, and Jack proudly responded, "That's what I was just saying!"

Writing the book was an act of faith. After Jack died, my survival seemed too much to bear. The thought of completing a daunting project like a book was fanciful. Yet, buried somewhere in my intense emotions was a nagging sense Jack would have been disappointed if I gave up on the book. As an internal compromise, I decided to quietly write knowing that while I would quit before it was finished, I could tell myself I tried.

Gingerly, and with low expectations, I started to try to piece together a different life and write the book. With the help of an extraordinary group of loved ones, I was able to slowly do that. My sisters, Sarah, Mary, Brienne, and cousin Kate, along with their beautiful children, reminded me in direct and indirect ways that I mattered. The ever-expanding Mannion clan were a constant positive presence and, I realized, another gift from Jack. Layered through my families were the most exceptionally kind and caring friends—Terri Bright, Michele Gerroir, Andrea Banda, Bill Ryan, Beth Rougeux, Michalle Harmon, and Rosemarie Nelson. Without fail, each made me feel better.

One fateful day, I received to an email from David Rubin, the former dean of Syracuse University's Newhouse School of Communications, a one-time professor of mine, and a friend. In responding to his query, I was unusually candid that I was struggling but had decided to write a book. When I asked for advice, he volunteered to read my work. Thus started a lengthy process where I would send a complete chapter to him, and he would respond with multiple single-space pages of detailed thoughts. I would think about his reactions, rewrite, and send revisions back to him. It was a seemingly perpetual process of which I was the sole beneficiary. His insights were invaluable in helping me organize my thoughts and making the material stronger. I knew I was making progress when he would tell me he thought a chapter was good enough to share with his lovely wife, Tina.

Beth Rougeux around this time laughingly reminded me she was "good with boring stuff" and volunteered to help. She chased facts, articles, citations, and read every version, often telling me to add more stories. Her never wavering support, work, and good cheer were invaluable. Grant Reeher, too, read the chapters and followed up with tips not to bury the lede, and Carol Dwyer took the first copyediting cut.

Rounding out this select group of readers was Tim Byrnes. Tim told me early, "Good news, you can write. Bad news, writing is hard." While that information was welcomed, the most important thing Tim did was introduce me to the Brigadoon of Colgate University. Through that introduction, I have been able to teach the most amazing group of students who rekindled my love for American government. Similarly, Colgate allowed me to work with the smart, supportive, and generous individuals composing the Political Science Department. I feel fortunate to be associated with them and am in awe of their commitment to a rigorous, rich learning environment. Among the many opportunities the department shared was the ability to access Louis Rakin Foundation funds, which helped make the book a reality. An integral piece of my childhood reentered my life as an adult when I joyously reconnected with my childhood friend Jonann Brady and, as a bonus, discovered she was a professional copy editor. Her skills and, most important, our relationship made the copyediting process constructive and reassuring.

All along this journey, my City Hall team—Mary, Frank, Shawn, Stephanie, Joe, George, Adria, Joel, and others—fact-checked and cheered. The "Team of Kids"—Andrew, Dan, Elizabeth, Kate, Lindsay(s), Sam, Mick, Maria, and Alex—from across the county reminded me of stories and talked though ideas. Despite the fact we no longer work together and they are now fully grown adults, we will always be a team and they will always be my "kids."

While the book would not have come to fruition without the help of these individuals, I would be remiss if I did not thank the employees of the city of Syracuse for their dedication. I will always be in awe of the quiet and caring acts of sacrifice they routinely make to meet the mission of public service. Finally, I want to thank my parents for, among innumerable lessons, instilling in me a sense of integrity, even when the vocation I applied it in baffled them.

www.ingramcontent.com/pod-product-compliance
Lightning Source LLC
Chambersburg PA
CBHW020721310525
27529CB00008B/112/J